Tales
FROM THE Sky

AVIATION ADVENTURES
FROM AROUND THE WORLD,
AS TOLD BY THE AVIATOR

Roger Blair Johnson

Published by: Road Scholar Publishing Group LLC
P.O. Box 25243
Scottsdale, AZ 85255
Reboh@cox.net

Paperback ISBN: 978-1-7374284-0-4
ebook ISBN: 978-1-7374284-1-1

Book Cover & Interior Layout: Fusion Creative Works, fusioncw.com

Every attempt has been made to properly source all quotes.

Printed in the United States of America

First Edition

2 4 6 8 10 12

Dedication

To my father, Kenneth Blair Johnson.

You flew an aircraft as if the Angels themselves took delight in watching you and I am sure they learned a thing or two about your shared craft.

You were my hero, my mentor, my instructor, and my Captain. Words cannot express my gratitude in your selflessness in teaching me all you knew when we flew together. On sultry summer evenings you told me of your adventures of flying around the world, paving the way for other aviators to follow, including your son. You showed me the meaning of the stars, where God and the Angels abound, and how those diamonds in the night sky direct aviators to distant lands, how they give us hope and wonder of a better world.

I miss you Dad. I miss our weekly talks of flying. And though you are now in heaven, soaring with the angels, you are also in my soul. When I fly my airliner, you whisper to me when I begin to take my position as a Captain as routine, or do not see, with my heart, a beautiful view out my office window, that flying is not just a job, it is life itself, a gift beyond measure, and to never take what Aviators do for granted.

Table of Contents

Rick Henry 7

The Hero 43

Out of Control Phantom 55

The Mist 69

Stuck Mic 73

Night Flight... still my strangest flight. 77

Aircraft Down 87

Phantom Fires 97

Small World 121

Buzzing the Beach 129

Vampire Pilot 141

Near Death Experiences 145

Bob Grace 159

Washington Center 167

The Light 181

My Finest Flight 187

Kite Wars 197

Jack 207

Last Flight   239

Flight to Berlin   263

Sky Rage   271

Smoking Hot Jet   283

Of Fighters and Thunderstorms   289

Landing Blind   311

Rick Henry

The story that follows was written over a period of many weeks back in the mid-1990s. Admittedly, it is long. I wrote it with the intention of describing to the layperson what it was like flying the F-4 on a ground attack mission in the Nellis AFB bombing ranges during the mid-1980s.

Many years ago, I received F-16 flight training in Klamath Falls, Oregon. One day my mates and I were attending a classroom lecture on how to do no-lock intercepts using the F-16's radar. The instructor giving the brief was named Rick Henry, and at that time, Rick was one of a very few number of IWSOs (Instructor Weapons System Operator) remaining in the USAF. If a U.S. Air Force fighter aircraft had two seats, the front (F-4) or left (F-111), seat was occupied by a pilot. The backseat or right seat was occupied by a weapons system officer. The WSO, "whizo," operated the radar and bombing computers. IWSOs "eye whizzos" were instructors to WSOs and, in my case, fledgling F-16 pilots.

IWSOs and WSOs were an endangered species of sorts back then. The USAF was converting its two-seat F-4 and F-101B squadrons (Rick used to fly as an IWSO on the F-4) to single-seat F-16s, and this transition was leaving a lot of WSOs and IWSOs scrambling to find jobs within the military structure. It was heartbreaking to see these men's lives and families so disrupted by this modernization of the force structure. Many guys (it was a males' only business then) went into "desk" jobs in either the maintenance or personnel departments, many more got out of the USAF "proper" and went into the Guard or Reserve, and still others left the military altogether. The "lucky few," IWSOs that is, were given instructor opportunities in positions in which they were well-acquainted. They would most likely spend their remaining military life teaching fledgling F-16 pilots how to employ their weapon's system radar. Far too many good men were put out to pasture when their squadron went to single-seat fighters, and Rick was one of them.

As I listened to Rick that day, I could detect a sadness and a longing in his voice. He missed flying. He missed what he did best, and a very part of his soul was lost when the F-4s left. He had devoted his career to perfecting a profession that technology was able to surpass before he was able to fully express his own capabilities. It is believed that technology is able to detect, receive, process, diagnose, warn, display, direct, and defeat just about anything to allow the pilot to be free to fly the aircraft . . . but is that flying?

While Rick continued with his lecture, my mind daydreamed of the old days . . . I could see the days when Rick and I both flew F-4s. They were hot jets to us, a waning pinnacle of leading-edge technology. When I began to fly the F-4, it was the old man in the sky. It didn't turn tighter than the newer F-16s or F-15s, it wasn't quicker, it burned more fuel, and it "broke" more often. And according to some, the F-4 wasn't exactly the best-looking fighter on the ramp. But for what the "Phantom," nickname for the F-4, may have lacked in technical attributes, its shortcomings were balanced by the "street-smart" crews that flew it. Many a tired F-4 equipped with outdated and aging gadgets would kick the tar out of the wonder jets; wisdom has a way of balancing the scales.

There was a distinction about the F-4 that went beyond sheer technical numbers when compared to the latest "Mattel" toys (F-16/15). It had an aura, an ambiance that permeated the whole community of Phantom personnel, from the crew chiefs to the pilots to the admin clerks. The Phantom was beautiful, in an ugly sense, such as a Mack truck is aesthetically appealing to a truck driver, for the form bestows the function. Through the years, the Phantom fought in many conflicts around the world and was a proud veteran with a noble spirit that, on many occasions, flew beyond its designed abilities to bring its biological masters back to safety.

The cockpit smelled of fuel, ionized air, and sweat. Unlike the super efficiently cooled cockpit of the F-16, the F-4's air conditioner was just a placebo, intended to psychologically fool the aircrew into thinking that it served a useful purpose. In the winter, you did not lack for heat, and temperatures were mild. But in the summer—on a hot summer day, you were drenched in sweat twenty minutes after strapping into the cockpit. While airborne and flying a low-level, drops of sweat beaded down your face and onto your oxygen mask. Sometimes your eyes would take a drop or two, and you would lift your visor and take a quick wipe of your brow with your gloved hand, cursing that damned air conditioner and its old, impotent plumbing.

Unlike the automated systems in the newer fighters, flying the F-4 took a lot of manual labor and deliberate, calculated thought. At 500 knots, it took a relatively strong pull on the stick to turn it and the G forces, while turning at 500 knots, tried to keep you glued to your seat. You huffed and puffed, straining with your arms, neck, chest, and stomach muscles, using each group to either pull your head and upper body off the seat back so as to perform your requisite duties, or to keep your arms in place to operate the stick and throttles; conversely at 100 knots, it took a sensitive, delicate feel to keep it from going out of control. The ailerons and rudder demanded special attention in the F-4. At low angles of attack (AOA[1]), the ailerons were used to roll and "turn" the aircraft and the rudder was somewhat ignored. But as the angle of attack increased, the ailerons were used less and the rudder took center stage as the flight control of choice. The ailerons, if used with reckless abandon at higher AOAs, could cause the Phantom to, quite violently at times, depart controlled flight; therefore, they had to be left alone as much as possible. But even the rudder, if used without respect for your current flight envelope, could impart an out-of-control situation, so its input, too, was not abused unless you were certain of its affect upon your flight path. On the flip side, the engines (there were two of them) were always willing to be abused and were as reliable as the watch on your wrist; the military issued one, of course! Finally, flying a low-level, like the flight controls previously mentioned, demanded much of the rest of your "undivided" attention to remain on course and on time.

Unlike the super accurate inertial navigation systems of the newer fighters, the F-4's INS would usually fix your position within the state or country (depending on size) over which you were flying. The Phantom's INS was only accurate on rare occasions. The INSs of the newer fighters allowed those pilots to confidently fly to their targets, thusly freeing the crews from a lot of map reading and also allowing them to concentrate more on threat detection (both visually and with the radar).

The "INS," Inertial Navigation System, uses a gyroscope, either mechanical or ring laser, to measure movement and position of the aircraft. In its most basic form, it tells the crew where they are and the distance and ground track to a manually selected latitude and longitude, corrected for wind. It literally can guide you to any point in the world. It also tells the crew their ground speed and their magnetic ground track, as they fly over the ground. Finally, the system can be tied to the aircraft's weapons system to more accurately drop either conventional or nuclear weapons. In older fighters, the INS was reliable but tended to drift in position. It was not uncommon in the F-4 for the INS to be two miles off after forty-five minutes of flight. In the F-16s that I flew after the F-4, after two hours you might be off by a tenth of a mile, but, in either aircraft you could manually update the INS's actual position whenever you wished. An accurate INS helped to relieve pilots and WSOs of the stress of accurate map reading while flying at very low altitude.

No such luck in the Phantom. Since the F-4's INS wasn't the most precise, we rarely used it as our primary reference for navigation along the low level routes. Instead we "Phantom Phlyers" preferred (prepherred?) to navigate in much the same way as Lindbergh did on his flight to Paris in 1927, using dead reckoning (dead reckoning, a.k.a. DR. Where the dreadful name came from, I do not know, but I suspect from the early pioneers of aviation, some of whom did die trying to get from A to B using the following procedure. To "DR" in aviation speak means to navigate with reference to the aforementioned tools. You preplanned your intended route of flight on a map. You figured out the headings you needed to fly, from turn point to turn point—you rarely flew a straight course to your target—the times to each turn point, based upon a ground speed that you intended to fly, and the overall time of the low-level. Also, you studied the route of flight to learn its terrain features and to look for prominent landmarks that may help you to stay on/get on course. More often than not, "DR"-ing worked, but you had to have faith that it would.).

In fact, we used the same tools—a map, a clock, and a compass (we didn't really use a compass, per se, for everyday flying, instead we used an HSI . . . horizontal situation indicator) as Lindbergh.

However, unlike "Lucky Lindy," who just needed to hit a continent on his trip over the "pond" and wasn't too worried about a time schedule, save for his fuel, when we flew our low-levels, we had to be accurate and on time, particularly when it came to finding and bombing a target. (Usually, you were given a time "window" in which you had to hit your target.) Low-level navigation could be very difficult, particularly if flying over featureless terrain. Nature wasn't always cooperative when it came to positioning landmarks where you wanted them, particularly when the visibility was poor, hence trying to find some low-level turn points demanded most of the pilot's attention.

Because so much had to be considered by the pilot, flying the aircraft had to be done by unconscious thought, and while the WSOs/IWSOs did help with some navigation, normally you wanted him "in the radar" searching for possible threats, or in concert with checking the radar, he would "be outside," visually checking the flight's "six o'clock" for bandits. In all fighters, new and old, you had to learn how to multi-task; but in the Phantom, you had to learn how to prioritize the many tasks required and, in essence, you really had to learn how to prioritize the multitasking of multitasking! In any jet, it's an adrenaline-producing environment; in the F-4 however, since so many things had to be done either physically or mentally in a short amount of time, and done accurately, it was sweat-producing and gut-wrenching work!

But it was satisfying "work," particularly if it was a hard mission. One time, while on a TDY (Temporary DutY) to George AFB, in California, I was tasked to lead a strike package of twelve F-4s against targets in southwestern Nevada.

The challenge was formidable. I was leading "my" four-ship of F-4s from my home squadron, plus an additional eight F-4s that belonged to the Luftwaffe Fighter Weapons School (because the weather was so good in Southern California, the West German Air Force [at that time, there were still two Germanys] based its Fighter Weapons School at George AFB, in Victorville, California). My four ship's target was an airfield in the Nellis AFB Range Complex.

The Nellis Range Complex, where the Red Flag air wars are fought, also contains "Area 51," of alien spacecraft and top-secret USAF aircraft fame. It is about 150 miles wide, east/west, and fifty miles or so "high," north/south, and starts about sixty miles north of Las Vegas, Nevada. The area contains many bombing targets such as airfields, industrial complexes, air defense sites, and railroad-type facilities and it also has "very active" and realistic manned air defenses that "simulate" shooting surface-to-air missiles at ingressing/egressing participants. Not only does your aircraft indicate that a missile has been launched at you or is about to be launched, via the electronic displays in your cockpit, but "Smokey SAMs," real, unguided, but very visible rockets, are launched to add even more realism. Aircraft have crashed and crews died trying to evade detection from these sites, or, if detected, the crews have crashed trying to break the radar lock from the offending SAM site. At the end of a day's Red Flag mission, the sites would send video footage of aircraft that they tracked and the countermeasures that that aircraft used to try and defeat either radar lock or missile tracking guidance. It was an excellent training experience, but it was pretty embarrassing to be a "movie star" at the end of the day's mass debrief where about 300 fighter pilots and support personnel might see your aircraft, on a huge movie theater type screen, doing the "funky chicken," jinking up and down and left and right very deliberately and abruptly, very close to the ground, trying to evade a "simulated" SAM (surface-to-air missile). You really worked hard to avoid "stardom"; peer pressure can be hell as a fighter pilot!

The mission frag (a frag is an order from the upper echelons of the command structure detailing which targets are to be hit, at what time, with what ordnance, and by what aircraft (squadron and or wings). Other restrictions pertinent to the mission will be put on the frag, such as other assets in the area and possible ingress/egress restrictions) ordered us to destroy aircraft on the airfield ramp, cut the main runway, and destroy ops buildings as well as other targets in the immediate area of the airfield. Also, because of mission tasking, we had to fly a circuitous route to the target that was at least 300 nautical miles in length. Another constraint was the target defenses; the surface-to-air threat surrounding the target was the most advanced anywhere in the world, particularly the SAMs. Finally, to make things that much more difficult, F-16s and F-15s from Nellis AFB were trying to intercept us, either en route to the target, at the target, or while on egress from the target area.

The terrain over which we were to fly was typical Southwestern desert—distinct, prominent mountains and their associated ranges, their features still chiseled and sharp in appearance, gave way to equally distinct, owing to how flat they were, sagebrush-covered valleys. There were no major population centers anywhere along the route of flight, and any smaller towns that could have posed a problem were avoided during the planning of the low-level. The weather was forecast to be sunny with the temperature in the mid-nineties.

After planning the mission the previous afternoon, we took off from George AFB about three hours after sunrise the following morning. We lined up on the runway, all twelve of us, in groups of four, with 500 feet between the groups, and with my four-ship being the farthest down the runway. We were loaded with six 500-pound nonexplosive practice bombs, three under each wing, and two 2,500-pound external fuel tanks, one on each wing. Because we were carrying bombs (actually cement-filled bombs, which we used to simulate the real thing), I briefed the flight of twelve to take off single ship, in twenty-second intervals, hence with twelve aircraft, it took three minutes and forty seconds before we were all airborne.

Once I was airborne (I took off first), I turned my aircraft to the north and proceeded to climb to twenty-six thousand feet (FL 260). I kept my speed in the climb at 300 knots (normally it's 350) to allow the trailing aircraft to join up.

By the time we reached 26,000 feet, all twelve aircraft had "joined" up . . . if you could say seven to ten miles between the lead two aircraft and the trailing two aircraft being joined up; some things in life are relative. From takeoff to landing, I had briefed that we were to fly in "tactical formation" (to allow fighter aircraft more survivability and maneuverability in high threat areas, we flew our aircraft pretty far from one another; in the ensuing paragraphs I will describe the distances and positions of each aircraft involved when "flying tactical"). Normally, this meant we flew two by two by two, each two-ship behind and slightly offset from the other two in front. (In a world without air traffic controllers and their control, we would have been flying at grossly different altitudes whilst en route to the low-level start point so as to make the formation harder to see, but the realities of flying in civilian airspace necessitated that we fly, all twelve of us, at exactly 26,000 feet.)

The first 100 nautical miles of the trip were flown at medium altitude to conserve fuel, and it was also considered "friendly" territory. Our route of flight took us over Edwards AFB and to the eastern border of the Sierra Nevada mountains. From just abeam Mount Whitney, in the Sierra Nevadas, I turned more north and east to fly to the northeast shore of a dry lake bed called Owens Lake; this is where the low-level portion of the flight was to begin.

The weather that day was beautiful, and since it was so clear and there were no pressing duties while cruising to the start of the low-level point, I chanced to glance at the world around me . . . I was not disappointed. To the left, west, and just immediately below me was Mount Whitney, California's highest peak. The morning sun's golden rays cascaded onto the mountain's eastern flank, causing the snow-crested mountain to appear to stretch to the heavens as if it was just waking up and performing a morning yawn. The lesser mountains, west of this imposing granite monolith, and in its shadow, were still enjoying their slumber, nestled up with white blankets of low-lying clouds. Beyond the mountains, and still farther west, I could see the blueness of the world's largest ocean, the Pacific. In direct contrast, to the wetness of the Pacific and the snow adorning the mountains immediately below me, the view to the east afforded me the opportunity to see Death Valley and the bleakness of the Mojave Desert beyond. And in front of me, as if meant to separate the two extremes, was the eastern side of the uprising Sierra Nevada mountain chain. This imposing wall of mountains, all sporting crowns of snow and, in their lower evaluations green wraps of pine, seemed to be nature's sentinels, standing guard against any intruders from the east. It was on mornings such as that, with views such as the one I just described, that I can understand the reason why birds sing the sweet melodies they do, as I caught myself many times whistling some unknown tune while cruising the skies.

As we approached Owens Lake, it was time to descend into the low-altitude environment in preparation for the start of the low-level portion of the mission. So, I asked Los Angeles Center for a descent to an altitude below 18,000 feet. Once below FL180 I cancelled my IFR clearance and sent the flight of twelve aircraft to our tactical radio frequency for the rest of the mission's ingress and egress. Once we began the low-level we would never really climb above 500 feet above ground level, except to enter the traffic pattern at George AFB upon our return.

To descend to low altitude is not as simple as it might seem. Firstly, you don't want to go into a screaming dive because your ground speed has to be kept to the speed at which you planned to fly the mission ingress, which included the medium altitude segment (to include the takeoff and climb to altitude), the descent to the low-altitude structure, and finally the low-level itself. Starting the low-level at the correct time was critically important. Secondly, you don't want to be sixty degrees nose low 2000 feet above the ground because your turn radius is so high that you would impact the ground trying to pull out. So, you descend in stages, starting at sixty degrees of dive angle, while at the higher altitudes, and as you got lower, you shallowed out to forty degrees and then twenty degrees and then ten degrees and then level flight.

While Rick Henry wasn't in my aircraft on that day, I knew that he'd flown on many missions like it. The heart pounds and sweat soaks you as you get closer to the target. As you near the start of the low-level, the backseaters stood by to update their old INS in the hope that it may help its accuracy. As previously discussed, the pilots in the newer fighters rarely worried about their INS being off course or in error, and even though F-4 crews viewed their INS with a healthy distrust, WSOs would still update the INS's position over the low-level start point in the hope that it might guide pilots unfailingly along their low-level route.

Since you didn't trust your INS's accuracy, you navigated, as previously stated, with a custom-made low-level map, clock, and compass. Whereas an F-16 pilot's INS automatically tells him/her when they'll get to the next turn point and what ground speed to fly to get there and at what time they will arrive at that point, we F-4 guys had to calculate it ourselves. Assuming you were on time at the start of the low-level point, the lead aircraft adjusted his ground speed to match the flight-planned ground speed. The ground speed planned for low levels varied from mission to mission, based on a multitude of factors, but on today's mission we planned on flying at 480 knots until two turn points before the target whereupon we would accelerate to 540 knots for the target run and then go as fast as we could after we dropped the bombs. In between all this navigating and map reading and calculating time, you were visually checking all around you for bandits (usually you are looking inside the flight toward your wingman or lead, depending upon whom you are). And while you are map reading and navigating and checking for bandit aircraft, you are flying your aircraft and dodging rocks and hills and valley floors and trees and generally trying to fit the F-4s flight profile to match that of the terrain. At times you'll fly for minutes not really knowing where, exactly, you are, and, at eight to nine miles a minute, that can be a lot of uncertain ground. You learned early in the F-4 to become proficient in dead reckoning. Because of route study before the mission, you know which "get well" points to look for, landmarks that are like sirens in the night, guiding you to your turn point. At each turn point you checked your actual time there, versus when you were supposed to be there and adjusted your speed to either gain or lose important seconds.

Before I move on, I would like to make one thing perfectly clear with regards to flying at low level . . . when I say you are looking at the map and checking your ground speed or doing anything that involved looking in the cockpit, you usually looked very quickly at whatever it is you wanted to look at and then you looked back out again. You memorized what you looked at and then comprehended it as you were looking back outside. Hitting the ground was a serious consideration at 100 feet and 500 knots, and looking too long in the cockpit (we're talking one to two seconds) was the absolute max, down that low. You might have to take several glances to accomplish a task, but so be it. The PK, probability of kill, after hitting the ground was about 99.5 percent (I know of three guys who brought that down from 100).

While the pilots are reading their maps and calculating the times and doing "that pilot stuff," the WSOs are "tweaking" their radars, adjusting the electronics and manually fine tuning their old equipment to better search for hostile aircraft. The F-4's pulse radar didn't have the ground clutter rejection capability that the F-16 and 15 have. It showed everything that was "solid," be it a mountain or airplane or thick flock of birds. So, the WSOs must finesse and cajole their antiquated black boxes to get the most from them and to be able to decipher the difference between geese migrating to a summer home or bandit aircraft intent upon shooting us down. They must also know the strengths and weaknesses of their own equipment, and the enemy's, to capitalize on the situation. And when they do suspect they have acquired an enemy aircraft on their radar, they will direct the flight to either turn left or right, off the center of the low-level corridor, to avoid that threat, thus compounding the pilot's navigational problem. The WSOs, too, in addition to checking their radars and visually checking six, are also helping to navigate and keep abreast of the flight's progress.

Because each aircraft had its own radar and pilot and WSO and bombs and air-to-air missiles and twenty-millimeter, cannon it was its own military arsenal with pilot and WSO trusting that the other would perform their respective duties with 110 percent of their ability. If either guy lets his performance slip, it could mean the difference between life or death. We were a team that was so finely honed that one word could have much meaning. We listened to the radio, and each other, with prejudice and spoke only for the express purpose of accomplishing a specific task.

And beginning with this single aircraft, you add two and then four, or more, and you now have a machine, a formidable war machine, in the singular, that is moving en masse to its destination. And if attacked, this machine can defend itself and if it loses a part of itself, it can still continue and it can split up and divide to survive to continue to its target. Like a column of ants on a mission, you can step on some, but their independent nature allows the others to doggedly continue on their quest, undaunted, deviating if need be, but unstoppable. However, unlike an ant, the F-4, now being more like a bee, had a sting to it; trying to swat it could extract a certain measure of pain.

The goal of this "machine" was to destroy whatever it was ordered to destroy, and the sheer beauty of the land that we were flying over went unnoticed in our singular design to accomplish our goal. The mountains were noticed, not because of their beauty, but by the question, "Is that my turn point?" Or, is there an enemy aircraft lurking behind that mountain? Old ghost towns passed underneath, the sounds of the spirits in them drowned out by the scream of afterburning wagons and the voices of still living souls in them, urging their fire-propelled chariots on to distant lands.

As hard as it may seem for the lead aircraft, in this case today my WSO and me, who were navigating for the whole flight of twelve, the trailing fighters, spaced every one and a half to two miles behind each other in pairs of two, have the difficult task of trying to maintain a "visual" on the aircraft in front of them. They curse the purple mountains' majesties, as they compound their problem of trying to keep track of the preceding fighter, as well as possibly hiding a bandit aircraft or two. As the lead aircraft flies a sinewy flight path through the mountains trying to terrain mask, so too do the trailing aircraft try to fly the same terrain-matching profile. But at times the visual between the leaders and the trailers is lost and the trailing aircraft "DRs" where he thinks the preceding aircraft is. It could be a nerve-wracking wait, guessing, hoping, and sometimes praying your leader would come into sight. In the meantime, the pilots and WSOs in the trailing aircraft are assessing their maps and compasses and clocks and radar and the sky and the ground to check on their progress to the target and for any sign of hostile aircraft.

It must be understood that all the pilots in all the aircraft had the innate responsibility (innate because it was in a pilot's personal code of ethics, or should have been) to know where he was on the low level so that if his lead should either crash or have to abort the mission, then each aircraft could continue to the target. Also, if the lead had a system failure of some kind, he may pass the navigation lead to another aircraft, his wingman for example, so knowing where you were, at all times was essential for your situational awareness. However, if you were over hostile territory and your wingman aborted, had to go back to base, then you went with him. In the USAF, the basic, or minimum, fighting force consisted of two aircraft, which was called an element; formations of twenty to 100 fighter aircraft or more were built upon this two-aircraft concept. Visual mutual support was of paramount importance in those days, and having each aircraft flying a line abreast formation, even as a two-ship, offered both aircraft the ability to maneuver and visually watch over each other. As the Ice Man said in Top Gun, "You never leave your wingman."

Wingmen, who are flying abreast of their leaders, flew on one side, or the other, of their leader, and would try to maintain a 6000- to 12,000-foot line-abreast position. As their lead maneuvers through a canyon or mountainous area, he/she might "close it up," bring their aircraft closer than normal to their leader, to maintain better mutual support. If the flight was approaching a ridgeline running perpendicular, or almost so, to its flight-path, the wingman would look for a low-point, or saddleback, as would lead, to fly through. Just before reaching the top of the opening of the ridge, each aircraft would roll inverted, and the pilots would begin to pull the aircraft down so as to conform to the mountain(s) and not fly too excessively high above the surrounding terrain. There are times where you are "pulling" through a notch and all that you can see to the left, right and "above" (remember . . . you are upside down) are hard, impact-resistant boulders, and maybe you are fifty feet away from them as you flash by at 500 knots . . . all the time "pulling" the aircraft "down" to conform to the mountain's contour. Over a wide alkaline valley or above a plateau, or any expanse of flat earth, assuming good visibility, the wingman will fly wide of their lead, spreading the formation out, so as to not highlight both aircraft if there is an enemy lurking about looking for flashes of sunlight off of a canopy or a shiny wing of a fighter as it maneuvers. The wingman has a tough job, for he is literally trying to "hang on" to his lead, and in the process of "hanging on," he is also navigating and visually checking the formation for enemy aircraft and trying to spot any aircraft flying low level in front of him, so as to avoid a collision within the formation, and in general, the wingman is trying to maintain mutual support. In the purest form of flight lead-wingman covenants, his sole job is to keep a visual with his lead and fly off that lead while trying to have a clue as to where he is on the low level. Often the inexperienced pilot's situational awareness was so out to lunch (screwed up!) that he didn't realize he was at the target area until lead was popping up in preparation to drop his bombs or was dropping them!

Approaching the target, the WSOs search their radar with even more conviction and the pilots readied their bombs for release by selecting switches that tell the aircraft which bombs you want to drop, in what millisecond interval, and then setting the master arm switch to "arm." Additionally, in-between performing all the aforementioned navigation and formation maintaining and bandit lookout duties, the crews rechecked the attack plan with its associated headings, times, airspeeds and bomb delivery parameters, as well as reminding oneself of what the specific target is. (When a large target area, such as an airfield, is to be bombed, individual targets on the airfield are singled out, such as aircraft parked on the ramp or fuel storage tanks. The mission frag is what identifies the target complex and the DMPIs on it (Desired Mean Point of Impact... the individual targets), but it is up to the mission commander to determine who bombs what, and in certain cases, special ordnance is requested for specific targets, such as cratering bombs when bombing a runway.)

On this particular day, my twelve-ship was attacked from behind by two F-16s, which caused the four trailing aircraft in my flight to perform a 180-degree turn to defend themselves and to try and bring some weapons to bear on the attackers. And then two more F-16s "tapped," pounced upon, the other four German aircraft! In short order, it was like a mini Battle of Britain with aircraft everywhere! Break turn calls were heard on the radio, aircraft were calling shots on the bandits, and the bandits were calling kills on the good guys. And as if this wasn't enough excitement, the surface-to-air missile sites were locking their radars onto the F-4s with the intent to shoot them down.

So, in addition to the constant radio chatter of the other aircraft and the intercom communications between you and your WSO, you also had the "bell and whistle" sounds emanating from the radar, warning receivers telling you that enemy radars, either from an aircraft or surface-to-air missile site, were looking at you.

Through all the chaos and mayhem that occurred as we neared the target, my wingman and I made it, seemingly unscathed, so far.

Because I had been turning so much enroute to the target, due to the hard reality of the bandits behind me and the paranoid calls from the WSOs in my lead four-ship who were seeing "mirages" with every sweep of the radar, I had gotten considerably off course. Believing the enemy behind me was either dead or satisfied with its meal of German F-4s and not coming after my four-ship, and ignoring the delusions of WSOs calling for turns when my WSO had no target in sight, I made a sharp left turn to a rather prominent mountain that was at my ten o'clock position and about twenty miles away. This mountain was a get-well point for me and immediately gave me total SA (Situational Awareness) as to where I was. Believing that no more F-16s existed in the world, but still not sure about the F-15s' whereabouts, I increased our speed to make up for lost time. In a little over two minutes, I was in a right turn, rounding the north side of this rather tall mountain, when my WSO said he had a radar contact on a possible bandit!

We had been flying at an uneven 100 feet above the ground due to undulating terrain and were zipping along at 500 knots. We were about halfway through the turn when the WSO said he had a radar contact. We were pretty low to the ground and turning at fairly high G, so I can't say I was looking too far in front of me since I really didn't want to hit the ground, so my bandit lookout wasn't as detailed as it should have been at that point. We were also about two minutes from our target, and I was getting ready for the bomb run, so you can imagine that the bandit call from my WSO as we were turning around the mountain really caught my attention!

I briefly looked inside the cockpit at the radar (normally, the WSO tells you where the bandit is verbally, so all you have to do is look to the position where he is directing your eyes, but since I had been looking in the cockpit, briefly, to check my map, as I was going outside with my eyes, I glanced at the radar scope to save the WSO some words) for the relative position of the target—the front cockpit of the F-4 has a radar scope—and then looked outside to where I thought the bandit was. Sure enough, there was another F-16 . . . man, the USAF sure bought a lot of them! He was about three miles away, a thousand feet or so higher than us, and in a fairly hard (turning rapidly but not at the maximum capability of the aircraft) right-hand turn, but his turn was taking him through a nose-on position where he was about to go belly up to me! My WSO was screaming for me to shoot a missile, particularly since he was locked on to the "Viper" (nickname of the F-16).

We were loaded with two radar-guided AIM-7Es and two heat-seeking AIM-9Ps. In reality we had "simulated ordnance." In place of the AIM-7 missiles were AIM-7 plugs that told the aircraft's weapons system an AIM-7 was loaded in one of four AIM-7 weapons stations. The AIM-9s were a bit different. We had four AIM-9 stations, two on each wing, but we did carry a full-size AIM-9P missile, sans warhead and rocket motor. The seeker, though, which gave guidance commands to the missile's autopilot, was there. That was required because we needed to know if the missile was "seeing" the heat source of the intended target and the only way to know that was to have an actual seeker on a dummy missile. When the seeker head "saw" the heat source from the hot exhaust of a jet engine it would emit a growl-type noise that we heard through our intercom, so when you armed up the system, you saw, via your weapons panel, two AIM-7s—we had two "plugs" on this aircraft—and one AIM-9P (we limited ourselves to two AIM-9P shots). When you "fired" your missile, the system "stepped" automatically to the next loaded AIM-7 station, or went right back to the AIM-9 if that missile had been selected.

My missile of choice while flying that low was the heat-seeking AIM-9P, but the F-16 was coming straight at me, and the AIM-9s we had were not all aspect, meaning I couldn't shoot him while he was nose on to me. I needed more of a tail aspect; however, the more he turned, the sweeter the shot got. I was very low, so I had to climb a bit to fire the AIM-7. (An AIM-7 is kicked off the bottom of the aircraft and drops a bit before the rocket motor fires, about forty-eight inches. While it doesn't need more than twenty-five feet for this whole process, I always felt that a couple of hundred feet was better than 100.)

I "fired" (I pulled the trigger, but obviously, no actual missile came off!) one AIM-7 and waited as the F-16 continued his right-hand turn. My WSO and I continued to close in and with about a mile separating us, and with him heading away from me, I switched to "heat" on the weapons control panel. With a good look-up angle—his aircraft was framed by only the blue sky—I put the AIM-9's seeker head aiming reticle, which is illuminated on the front windscreen of the F-4, on the target. The growl from the AIM-9 was instantaneous, like a wild child being held back by a parent. I waited a second, there was no warbling of the tone, and then squeezed the trigger to let the little varmint loose. The hunted had killed the hunter.

There were rules of thumb that we used to determine if we had killed this or that bandit, based upon the distance, altitude, and speed. On the F-4 we didn't have a heads-up display [HUD] or any VCR tape recording the actual shot. We could record, using an onboard VCR recorder, the radar scope image, to verify the radar lock-on, and the VCR tape also recorded the intercom communications as well as transmissions from the UHF radio and the RHAW's audio emissions. In addition, the VCR tape recorded the sound of the AIM-9's seeker head growl as it tracked the heat source from the target. Finally, in some cases, like in Red Flag wars, when an aircraft took a missile shot, a signal was sent to the Red Flag computers, and they computed, based upon actual archived missile shots and the parameters of the aircraft and their weapons systems and the missiles they were shooting, as to whether or not the shot was a kill. In the end, though, nothing was absolute, and unless the missiles really started flying, you had no idea if your missile shot[s] would have been good or not.

After the kill, there was no time for a victory roll or a celebration yell because just as the missiles had timed out and my backseater and I called a kill, to record on the tapes and also to let GCI (Ground Controlled Intercept) know of the kill, our RHAW lit up with video and audio.

RHAW—Radar Homing And Warning. Ever since the latter stages of the Vietnam War, and due to the widespread use of SAMs, fighter aircraft were being fitted with onboard receivers that told the pilot and WSO if a SAM radar was either tracking them and/or had shot a missile at them. The early RHAW gear was very basic but quickly became very sophisticated and included the ability to detect airborne radar from other fighter aircraft. On my F-4 that day, we had an ALR-46 RHAW set. When a new/different ground radar began to track us it gave what we called "new guy" audio, beeping about three times to say, "Hey, someone new is looking at you!" You'd check the RHAW gear to see what the beeping was about and from what direction the radar was located. To find this direction, you looked on a smallish, round CRT visual display mounted, on the F-4, just on the forward, upper right of both cockpits. A symbol for the type of SAM, SA-2, 3, 4, 6, 8, etc., would illuminate at that position on the scope relative to the actual o'clock position of the missile site, and the distance that the symbol was from the center of the scope was the "black box's" best guess on its relative range. What would really get your attention with the RHAW system was a missile launch. When certain missiles were launched, that bad boy (ALR-46) would detect it and start howling! There was no doubt about the launch unless you had the volume for the system turned down and even then your backseater would be screaming at you to maneuver to either break the radar's lock or cause the missile to miss. Additionally, the system, as I said earlier, could detect the radars from other fighter aircraft, as well as our own. So, if an F-16 locked on to you, you knew it! The F-15 was different. In certain modes, the explanation of which exceeds what I want to convey in this story, you could not tell if they were locked on to you, and when you could, it usually meant that they had already shot a missile . . . not good.

Since I had highlighted myself by coming out of the low altitude environment (if you can call 300 feet above the ground highlighting yourself), a SAM site had locked us up and was about to fire! The "new guy" audio yell in my ears of the SAM site's missile tracking radar locking us up was unmistakable, as was the symbol indicating what type of missile it was on my radar warning receiver's scope. In addition to the type of SAM, its relative position, and estimate of range were also indicated on the radar warning display. The RHAW showed the offending site was at my twelve o'clock. I immediately asked the backseater to "drop"—actually it is ejected—chaff, (*Chaff…very tiny bits of varying length and very thin fiberglass rods, coated with metal. The chaff cartridges are a bit bigger that 12 gage shotgun shells and when fired the cartridge explodes, scattering the hundreds, if not thousands, bits of rods behind the jet. The varying lengths of rods is for deceiving varying frequencies of radars. The puff of the rods blooms quickly behind the jet and is intended to cause a radar to either break its radar lock on the fighter, or two cause the radar operator to think there is more then one aircraft…it's not very effective on pulse doppler radars)* and I started a very hard left-hand descending turn. At 300 feet above the ground, I can't say I descended too rapidly, but I had to turn to put the missile site at my three or nine o'clock. In this case I turned left to put it on my right side, and I wanted to get low to try and terrain mask. *(Terrain Masking—there are two types of terrain masking: direct and indirect. Besides dispensing chaff, another way to try and defeat a missile tracking radar, or, well any radar site that was trying to find or track you, was to hide behind the ground, or buildings . . . if there were any big ones nearby. Usually, mountains were the best, as they were the highest; hills would work, too, anything with vertical development that you could put between your aircraft and the radar. Indirect terrain masking was the opposite; you put vertical development "behind/next-to" you, but you wanted to be close to it. In other words, you put yourself on the nearside of the mountain but still used the mountain as a "noisy" backdrop to camouflage your aircraft from the radar. With newer radar sites, which have pulse Doppler radar*

or have moving target indicators, indirect terrain masking is not nearly as
effective as direct.)

I wanted to get the missile to the beam (beam, meaning put the
missile directly at my three or nine o'clock position) so I could see it
and then maneuver against it. As I got the missile site on my beam,
I saw a "Smokey Sam" going up in the air; it looked to be about four
miles away. I headed for the dirt when I saw the missile as I knew the
SA-3 was good down to 100 feet, and I intended to "blend" with the
local vegetation . . . of which, seeing that I was flying over a desert,
there wasn't much. There was a fundamental rule when flying near the
ground though, that I never forgot as I neared it. The "PK"—probability of kill—of hitting the ground at 500 knots was almost 100
percent. As I said earlier, I know a couple of guys who had brought
that statistic down to 99.5 or so, but I was never one to want to screw
with trying to change a statistical model. Also, the odds of the missile
not hitting me, based upon my maneuvering and other factors, was a
much safer bet, so I wasn't going to kill myself for the sake of worrying
about being on the "evening news," however you looked at it.

Beam. The idea was to "beam" the missile, put it on your left of right
wing's side, pop chaff to confuse the tracking radar, and then start
maneuvering up or down—fighter pilots call it using the vertical—
to try and get the missile to miss your aircraft. Your goal was to get
the missile to miss your aircraft . . . the farther the better since the
warheads in some missiles were pretty big. The earlier missiles, SA-2,
3, 4, were fairly easy to out-maneuver . . . assuming you saw them.
However, the older missiles were big, relatively speaking, and their
booster motors [for initial launch] and sustainer rocket motors [to
give them range] made a lot of flame and smoke. The SA-6 and 8

were newer missiles and were more difficult to both see and deceive. But as I was saying, if you could get the missile going up, and then you go down, or vice versa, and you did this a couple of times, you got the missile out of sync with your movements and sometimes the missile would tumble out of control, or the radar, because of chaff, may break lock and the missile "went stupid." At the least, you hoped the missile would miss you by a lot, and then you could be on your way. However, the enemy usually shot more than one missile and then may shoot from more than one missile site! You could have your hands full if you were the target of a couple of SAM sites! Sometimes, you carried a jamming pod that would jam either the enemy's tracking radar, acquisition radar, or missile guidance up-link. When they worked they worked well, these jammers, but they weren't a panacea, and they had their limitations.

As I neared the ground, I turned my tail away from the missile site and continued in a hard left turn.

Non-pilots have often asked me how I turn at so low an altitude . . . do I look at the instruments, the VVI (vertical velocity indicator), the artificial horizon indicator—what? At very low altitude, where hitting any obstacle is a very real and immediate threat, my eyes are glued to the outside world, specifically in the direction in which I am turning. I judged altitude based upon experience, occasional looks at the radar altimeter, relative motion of the ground (going by the size of vegetation/dwellings, which in itself can be dangerous). When you're pulling five Gs at low altitude and turning, and covering three football fields in a second, you need to look into your turn to make sure you will clear any terrain you might be turning into, so it is imperative to keep your eyes outside. Also, you need to clear the sky in front of you to make sure you don't hit another aircraft, be it your wingman, another friendly, or a bandit, smacking any of the aforementioned could definitely ruin your day. Finally, while turning, you had to be very careful where you put your lift vector. In a turn you could easily develop very high descent rates, so you had to be careful to not over-bank for too long, or else that too could ruin your day.

It is hard to imagine, as you read this, the environment that you are in when all of this is going on. My WSO and I were turning at five times the force of gravity, 5 Gs, all the while as the ground was moving by in a blur at 840 feet per second about 100 feet below. While turning at such a low altitude and trying to avoid the rocks so as to not make spam out of the WSO and me, I was looking for landmarks so as to get us back on course and get to the target. And, adding even more stress, I was looking for enemy aircraft and other SAM sites not to mention looking for my wingman. I could have pulled more than 5Gs if I needed to, but with the bombs and fuel, etc., pulling more could have over-G'd the aircraft, depleted my airspeed/energy state, or both. Nope, 5Gs was the norm for that kind of maneuvering, unless of course you had to do what it took to save yourself/aircraft/both.

The WSO too was looking for the wingman and visually checking for bandit aircraft in addition to using his radar to scan the area ahead and to the left and right as we turned.

Sweat was dripping from the top of my helmet, just above my eyes and I raised my visor to wipe the saline solution before it stung my eyes and made seeing more difficult; however, the eyes are not the only sense that was being assaulted.

My ears were acutely aware of any audio emanations from the earphones built into my helmet. I remember hearing my second element, numbers 3 and 4, call "split" over the radio as I maneuvered against the SAM site, meaning they are not being attacked and are continuing on the low level to the target, thusly leaving my number 2 man and myself to fight our own way out—that's a "standard" for most missions, nothing cowardly about that, and I expected his call as soon as I started fighting against the missile. I was definitely spring-loaded for any new guy audio sounds from the RHAW gear . . . not wanting any! Also, I heard GCI broadcasting in the blind that there were bandits just west of bull's eye and moving east. Finally, as if the previous "decibel deluge" wasn't enough, my WSO was telling me the SA-3 site's radar had broken lock and that the "IP"—initial point, the last point on the low-level from which the bomb run begins—was in the INS.

I didn't consciously notice the extra weight of five bodies on me as I held my head slightly forward and tilted so as to look in the direction in which I was turning; after flying fighters for a couple of years, you get used to pulling Gs. In fact, I kinda missed the "feeling" when I hadn't flown in a while.

I continued my turn to head toward the south, toward where I thought the IP was located. The SA-3 site was now at my six o'clock, moving to seven, and we were still at very low altitude, since I didn't want to become the poster boy for the SAM missile sites in the area. And all the while, as I continued this turn, I was dodging small hills and big rocks at almost 600 mph. I continued the turn to aim where I visually "thought" we should be heading and as I rolled wings level, to my surprise, I saw my wingman in perfect line abreast tactical formation!

After 200 miles of flying a twisty low level and flying in valleys and canyons; over mountains and hills; after performing defensive break turns to avoid being shot by surface to air missiles; after speeding up to 600 knots and then slowing down to 400 knots; with all of this maneuvering being done with very little consideration for my wingman and without a single whine from him over the radio, there he was, my number 2 man, in a perfect line abreast position for the attack. Awesome.

I just needed to make sure I was headed in the right direction for the attack! Quickly checking my map, I confirmed that the edge of the small hill, next to the dry lake bed with a dirt road coming from its northern "shore" was indeed the IP. I then looked at the clock in the aircraft to make sure we weren't too early or late for the attack. I had hacked the clock at the start of the low level and was referencing it for total time on the low level. If we were too early we would have done a big 360-degree orbit to kill time and if too late, well, we had a "dump target"—a backup target that was more lightly defended than the primary . . . a.k.a. desert—and we would have proceeded to bomb it.

Amazingly enough, as we overflew the IP, I glanced at the INS distance-to-go window and it showed us two miles off, which wasn't too shabby given the older technology.

With my wingman in position for the attack, about a mile to my immediate right, I proceeded to stabilize our ground speed at 540 knots, the speed planned for our bomb release. We also had to "climb" to 200 feet above the ground, as this was our delivery altitude: we were dropping six parachute-retarded bombs, military designation BSU-49, from a level delivery (The BSU-49/Mk-82 drag unit/bomb combination was used to deliver 500-pound bombs from very low altitude. When the bomb is released, a wire on the aircraft pulls an arming wire on the bomb fuse, arming it, and another wire pulls a release for the "drag chute" [ballute]. This ballute quickly slows the bomb to provide safe separation between the delivery aircraft and the exploding bomb). A quick glance at my thigh, upon which sat a piece of paper—in fighter pilot lingo we called it a "lineup" card— which had, among other things, my bombing parameters and target info. Looking at the card reaffirmed my own memory of our targets (aircraft parked on the airfield ramp) and reassured me that my flight was indeed heading for the correct target area, and, lastly, was in the proper position for the attack.

Once on the target run, a lot of attention is paid to being exactly on parameters, which requires flying the correct airspeed, radar altitude, and drift angle. You want to destroy the target on the first pass and do not want to come back tomorrow, or worse yet, not get your bombs off on the first pass and have to reattack (if a reattack was briefed).

Reattacks were "bad" as the enemy now was wide awake, if they weren't on your first pass, and if one of your wingmen got some bombs off, they were most likely pretty pissed off that you were bombing them, and I am pretty certain they would want a piece of you and your WSO's butts.

WSOs were of supreme help during those vulnerable seconds on the bomb run as they kept a visual lookout for enemy aircraft and SAM launches. Up until the actual release of the bombs, if you had to save your aircraft, or flight, from attack, you would do so . . . you had to stay vigilant!

That day, the actual IP to target run was almost uneventful, given the hell we had to fly through just to get here. Flying as well as I could to maintain the aforementioned bombing parameters, I would alternately look at the airspeed, radar altimeter, and bombing reticle, which is a red illuminated circle with a little dot (pipper) in the middle of it. This reticle is projected onto a slanted piece of thick glass, "combining glass," and is directly in front of your face, but over the instrument panel, and right behind/below the front part of the canopy. Looking out the front windscreen/canopy I could see both the pipper and the ground beyond it. I let the pipper run along the ground, and when it touched the target, assuming my airspeed, altitude and aircraft pitch attitude are correct, I released the bombs via a "pickle" button on the flight control stick. On the weapons release panel, before takeoff, I set the bomb fall interval so as to allow fifty feet spacing between each bomb impact. Thusly, when I "hit" the pickle button I needed to hold it for a couple of seconds as the bombs release in microsecond intervals and if you release the pickle button too early then all of your bombs my not drop-off (you can actually feel the bombs as they thunk off the bomb carrying ejector racks).

Between my wingman and I, we dropped twelve bombs on an "enemy" airfield. My bombs landed on an airfield ramp loaded with aircraft, and number 2's bombs were dropped on some ops buildings. According to my timing, all the bombs were released within our TOT window (Time Over Target). There was not another aircraft or Smokey SAM in sight as we screamed along at 200 feet and 600 mph over the targets, disgorging our venom.

Once the bombs were released though, we weren't home free yet!

I went into "min" afterburner—that's when you see flames coming out the back of the jet engine's tailpipe, purposeful flames that is, not your "Holy crap, I'm on fire!" flames—accelerated to six hundred knots plus, so as to quickly exit the immediate target area, and turned the flight to the egress heading.

We were now only a two ship. As crowded as the skies had just been, they were now empty, but listening to the number of bandit calls on the radio, it was obvious to my WSO and I that there were still plenty of bandit aircraft in the area.

We had exited the target area to the southeast, initially, and were still in the western areas of the Nellis range complex. I had Beatty VORTAC tuned into the TACAN receiver and was headed for it when we caught up to a lone RF-4 from who knows where. (The RF-4 was built for one purpose—to take pictures of potential targets, take after-strike photos of targets that should have been bombed, and snap pictures of various other things that the higher ups wanted photographed. They were generally faster than bomber F-4s because they were more aerodynamically sleek and they were lighter.) We were flying at about 300 feet AGL and the RF-4 was slightly higher and about three miles in front of us. My WSO locked onto the aircraft with our radar and with that, the "RF" lit his afterburners, dropped down to less than 100 feet AGL, and literally left us in the dust! Garry, my heretofore unnamed backseater, and I were laughing our butts off, thinking how much we must have scared that guy when an F-15 locked onto us from our six o'clock; now it was us who were scared!

After my call to the wingman to push it up due to a bandit RHAW strobe at our six o'clock, Garry spotted an F-15 about two miles or so behind us, quite a bit higher and not closing which wasn't surprising since we were accelerating past 650 knots and low enough to scorch the desert cacti with the heat from our afterburners. In conjunction with increasing our speed and descending, number 2 spread out even wider on me in order to make the bandit commit to just one of us.

We were only chased for a minute, at most, when the Eagle pulled up and turned away and since we did not hear a shot or kill call from GCI we figured we had not been shot. As before, after the initial flurry of activity it got quiet on the radios and once again we, our flight of two, was alone.

After the Eagle left us I switched our flight to a different working frequency so we could talk, if we had to, in private.

With 140 miles to go to the base, according to the INS, we were back in "good guy" territory and since I didn't expect any more threats attacking us I told my wingman to go chase and with that call he dropped into a one mile trail position. We had some extra fuel to burn so I decided to enjoy the morning and told number 2 we were going to do some sightseeing.

A southeast-northwest running set of mountains stood tall, as we approached them rapidly from the north, their chiseled crests illuminated by the undiluted rays of a desert sun still well below its zenith. As soon as I cleared the mountains I turned hard right, flew for a few miles and then cranked in a hard left turn and entered Death Valley.

I was favoring the west side of the valley and had slowed the formation to a rather sedate 400 knots indicated when I spotted a couple of large RVs a few miles ahead. I decided to give them a close visual inspection so I pushed the throttles up to military power as we approached at very low altitude As I got right over top of them I rolled on a knife edge and looked down. I saw four people standing side by side, looking up and waving! We, were smoking along at close to 600 mph so even though my F-4 passed overhead in relative silence, just a short distance behind me, and furiously trying to catch up, was the absolute shrill scream of a Phantom in near full grunt! As my wingman passed over the same two couples he said they had their hands over their ears but were smiling!

After the RV encounter, we flew over "Skidoo," an abandoned gold mine and from where the term "23 Skidoo" comes (twenty-three miles was the length of the aqueduct that brought water to this old desert ghost town and mine area).

From Skidoo we continued south with the Panamint mountains just to our right. Before crossing into Panamint Valley, I decided to fly near the tops of the mountains just for the heck of it. As I cruised along, admiring the view all around me, I would occasionally see a little spot of trees and plants, nestled in tight little rock folds near the peaks. In contrast to the aridity of the valley floor, these mountain redoubts were like little ecological islands unto themselves. With their green vegetation and tiny streams, they looked so inviting and cozy and yet, owing to their remoteness above the valley floor, I suspect the only visitors to these sanctuaries were less than human. I have always been fascinated by these nature hideouts, and I swear that one day, I will visit one of these "castle keeps" of nature.

After admiring the Panamint Mountains, I took us into the same named valley barely clearing the mountain peaks as we dropped into the narrow and very flat valley. What number 2 did behind us as we were sightseeing I have no idea. Occasionally I would glimpse him in the mirrors, or Garry would make mention of his position as he maneuvered from side to side.

Eventually the valley played out and with fuel now getting low, I climbed the formation to a few thousand feet and slowed down to 300 knots so my wingman could join up in preparation for recovery at George AFB. Coming up initial, we pitched out over the numbers and flew as tight an overhead pattern as we dared; my wingman and I were the first of the twelve to return.

During the mission debrief, we learned that six F-4s had been killed and that four F-16s had been shot; though in reality, unless real missiles are flying those "electronic" kills are always taken with a grain of salt. The one F-15 that chased me, after coming off the target, couldn't get close enough to shoot before his fuel supply got too low. The optical scorers, who scored the bombing accuracy, indicated that 60 percent of the bombs were on target and all bombs were dropped within the TOT window. As for the lone RF-4, no one knows who he was or where he came from. Finally, the SA-3 site that engaged me as I approached the target said that between my maneuvering, chaff, and indirect terrain masking, the odds were less than 10 percent of a successful guide by the missile.

That night at the bar the Germans were buying. They had passed their fighter weapons course, and they were going back to the fatherland. All in all, it was a good mission, a great mission in fact. We went in, hit the target, and yeah, we "lost" a few airplanes, but considering the difference in technology between the F-4 and the wonder jets, we should have been decimated. Instead, we "shot down" a few of the F-16s and due to the wisdom of deviating "a bit" when coming off the target, the F-15s were hard pressed to catch us.

I'll never forget that flight. It represented what flying the F-4 was all about—tough, macho (this was the '80s and "macho" was still in vogue), and with a street fighting mentality. We busted our butts to fly well, and we loved every minute of it. As much as I sweated, I'd sweat some more, and I loved it more. The Phantom was the last of the stick-and-rudder airplanes, and the kinship that I had with my backseaters will never be replaced. At 500 knots and 100 feet, he trusted me with his life, and I trusted him when he would tell me my "six" was clear or scan the area ahead with his radar.

I often wonder, "What is the measure of a man?" Is it by what he does? What he did? Or is it by what he thinks and feels, or what is in his spirit or soul? Everyone has his own answer. One of my favorite sayings about this is from Martin Luther King Jr., who said, "The ultimate measure of a man is not where he stands in moments of comfort and convenience, but where he stands at times of challenge and controversy."

There is no doubt that Rick Henry had faced many difficult trials and challenges while flying fighters. And though time's march and life's unpredictable erosions have taken Rick out of the cockpit, the memory of his valor and devotion in those trying times didn't go unnoticed by me in class that day, and no matter what distance we may be from "where we have been," in both time and/or geographical miles, what the heart holds dear is never very far from us and the examples we have set.

The Hero

Many years ago I got the chance to fly with a true hero. Steve Lawrence was my First Officer on a fourteen-day international trip with our airline and which hopped around the Far East. Before getting in the airlines, Steve was a teenager and Warrant Officer in the Army, flying in Vietnam as a Huey gunship pilot.

We began our trip in Memphis, operating the dreaded red eye flight to Anchorage. With a refreshing overnight's stay in beautiful Alaska, we then blasted off and pressed on to Tokyo the next day. As we flew westward, taking the short way to get to the Far East, Steve totally captivated, amazed, and fascinated me with his stories of combat flying the Huey gunship in Vietnam. With 2 tours under his belt, he was able to fill the sky miles to Tokyo with remarkably dangerous close encounters of the Vietcong and North Vietnamese Regular Army kind. The most amazing story he told was one in which he was nominated for the CMH, Congressional Medal of Honor, the highest military award possible in the United States Armed Forces.

Steve's most harrowing adventure in Vietnam actually occurred in Cambodia, although the Army doesn't want to admit that. On this day, during the waning days of both Steve's second tour and the

Vietnam war, the American and Vietnamese forces entered Cambodia with the intention to stop the flow of North Vietnamese Regulars (professional army soldiers of North Vietnam, vice the VC, which were Southern Vietnamese partisans) from using Cambodia as a safe haven for the build-up of war fighting supplies and the massing of North Vietnamese troops. Steve's flight of 4 Huey's were tasked to fly cover for medevac helicopters that were being used to evacuate wounded American ground troops that were actively engaged with North Vietnamese troops in a small village on the border of Cambodia and South Vietnam. As the day's combat unfolded a Huey Gunship was shot down near a small village that was occupied by North Vietnamese Regulars. The helicopter crashed in a rice patty and very near the hamlet. All four of the crew were unscathed in the initial crash but were hopelessly pinned down by withering and unrelenting small arms fire coming from the village. There was one narrow and elevated (above the rice patties) dirt road that led due east out of the village and the downed helicopter was on the southern side of this road. On the north side of the road there too was another rather expansive rice patty. The boys in the downed helicopter had little to no protection and had to stay low to keep from being shot.

Steve told one of the medevac helicopters to go in and land on the small road and pick-up the downed crew while Steve and the other gunships provided cover. The medevac pilot refused. In fact not one medevac helicopter would attempt the pick-up stating that it was too dangerous and that they too would get shot down.

With that pronouncement and forgetting his own safety Steve said he would get the guys. On his first and second attempts he was unsuccessful if only because the crew from the stricken helicopter couldn't get to Steve's chopper because the small arms fire from the village was so accurate, intense, and non-stop, they dared not run in the open to reach it. After the second pick-up attempt Steve and his boys lifted off and came around yet again for a third attempt. As Steve approached the other two gunships provided as much covering fire into the village as they could muster. The dirt road that led east from the village was so narrow that Steve could put only put one skid on the path while the other was over the rice patty, hence Steve actually had to hover while waiting for the downed crewmen to climb aboard the chopper. This time the pinned downed boys, figuring they'ed die if they didn't chance it, literally ran for their lives through the rice patty. With bullets splashing in the shallow water all around them they finally reached Steve and clambered onto his helicopter. Steve said the small arms fire was pelting his helicopter as if he was in a hail storm, which he really was, but the lead kind. Finally, the last man getting to the helicopter jumped onto the Huey's skid as it lifted off, with the copilot reaching out the door and holding the man by one of his arms and clothes.

As they flew eastward away from harm, they took stock of themselves and not one of man was hit by a bullet or shrapnel. God was providing the ultimate in protective cover that day.

The helicopter however was not so lucky, taking the brunt of the battle. It was written off as destroyed because of so many bullet holes and the fact that one of the skids collapsed upon landing, causing the chopper to roll onto its side while the blades were still turning. But the war horse protected its crew at the expense of itself, just as Steve was willing to do with himself for the downed crew.

While the previous battle was probably the magnum opus of Steve's Vietnam days, it was just one of many exciting stories this amazing man told me as we flew.

A captain once said to me when I was a flight engineer on the DC-10 that I reminded him of Larry King (Talk Show guy) because I asked him and the first officer so many questions about their lives. I guess I am naturally curious of people's past and present lives; in my interrogatories with Steve, I had hit a virtual gold mine.

So, as Steve and I flew further west from Tokyo, again after a night's rest and onto Beijing, I continued my interrogation of this wonderfully humble pilot who has lived a million lives and certainly a cat would be jealous of him since I'm sure Steve has at least 100 lives.

After the Army Steve joined the Coast Guard and there too he encountered harrowing conditions, although in this case it was Mother Nature who was attempting to kill him and not the VC.

Steve said that he felt his time flying helicopters out of southeastern Alaska was even more dangerous than his time in Vietnam. The one example he gave was the time he he got launched at night, dead of winter, out of Ketchikan, Alaska. There was a gale blowing at the time. A fishing boat fairly far off the coast had a severely injured crew member that needed to be evacuated and taken to the hospital.

Upon arriving over the large boat in his helicopter, they dropped a basket to the deck of the boat for the stricken man to be loaded into. Steve said they had to wave off from the boat a few times because the swells were rising and falling so much that there were times that the mast on the vessel was level with his cockpit and then it would drop forty feet lower. All this time though the fishing boat was moving too, so he said they had to time the pick-up to be in sync with the waves and the boat's movement. Now remember, it's pitch dark, gale force winds, rain....I honestly don't know how he did it.

But, after picking the man up, they used so much fuel they couldn't fly directly back to base. With foresight no doubt, the Coast Guard had stashes of fuel, medical supplies, and survival equipment at various locations along the coast for just the reason as Steve's in this case. Flying low, because of the weather, they got to the coast and found one of the emergency caches of the aforementioned and got enough fuel for their return to Ketchikan. The injured fisherman survived.

So now Steve and I are in Beijing, and low and behold in another previous life Steve briefly worked for Boeing and spent a lot of time in China, Beijing being one the cities to which he frequently traveled.

For dinner, the evening after our arrival in China, Steve said instead of eating at some restaurant frequented by expats, he said "let's go feral" and go into an area of Beijing not frequented by Westerners. I said I was always up for an adventure so, off we went. We took a taxi to an area that Steve said he had been into with Chinese businessmen when he worked for Boeing. I did grab a local Beijing map from the concierge before we departed, just as a matter of habit back then.

After being dropped off by the taxi, we walked a short ways into an area of Beijing which I never knew existed and to be honest it was an area in which I wondered if Westerners were even allowed; I mean China is Communist. Steve kept poo pooing my concerns saying I worried too much as we continued walking while Steve tried to find that "magical" restaurant.

And we did. There was not ONE word of English on the menu of this place and not one person could remotely comprehend what we were trying to say. So communication turned to pointy, talky as we looked at the menu which, thank god had pictures of the various food dishes they served. To this day I still have no idea what I ordered and ate. Steve claims he knew what he ordered but I didn't believe him.

Getting something to drink was easier since beer and vodka seem to be universal words in all the world.

As Steve drank his beer and me my vodka tonic, the bartender, (we sat at the bar instead of a table, since the place was so small and full of patrons when we got there) put a shot glass full of some liquid in front of each of us and pointed to a table of four men who were all looking and smiling at Steve and I and yelling "Gombey!!!" (literally means "dry cup" in Chinese... "Cheers" to you and me).

It didn't take a rocket scientist to figure out that the guys bought the drinks for us to drink, but Steve said that we had to "save face" and drink whatever was in the shot glass and then return the favor, ie. buy them drinks. Before going any further, let me inform you back in this period of time almost NO ONE took credit cards for payment in Beijing unless you were at a place frequented by Westerners.

So down the hatch goes whatever crap they were serving up and then I bought the four guys a shot of the same hootch they just served us. Steve thought this was great sport, us yelling "Gombey!" as we bought them drinks, and then they yelling "Gombey!!" as they served us again....and again....and again....etc, etc.

I cannot tell you how many times we went back and forth on this "save face" game of International intrigue and diplomacy as my wallet was rapidly being emptied since there were four of them and two us; liquid assets took on a duality of meanings that night. Finally, the four men got up from the table after they downed the latest round from Steve, and visibly stumbled out the door, waving and smiling as they did. I felt incredibly relieved, victorious, and oh so drunk as they left.

Right. Now Steve's and my turn. I was actually afraid to try and stand, but amazingly enough, my legs did support me and my semicircular canals (used for balance and in the ear area), though embalmed with whatever alcohol we were drinking, did continue to function reasonably well enough to allow me to stately walk out of the restaurant without falling flat on my face.

After getting outside Steve said we needed to flag a taxi to get us back to the hotel. I put my hand in my pocket and pulled out the equivalent of maybe two US dollars. Not near enough to get us across town. Steve had even less.

Drunk, broke, in a foreign city where they barely speak English, and with no clue as to where we were and it was 1 AM….how are we doing so far?

But, then I remembered I had "the map." I pulled that bad boy out of my back pocket and then Steve and I plotted a course back to the hotel. We must have walked for two hours, I'm sure it wasn't nearly a straight line, but we eventually got to the hotel, but to be honest I have no idea how we found it we were both so inebriated. The good news is we had another 30 hours before our next flight so I slept the entire day away.

Arriving in Shanghai on a Saturday evening, and being totally refreshed, it was my call on the dinner venue that night. I chose "The

Big Bamboo" a well known expat place and akin to an American sports bar. It was, thankfully, an uneventful dinner and we weren't challenged with any "Gombeys".

The next morning, Sunday, I woke up early, had breakfast at the hotel buffet and then took a walk. It was a beautiful morning as I decided to walk no where in particular, just to walk for a couple of hours before being picked up in the lobby about mid afternoon for mine and Steve's flight to Hong Kong.

As I walked by a somewhat small building with a storefront that was predominantly windows I saw a few globes in those windows. I always wanted one of them but the ones in the states were always too expensive so I never bought one. Since the globes were probably made in China, I thought I'd take a look at what this store was selling.

The first room I walked into had a few globes for sale. I looked at one and as I did the proprietor of the shop asked me if I wanted buy it. I said, "How much?"

He said, "1200 dollars," I about choked.

"Ahhhh no. I'm good," I said, "too much."

So he says, "How much you pay?"

"250 dollars," I said. I then added that I really wasn't out to buy anything that day, I was just taking a walk.

When I said $250 he choked....Now I can't do the Chinese accent in typing the way he was actually speaking, but think of that accent as you read what follows and that's what I was hearing as he and I went back and forth on this globe.

"I give you special deal, you number one customer, 1000 dollah!"

"Look sir, I don't want it! I'm serious I wasn't out to buy anything today." I said with sincerity.

"No, how much you pay, you first customer, must sell to first customer," he said with conviction.

"250 dollars," I bluntly said, adding, "I'm telling you I don't want it."

"Ha, ha, ha,....you funny man. I give you best price 800 dollah!"

And on it went.....me staying firm at 250 dollars and him complaining I want to pay too little, but since I was the first customer, he needed to sell to me because if he did it meant good luck for that's day's business.

The poor man was beside himself with my intransigence. I would not come off 250 dollars because quite honestly I really wasn't wanting to purchase anything that day but he certainly wanted me to. In the end, he agreed to 250 dollars. He was happy, he made a sale to his first customer of the day and I got a beautiful globe that I always wanted but was too cheap to pay for in America.

The globe was nicely wrapped in styrofoam, put in a box and then put in a easy carry plastic bag.

At showtime in the lobby Steve saw me with the package as we got into the limo for the airport and asked me what I got. I told him about the globe, that I always wanted one and once we got on the aircraft I took it out of it's box and showed it to him. He said he too liked those globes, and then he asked me how much I paid? I said 250 dollars.

At telling him the price Steve starting busting a gut laughing. He said I paid way too much for the globe. I said well they wanted 1200 dollars initially. He said it didn't matter, they always start way high, trying to judge if they have a stooge as a potential customer by the way he bargains. I will admit I was never very good at bargaining. This globe by far, I thought was my best Donald Trump, The Art of the Deal purchase I ever made and I was proud of myself until Steve started, and continued, to diss me, and I mean relentlessly, but in a goodnatured way about how I got ripped off.

We had like seven or eight more days of flying this trip together and every time I lugged that globe between the aircraft and the hotel, and back again, Steve kept asking me if it was getting too heavy for me to carry that overpriced globe. Steve was persistent in his good natured ribbing, but, I was certainly just as determined to not let it affect my belief that I got a good deal and that carrying the globe was not a big deal, and if anything, worth the trouble.

After many more flying miles of listening to Steve's wonderfully exciting helicopter flying life, we ended where we began fourteen days earlier, Memphis. Steve and I parted as friends and I could truly say I was going to miss flying with him as he and I went our separate ways to our abodes. He really made the time between departure and destination "fly by" as he filled the distance traveled with his stories of valor and humor.

Two weeks after Steve and I got back to Memphis from our trip, he called me. I was out having Lunch and I remember it was a Sunday.

I answered the phone. "Yo Steve, what's up?" (I had stored his name and number as a contact in my phone).

"Hey Roger, how's going? How is life in Memphis?" he asked, sounding suspiciously contrite.

"It's good man. Thanks. How's it in Tampa?" I asked back, wondering why he was calling me.

"That was a fun trip wasn't it?" he asked.

"Yeah, it really was, I enjoyed hearing of your life Steve. You really are a true hero, but I gotta say dude, cut the crap, what do you want?" I said laughing.

Then he broke down. "Ok, ya know that globe you. bought? Where was the store you got it from?"

"Why? Why should I tell you? You gave me so much crap about lugging that thing around and the price I paid, why would I tell you?" He knew I was joking.

"Ok. So about an hour ago my wife and I were walking through the mall here and we walk by a store that had one of those globes on display. It looked just like the one you got. As we walked by I casually mentioned to my wife about how you got ripped off in Shanghai when you bought yours. So, she asked me what you paid. I said 250 bucks. She pursed her lips, which is never a good sign for me to see, and then demanded I go check the price of the globe in that store. So I did. I couldn't believe it. 1350 dollars! I never knew. So now she wants one and wants me to get it on my next trip to Shanghai....ca'mon dude, do I have to beg? Where did you buy yours?"

"Ya know Steve, you are my hero, really, I mean that, but there is a certain pleasure in knowing you are eating crow right now given how much crap you gave me after I bought it. So big guy, let me savor the moment for a few minutes. I'll send ya the directions in a few minutes."

And I did. I actually don't know if he ever bought one though.

Epilogue

I can't begin to tell you how humble Steve was about both his Vietnam and Coast Guard experiences. I had to really press him on those years of his life. I can be relentless in asking a person about the intricacies of their life, though I'm not obnoxious about it. My father always said when meeting a person you don't know, always ask them about themselves, people love to talk about themselves and its a great way to break the ice.

When I flew with Steve and though he had been nominated for the CMH, he was not awarded it. Too much to say about that here, but after he and I flew that trip he was eventually awarded the Distinguished Service Cross, the second highest military award you can receive in the military, just below the Medal of Honor. Believe me, if you could have been privy to the stories that Steve told me on those flights, stories I pried out of him, you couldn't help but appreciate the fact that you were in the presence of a bona fide American hero.

Out of Control Phantom

I was just a "Butter Bar" (2nd Lieutenant) in 1981 and going through USAF Pilot Training when I read an article in a military safety magazine, written by some Colonel, about how he almost died one night while flying an aircraft. After all these years I can't remember what type of aircraft the man was flying and for that matter what actually happened other than the moral of his story was that he got complacent and this complacency almost killed him. Since I read a lot of aviation magazines back then and they all had their share of safety talk, I always found it odd that his one story seemed to always make its way into my brain when I went flying. I'm not sure if it's because back then, when I was brand new and an impressionable military internee, that when a Colonel spoke I listened and obeyed, or because the title of the story was "Complacency Kills" and that really made me sit up and take notice or, maybe both of the above.

Now, fast forward to the end of the 80's... I'm listening to Don Henley's song, End of the Innocence, – a song that Henley wrote to sum up the decade, or at least so the DJ says— and as I drive to work on this beautiful late summer morning, I'm thinking about my upcoming F-4 flight. It's a bit of a drive from Ocean City, New Jersey to McGuire AFB, where my Guard Unit is located, but I really don't care as most of the drive is through the country, the "pine barrens" (amazingly enough the South-Central part of the state has a lot of stunted pine tree forests and cranberry bogs) and on whimsically meandering two lane roads. It's actually a nice way to start the day, particularly if you drive a sports car.

I volunteered to take a military leave of absence from my full-time airline job so I could train the newest member of our squadron pilot ranks. Steve O'Neal was just a "butter bar" himself and was trying to get fully qualified in the F-4 before we transitioned to F-16s. Since most F-4 units had been converting to the Viper (the USAF's official name for the F-16 is the Falcon, actually though, amongst the guys who flew it, "Viper" was the more common nickname) the school that trained F-4 pilots closed while Steve was in his last few weeks of a 6 month course. Since I had been an instructor in that F-4 RTU (Replacement Training Unit), located in Wichita, Kansas, and had been qualified to instruct in every phase of the training syllabus, I figured I was a natural candidate to finish Steve's training at his home station and volunteered my services to do such. Evidently the Group Commander thought so too as he more than willingly said he'd cut 6 weeks of active duty orders for me to bring our young "weedhopper" up to war fighting standards. I was really looking forward to taking a break from my monthly airline's schedule of international flying and doing some hard core, full-time fighter flying again. I was living the best of both worlds aviation wise and knew it so I'm not whining. I was also looking forward to Steve's and mine first flight together, particularly since today's flight, our first, had been one of my favorites in the F-4 training syllabus…Advanced Handling.

Normally a green F-4 student would get this Advanced Handling ride relatively early in his (back then it was a males only community) F-4 transition phase of training, but since I had not flown with him before and he needed a couple of warm-up rides to "get his hands back" (he'd been out of the cockpit a couple of weeks shuffling between units and moving) I thought I'd give him a "fun" first ride as a way of saying, "Welcome to the world of fighters!"; as you will see…Steve got a weeeeee bit more than either he, or I, expected.

I arrived in the squadron parking lot, fully refreshed and invigorated from my splendid morning drive, and by coincidence, Steve had arrived at the same time. Since we had met a couple of weeks earlier at a Phantom "Pharewell" party at McConnell AFB in Kansas, our greeting in the parking lot was pretty casual. After attending the morning's mass brief, Steve and I moved to a briefing room to review the flight.

Since he had never flown out of McGuire AFB, I thoroughly briefed him on the standard stuff first: Ground ops, start, taxi, take off, departure and arrival procedures, divert fields and local area orientation. After that we talked about the meat of the mission, advanced handling, F-4 style.

It had been a while since I had actually briefed a green F-4 pilot, so I can't say my brief was as smooth as I think it used to be when I was a seasoned RTU (Replacement Training Unit) Instructor. However, since I was more concerned with what he actually saw in the aircraft, then how I briefed, per se', I considered the brief a mere formality at this point as the real learning was to take place in the wild blue yonder. And with that said, I briefed young Weedhopper on how to do: Loops (both high and low speed), pitch backs and slice backs, hard turns, guns break, slow speed flying and finally, the piece de resistance....my patented vertical zoom climb from 10,000 feet and 500 knots to 30,000 feet and zero knots…it was a real confidence builder!

From the briefing room to the classroom we moved and in no time we were 60 miles off the coast of New Jersey, 15,000 feet up, in "Whiskey 107" (a so designated chunk of military airspace off the Jersey coast in which military aircraft did maneuvers) on an absolutely glorious late summer day. Even though I was in the back seat of the F-4, I was happy to be flying fighters "full-time" again, albeit even if "full-time" meant a few weeks; it was still a nice respite from the globe trotting I'd been doing with my airline. And since it was such a nice day and I was doing what I so loved, I felt it just didn't get any better than this. And while you might think, since I was in the "back" of the F-4, "the pit", it would be lousy duty, it wasn't all that bad. I loved to teach, especially young, new guys, as they had such great attitudes. They were like little birds in the nest chirping, "Feed me…feed me!" (Feed me knowledge, teach me!)

Once we entered the "working area", we had to get right to work as the F-4 wasn't exactly the most fuel efficient of aircraft and we would be using "gas" at a pretty high rate because most of the maneuvers required high power settings so I ran down the laundry list of aerobatic maneuvers fairly quickly in order to cover them all. I wasn't looking for perfection in Weedhopper's flying skill as this was more of a demo and gee whiz ride than anything else. Real learning for everyone comes when the instructor is usually out of the aircraft and you are solo, with a "real" backseater, not an instructor. In the F-4 there were many esoteric nuances when it came to maneuvering the aircraft well in battle; trial, experimentation and some failure were required in order to learn.

As our total fuel on board registered 6,000 lbs we had done every-thing I wanted Steve to see, at least up to this point. If we were at cruise altitude, and "cruising", this amount of fuel would have equat-ed to roughly an hour of flight, but, since the throttle was usually in military power (100 percent rpm) or in afterburner (A/B, flames coming out the back of the engine), we were using up "dinosaurs" (we usually called "fossil" fuels dinosaurs) pretty quickly. Also, I waited until 6,000 lbs before the zoom climb demo on purpose. I wanted the CG fairly forward as it helps in bringing the nose down with more authority. Finally, with 6 grand of fuel in the tanks the F-4 weighed about 40,000 lbs at that point. Since the engines put out 36,000 lbs total thrust in full A/B, we were fairly close to a 1 to 1 thrust to weight ratio which helped to get this monster up to 30,000 feet while going pure vertical.

With Steve flying we accelerated to 500 knots IAS at 10,000 feet about 30 miles off the coast. I quickly reviewed to him what we were going to do and how to do it: Accelerate to 500 knots in military power; at 500 knots pull the nose up in an airspeed/energy conserving pull (light "tickle", buffet, in the airframe, about 5 Gs on the G meter) and as you are pulling go into full A/B, all the while continuing the pull. Once you reach 90 degrees nose high, vertical, hold it there, the nose, while maintaining full A/B. It was actually a pretty easy entry.

The hard part for most guys was holding the nose in the pure verti-cal…you actually had to push the stick forward to keep the aircraft tracking straight up, initially, and this was counter-intuitive to most guy's instincts. I usually had to give a continuous "dialogue" as we climbed to get the guys to keep the aircraft going straight up as they kept wanting to pull over into a loop. Having said that, on today's flight my young charge seemed to defy the conventional wisdom of most students and was pretty fearless in this part of the maneuver as he held a pure vertical climb with aplomb. As we approached 200 knots indicated airspeed, I told him to get ready to apply left or right rudder and deselect A/B, as I had briefed earlier, so as to get the nose moving one way or the other as we apexed. At this point afterburner was not needed as we had all the height we needed.

What was supposed to happen was for the student to apply this rudder input gently and not all at once –feed it in--so as to get the nose to begin to fall as the airspeed went to zero, since gravity would do the rest, both with the nose and aircraft trajectory. With the engines now in military power and the airspeed at zero, the nose would fall slowly earthward and as it did you went weightless, though it never really seemed you went fully zero G for too long. The altitude obviously stopped increasing and as long as the controls were then neutralized, and you weren't asking the Phantom to do anything, like fly, via the flight controls, it was a really nice transition from going straight up to straight down and a very gentle maneuver. Once the airspeed increased to 300 knots, while going straight down, I would have the guys pull the aircraft to level flight and level off. Altitude loss was usually around 10,000 feet; hence, if you topped out at 30k you'd be level at 20 on the recovery. I'm telling ya, it was a real confidence builder with the guys. Now remember, what I just said is what was supposed to happen.

On this day, as we dropped though 150 knots I asked Weedhopper to "kick" in left or right rudder…and he did as I asked…he kicked in FULL left rudder and without hesitation. Oh shit… I will tell you, my heart leapt out of my chest when I felt the rudder go full left and the aircraft responding. Having flown about 1500 hours in the F-4 at that point, I knew this was not good and as soon as he put in the flight control input I told him to take it out—the rudder deflection—and also to push the stick forward (a lot of times a rudder input, a big one, will increase your AOA, so pushing the stick forward will counteract this increased AOA). I did not want an increase in AOA at this point, given the rudder input, and we were entering a grey area in my knowledge of F-4 flight characteristics with regard to this attitude/airspeed/flight control combination.

Now, this leads me another article I once read in a safety magazine (I told you I read a lot back then!) and it was called "Temporal Distortions". It went into some pretty deep theory about how, under times of stress, the body/brain goes into a kind of hyper awareness state and time seems to slow down because the senses become more aware...a second seems like a minute, etc. I don't remember the body's biological cascade of hormonal production that caused this time warp, other than it happens, as identified by many accident victims' testimonies.

So, after the aircraft lurched to the left, I launched into a "temporal distortion" of my own. My first thought was to take the aircraft from Steve and fly it myself, but, since the airspeed was now dropping through 150 knots, rather rapidly I might add, I thought, "What's the use?" We were approaching 30,000 feet, the throttles were back to military power, airspeed was rapidly bleeding off, and so far the aircraft was just yawed to the left, what could happen? In fact, I even said to myself that we were too slow for anything bad to happen! I am telling you, these thoughts went through my head and as they did it seemed to me that we had been going straight up forever, like in super slow motion. So, there we were, yawed to the left, still going up and I was thinking, "This is a non-event, the nose is just going to drop any second." Though my wait seemed long, in actuality I'm sure it wasn't, and in short order I was rewarded with the ride of my aeronautical life.

What the aircraft actually did, as best as I can figure, and to give you a visual perspective, is this… Think of a springboard diver in the Olympics as they leap off the board and into the air. As they go up they start a twist—roll—and then start to flip. Very shortly after beginning this upward vector they apex and then they start down towards the water and all the while they are still twisting and flipping. In short, that is what Steve, the aircraft, and I did on that day…had we done it at low altitude during an air show I'm sure it would have been a real crowd pleaser.

But whereas the diver is in control of this motion, we weren't. (One thing I didn't tell you is that the F-4 has an "aural" AOA indicator in addition to a gauge and chevron lights. As you approach "on speed", optimum AOA, it beeps…the closer you get to optimum, the faster the beep, until you get to "on speed and then it is a steady, medium pitched tone. But, if you go slower than on speed, higher AOA, it begins a higher pitched, faster peeping that is really irritating, no doubt to get your attention. The volume is controllable though so you can turn it way down, but most guys kept it at least at some audible level as it was a nice way to know your AOA without looking "inside" the cockpit) So the AOA tone was screaming as we began our gyrations adding to the dramatic way in which the aircraft departed controlled flight and giving a sense of urgency to get things back under control. As the aircraft rolled rapidly to the left and the nose fell through the horizon I thought it, the nose, would stay "down" once it passed 90 degrees nose low. It didn't. I also thought the rolling would stop. Wrong again. The nose sliced through nose low and up again, as we continued rolling, and then went back to a nose high slice and still rolling. I must add, at this point that none of this rolling and slicing/ pitching was violent in as far as physical discomfort. Visually it was interesting, and no doubt a weaker stomach would have launched its breakfast from whence it came, but for the most part it was a very smooth and fluid ride.

Up to this point, in all of my years flying the F-4, every time I have unloaded, reduced AOA (pushed the stick forward), the jet responded immediately and whatever out of control gyrations it was beginning to do, once unloaded, it stopped. Not this time; I was now in virgin territory and had to resort to the F-4's Bold Face procedures for help. (The USAF taught you to commit certain time sensitive procedures to memory for instant recall if the need arose, they called them Bold Face Maneuvers. I'd say this was pretty much one of those times)

The out of control "Bold Face" maneuver for the F-4 was as follows: Stick forward, rudder and ailerons neutral, if not recovered, maintain full forward stick and deploy the drag chute; there was also a note in the manual that said unless at low altitude the throttles should be brought back to idle (as a note here, if they, throttles, were left in A/B and you deployed the drag chute you would instantly burn it off!) I can't say I wanted to deploy the drag chute...not yet, so I didn't tell Steve to pop the chute; that was akin to admitting failure and I wasn't ready to do that. I had done the out-of- control bold face a lot in the F-4, save for deploying the chute, as if you wanted to win dogfights in the F-4, particularly against F-16s or F-15s you had to max perform the jet and a lot of times you departed controlled flight. But, in every case in the past where I departed, popping the stick forward and neutralizing the ailerons and rudder brought me back into controlled flight. As Steve went through these memory items to confirm that he had the flight controls where they should be, the aircraft continued to roll and the nose traced an unpredictable arc through the morning sky.

It was pretty evident that the out-of- control procedure wasn't hacking it so we quickly moved onto the next Bold Face and that was for the "Aircraft in a Spin" verbiage. This directed you to: Maintain full forward stick, aileron full with spin/turn needle, aircraft unloaded, ailerons neutral (that's not a misprint with regards to "aileron" in the singular. The F-4's ailerons only went "down", not up, so in a spin, only one aileron was being deflected). As we spun and flipped from the wild blue yonder towards the deep blue sea, which was now 25000 feet below us and getting much closer with each complete gyration, Steve applied the spin recovery controls in an attempt to stop this madness. I can't say I was worried at this point as I was sitting on a zero/zero (zero altitude/zero airspeed needed for safe ejection) Martin Baker ejection seat with a fantastic survival record and I had no qualms about giving the aircraft back to the taxpayers, albeit not exactly in same condition in which we received it, in exchange for my life.

Since we were not under any real physical discomfort during all this, other than maybe some visual disorientation, I talked to Steve a bit as we descended. He asked if this was a normal result of "the maneuver" and I said "No", but, "I expect the airspeed to increase at any second and for the aircraft to pop into something more "normal". What I didn't say was how screwed up this was and that we may be swimming home, but I didn't want to scare him anymore than he already was. I also told him that once the airspeed did increase, it was firmly planted at zero, not to be too hasty to pull the nose up as it was really easy to enter a secondary stall/out of control situation at that point and we most likely wouldn't have enough altitude to recover from another out-of-control situation.

As we passed 18,000 feet the roll rate rapidly began to slow but the AOA was still pegged, read audibly screaming!, way too high and the nose still wasn't dropping like it should, thusly leading me to the third and final Bold Face in the series.

The last Bold Face was for Out-of-Control Flight. If the first two Bold Faces didn't work, this one stipulated, pretty bluntly… Passing 10,000 feet AGL, if still out of control- eject. Because of this edict in the F-4 Flight Manual I told Steve that we were going to have to eject if the aircraft was still uncontrollable passing ten grand. Almost on cue though, as if the aircraft was listening and didn't want to be abandoned, the nose stopped its slicing, the wings fully stopped their rolling and the tail pointed itself directly skyward with the opposite end going seaward. The airspeed went from zero to 250 knots about as fast as you are reading this sentence and at 300 I told Steve to begin a smooth pull on the stick and recover, which he did, leveling at around10,000 feet AGL.

"Wheeeeww,,," I sighed under my breathe.

It was now very quiet in the cockpit. We were headed south, 180 degrees out from our initial heading, and cruised for a few long and silent seconds. Steve broke the silence first with his announcement that he wanted to "Go home"…without hesitation I concurred and told him to RTB (Return To Base). The rest of the flight was uneventful.

In the mission's de-brief, I learned that Steve never realized he was supposed to slowly feed in the rudder. He said he thought, as he listened to my very inadequate brief, that he was supposed to go full left or right rudder passing 150 knots and this thought process was actually reinforced as we passed 200 knots when I said to him, "Standby to "kick in" left or right rudder."

So, what happened? Why did a maneuver that I had done so many times before get so screwed up on this flight, almost causing us to lose an aircraft and possibly die? I'm sure you've figured it out already… Complacency of course. The "voice of Cybil" that I'd heard so many times before as I was about to fly a mission, or was actually flying one, about how complacency kills, had abandoned me while I briefed and flew that day.

I can only think that all the elements that led up to this wicked departure from controlled flight, the proverbial links in the chain, had started with my lovely morning drive to work and my carefree, life is great, I can do anything attitude. This fed into every part of the day's events. When I briefed Steve, I was so full of myself! I had been an F-4 Fighter Weapons School Instructor Pilot and Steve was just a new guy. I had been at the pinnacle of F-4 flying and Steve had barely scratched the surface, I was going to show him how to really fly the F-4. At this point in my career, I considered the brief a mere formality. Most guys I had been briefing for flights, since I had left the Fighter Weapons School environment for the airlines and my part-time guard unit, were so used to the "standard" stuff, the same 'ole missions, that they barely listened to the brief and were experienced enough to catch whatever might be different and ask questions if they weren't sure about something. Because of this, Steve was collateral damage in as far as my brief was concerned. I had glossed over the most important part of the flight believing that he would know what I was talking about and figuring that I was good enough anyway to catch whatever errors he might make in flight and then instantly correct them (the errors).

Which leads me to the second area of my complacency...the actual flying. I had 1500 hours in the F-4 as we alighted from the runway that day and other than drop "nukes" (nuclear weapons) I had done so much in the Phantom that I considered myself bullet proof and figured that I had seen it all. I mean I had instructed green F-4 students for 3 years and had dealt with all of their self-destructive tendencies, the reward being theirs survival and mine. And after that foray into an alternate flying universe, I went into the F-4 Fighter Weapons School as an Instructor Pilot after having just gone through the School (same type of school as the movie Top Gun portrays, only USAF style) as a student...I really felt like I was somebody.

To be sure I almost was...somebody, but not in a good way. Had we put the aircraft and ourselves into the drink no doubt I would have had my 15 minutes of fame and a lifetime of regret. As it was, we should have deployed the drag chute when we were fully out of control when the initial attempts to stop the gyrations were unsuccessful, but, pride go'eth before the fall...a 20,000 foot fall to be exact. I had too much ego when we were out of control to admit defeat and deploying the drag chute was akin to defeat in my head, and this narcissistic trait could have cost us dearly...another lesson learned.

As I drove through the forests and cranberry bogs of South-Central New Jersey that evening, heading home and enjoying the breeze upon my face, the dimming of a late day's sun and the rock and roll tunes emanating from the car's stereo. Don Henley's raspy rancor, once again, pulls me out of my trance and reminds me, very bluntly, that today's mission was truly, at least for me, the end of my innocence.

The Mist

I was headed northbound at 250 feet and 55 mph towing a banner and just off the Atlantic City beaches. I was eating lunch and daydreaming of being on the beach with some of the bathing beauties below when I noticed that the view of the beach ahead was rapidly disappearing and that I could only see straight down upon the waves, and even that view was being obscured somewhat by fragmented wisps of clouds that were appearing below me. With Atlantic City's now unseen semi-high-rise buildings blocking a westward reversal of course and the lack of a discernible horizon, giving me pause to want to turn out over the water, I tried to climb above the ever-thickening fog while going straight ahead. No chance there either since the climb rate while towing a banner was anemic at best, and as soon as I began to go up, the waves disappeared, and I had no idea how high the top of this stuff was, so downward I dropped to 150 feet or so. A call on the CB radio to the banner kids at Bader Field Airport, which sits just off the beach and to the west of Atlantic City and from where I was towing my banners, told me the field was still clear, though the banner boys said they could see a fog bank mounting higher in the sky over the eastern edge of the city, no doubt it was massing for a final assault on the warm veil of air that separated the beach from the airport. I decided to follow the beach and turn inland as soon as I came upon the inlet that separated Atlantic City from Brigantine. The problem was that if I was at 150 feet or so AGL (above ground level), the tail of the banner was lower, maybe 10 to 20 feet (depending on airspeed), and as I flew farther north, the fog became even denser, and I had to go lower still.

Lord, my heart was beating like a hummingbird's as I kept one hand on the banner release handle, figuring, that if I had to, I would cut the banner loose over the waves of the beach and then I'd immediately, and rapidly, climb straight ahead, believing I could hold a reasonable wings level attitude until I popped above the stuff. As I reached the inlet, I turned ninety degrees left, went down to 100 feet, and had increased the airspeed to 70 mph to raise the tail of the banner as much as I could. I initially flew over the boardwalk on the Atlantic City side of the inlet, but the closeness of the people gave me huge pause in keeping this flight path, so I elected to fly over the middle of Absecon inlet. While I initially patted myself on the back for this decision, which I thought was a good idea, it turned out to be poor execution on my part since there were so many boats rushing into the inlet that if I had to drop the banner there too, I'd probably conk someone on the head. However, the even greater folly of this change of flight path would soon be revealed in even finer detail a few moments after arriving over the middle of the inlet.

It soon became obvious to me as I flew ever lower over the water that it was a race between me and my aircraft and the distance the fog had gained in its advance down the inlet as to how low I was going to have to go to stay in visual contact with the boats and the water.

Unfortunately, I had forgotten about the new seventy-five-foot-high bridge that had been built across the inlet. In an instant of horror I saw the upper reaches of the bridge appear out of the opaqueness of the fog and now I was eyeball level with some seriously wide-eyed beachgoers in their cars as they crested the roadway above the inlet. The drivers rapidly stopped on the bridge in the same immediate reaction as I "popped" the airplane up to pass over them. I had to fly just a bit higher than the bridge in order to make sure the banner didn't actually scrape on the bridge or on any cars that were now stopped at its apex, waiting for me to pass. I looked back to see the banner pass, at most ten feet over the roadway. Once the banner was clear of the bridge, I immediately nosed over to descend to the water below in search of better visibility. There is no doubt the advertiser of that banner got his money's worth out of that tow, as I'm sure the words of that banner are indelibly etched upon the memories of some of those who had to stop for both my aircraft's and the banner's passage.

As soon as the length of the banner cleared the bridge, the sky in front of me began to brighten, giving me hope that the fog would soon clear. As if on cue, after clearing the worst obstacle since I'd entered the fog, I flew into clear air—what a relief.

Stuck Mic

I was about 6 months into my scheduled 49 weeks of USAF Pilot Training, UPT it's called (Under Graduate Pilot Training) and in the T-38 phase of flight training. My instructor, Kevin, was in the back seat of the jet and we were entering the landing pattern at "Willy" (Williams Air Force Base). We had just flown a "Contact" sortie. Contact was the phase of training where you practice overhead patterns, loops, rolls, Immelmann, etc. Basically, it's meant to hone your skills at being comfortable flying the aircraft in all attitudes, altitudes, airspeeds (high and low speed), and in the traffic pattern performing overheads, closed patterns, no flap patterns and finally landings (We actually did touch and goes).

Kevin was an awesome instructor and he and I gelled well both when he instructed me and when we socialized with our respective girlfriends when not at work.

After arriving in the landing pattern Kevin directed me to perform a couple of overheads, followed by touch and goes, and then a closed pattern to a full stop landing. I was actually following another T-38 as I arrived on downwind for my full stop landing.

Upon Landing and turning left at the end of the runway, the T-38 that was in front of me in the landing pattern was now not more than 100 feet in front as we both, the jets I mean, taxied to parking under the direction of ground control.

Almost immediately after switching to ground control's frequency I hear two men talking on the same frequency as ATC's. The conversation went something like this:

Voice 1: "Hey, what did you think of the squadron party the other night?"

Voice 2: "It was fun! But holy shit did you see the size of the base commander's wife?"

Voice 1: "Yeah! Man she is a fat shit. Could you imagine going down on her?" Gag me with a spoon"

Voice 2: "Hey man ya know what they say, the bigger the cushion the softer the pushing'!!"

Voice 1: "Dude I wouldn't screw her with your dick!"

Voice 1 and 2: "laughter…"

As the two pilots talked I became acutely aware the transmissions were coming from the jet right in front of me and so I said to Kevin, "Kevin, we are close to them, obviously they have a stuck mic., do you want me to make a radio call and try to tell them they are broadcasting on ground?"

"Johnson," said Kevin, "If you want to pass this ride you will keep your mouth shut. I know who those guys are, they are check section evaluators and they think their shit doesn't stink and are arrogant assholes, let them hang themselves."

And so they talked, more derogatory remarks about the Base Commander, other women, other pilots, it was veritable feast of foul language, disparaging remarks about other instructor's girlfriends or wives or on a more positive note, other women, Kevin's girlfriend included, women who they thought were smoking hot and they would like to "bang."

I was dying inside laughing, thinking if they only knew….honestly it was about as close as you could get to being a fly on the wall and privy to a conversation that no-one else should hear.

So, I pull my jet into the parking spot from which we taxied out of an hour and a half ago. After deplaning Kevin and I hop into the crew van that took us to our PE (Equipment) shack where we left our helmet and other flight gear. After getting in the van I saw two other pilot's in there, obviously they had just finished their flight too, and I noticed that they had "Check Section" patches on their flight suits. Kevin surreptitiously nudged me and gave me the universal "keep quiet" finger to the mouth. My lips were sealed.

We drove a bit down the flight line and as we did Kevin asked the guys how their flight went….one check pilot was giving a check ride to the other.

"Fine" they said, "how did your student do?"

"Oh, he's from New Jersey, but trainable," Kevin said. They laughed, Kevin laughed, I didn't.

Then two more flight crews, two students, two instructors get in the van. This is going to be interesting I thought.

Everyone kind of smiled at each other as we slowly drove down the flight line to the PE shack. It is singularly the most awkward period of silence I have ever experienced in my life.

No doubt the other instructors and students knew who had the stuck mic but they remained silent. Then, last but not least a solo student, no instructor in his aircraft, got in the van and said, immediately, after sitting down, "Wow, did you guys hear those guys with the stuck mic? Can you believe the shit they were saying?"

I will never forget the look on those check airmen's faces. Priceless.

Night Flight...
still my strangest flight.

While in college, I managed the Chalet. It was a school-owned bar/restaurant and activities center, centrally located on the college's small campus. It was around 11:30 p.m. on a Saturday night and had been a slow business night and there was no one else but me in the establishment at that time. The night before, we had an awesome blowout party I had helped to coordinate with the all-girls' college located across town, so tonight was pretty much a health night (no drinking) for most of the guys on campus I thought, myself included (the drinking age at this time in the United States was eighteen in most states).

The dark wood-paneled bar area was warm and felt cozy as I listened to the rock music du jour blaring out of the jukebox while analyzing the abysmal sales numbers for the day. While busily counting money, lip-synching to the music and making mental inventory/ordering reminders, I occasionally glanced outside to look at the wilting snow piles on the wood deck, excited with the knowledge that a snowstorm was due to dump another eight to twelve inches the next day. As I was deep in multitasking thought, one of the college's few female students—a freshman, Tammy, who came from an exceptionally

wealthy family and who was both facially and curvaceously beautiful—walked into the bar and sat with a purpose right in front of me.

Since Tammy and I breathed air from different universes—social,
financial, and work ethic—we had a whole different idea of what we
each wanted to get out of our college years. We rarely crossed paths
except for when she was in the Chalet with one of her many suitors,
girlfriends, or an entourage of both. If that sounds like an innuendo
of dislike, not in the least—I did like her. However, I was very driven
back then and Tammy was, well . . . not.

As I sat doing the books and counting money, Tammy asked me if I
was sober. I said, "Yes."

She then said, "Well, what I mean is, have you had a drink at all
today?"

"No," was my very simple response because I was counting money
and didn't want to lose my place, nor did I look at her while answering
her questions.

"Well," she continued, in an exasperated tone, "my sister is leaving her
fiancé and wants to come visit me here on campus and stay with me
for a couple of weeks."

"Well, I am very sorry for your sister, I guess, though I don't know
her, but I guess staying with you would be a nice getaway. When is she
coming and what the hell does any of this have to do with you asking
me if I've been drinking?" I said out of breath.

"Because every boy on campus that I know that has a pilot's license is
either drunk or drinking and headed that way and can't fly tonight,

and my sister wants me to fly down now in my airplane and pick her up."

Collecting my composure and thinking there goes my theory on it being a health night for the roughly 400 guys on campus, or at least for whatever number of pilots Tammy approached, I said to her, "Tammy, we are under a winter storm warning, why in God's name would anyone want to fly tonight?"

"I checked the weather," she bluntly pointed out. "The weather guy said the snow is not supposed to start until around noon tomorrow, that's twelve hours from now. Right now, it's 5000 overcast, and it's gonna stay that way for another six hours at least and even then slowly get worse and the visibility is at least twenty miles and the winds are very light."

I then asked her the obvious question, "Tammy, are you, in a round-about way asking me to fly you down to Martha's Vineyard to pick up your sister?"

"Yes."

I sat and looked at her for a few tense and long seconds. It was my thought that the truly rich have a different comprehension of life. From the side of the tracks I'm from, I'd suffer with my fiancé and try to work things out until the storm blew over . . . and take your pick on the storm—the emotional one or the winter one that was about to hit, or both. Because either way, there's no doubt they were both gonna pass . . .

So, after looking into Tammy's beautiful eyes, which I could feel were desperately trying to seduce me into saying yes, I gave her a condition-al yes. I said if the weather was as good as she said, then I was willing to pick up her sister, but I needed to check the actual conditions and the forecast myself. Also, I needed to go get a buddy in one of the dorms who had a current set of aviation approach charts and maps and wanted him to come along since I figured two pilots on a night like this would be better than one.

Having had another victory over coercing a male into doing what she wanted, Tammy happily skipped out of the bar and said she'd meet us at the aircraft, which was located just down the street from the campus.

Indeed, the weather was as Tammy said, and by a little after midnight and with legacy snow covering the ground in large patches, overcast skies, and calm winds, three college kids took off from Boire Field, in Nashua, New Hampshire, in a Cherokee Archer.

I always enjoyed flying at night because it was usually smoother, turbulence-wise, than during the day. Oddly enough, that flight was, in retrospect, a prelude to my future airline flying, which would generally see me flying at night in a sparkling, gem-sprinkled sky, dark cloud, or a combination of both.

As anticipated, it was creamy smooth as we climbed in the frigid winter air to our cruising altitude of 2,500 feet. Though the clouds were a little more than 2,500 feet above us as we leveled off, the visibility was almost unlimited, judging by the fact that I could easily see the glow from thousands of singular or merged lights emanating from the city of Boston and its many attendant towns, which were to the left of the aircraft. I called Boston Center and asked for radar flight following upon leveling off on this VFR flight since I wanted separation from any other idiot that might be stupid enough to be flying on one of

Old Man Winter's Saturday midnights, and also for the security of having someone know where we were.

The "dark" of night on this flight took on a different hue than of those nights of my past. That previously mentioned layer of snow on the ground caused the residential and city lights to be reflected to the solid layer of clouds above me, and then from there it was re-reflected all around, thusly magnifying the intensity of the ambient lighting to the point that it was actually quite, and abnormally, bright, even though it was a little past the witching hour and no moonlight was available.

The shimmering of the lights from outside the aircraft and the subdued glow from the aircraft's instrument panel, combined with a warm cockpit, smooth air, the drone of the engine, and the occasional radio calls from ATC—made for an intoxicating cocktail of aviation character that never failed to seduce me into wanting to come back for more. On that night, the emotional rush from that previously mentioned blend of ingredients was quite exhilarating and surreal.

Since the island of Martha's Vineyard was only a hundred miles or so as the crow flies from our departure airport, and since we cruised at 130 mph, it didn't take long to get there since we were also flying as the crow flies . . . direct. The most dramatic part of the flight was the conscious disregard for the security and comfort of the bright lights of the city of New Bedford, Massachusetts for the possibility that Martha's Vineyard lay beyond in the shrouding cloak of darkness that greeted the three of us as we headed offshore.

I'd never been to Martha's Vineyard before this flight, but I wasn't particularly worried about getting to or finding it since the island had a VOR that would electronically guide us to the field and the weather, upon flying over top of the airport, was good and the runway lights were all illuminated. The tower was closed due to the late hour and the time of the year so I did one turn over the field, checking the lighted wind sock for the prevailing wind, and then set up for an uneventful landing on the runway most aligned into the wind.

After shutting down on the ramp, Tammy jumped out of the airplane and literally ran into the night and disappeared.

Being alone with each other now, my heretofore unnamed friend, Dan, and I walked up to the airport's main terminal building to see if we could get inside and stay warm. The moist sea air that surrounded us when combined with the freezing temperatures made it feel colder than Houdini's weenie, and we had no idea how long it would be before Tammy came back since she ran off without saying a word.

Since we had time to kill and were cold, Dan and I walked around the terminal looking for an open door. I chanced to peek into a windowed door that showed some promise of life, if only because I saw some light sneaking out between the shutters. I had my face pressed against the window, trying to look through slits in the shutter when I noticed a man inside looking back at me! Crap! I was so creeped out that I fell on my ass, and as I did, my buddy started laughing hysterically. The creepy man inside opened the door and asked if we had flown the aircraft that just landed. I said yes, rather cautiously, not sure if he wanted to make us a midnight snack or actually held some official capacity with the airport.

Being invited in to stay warm and answer some general questions, we sat on a sofa in his cozy little room while he sipped on what I believe was an Irish coffee. He watched TV in between glances at Dan and me while he was either talking or listening. Though not a whiskey or coffee drinker at that point in my life, I could seriously have used a belt right about then due to the still recent memory of that face staring back at me in the window. As the conversation warmed, and our bodies, too, this delightfully odd, old man explained that he was born and raised on the island and was the caretaker of the airport during the off hours of operation, though what his actual duties were I never could ascertain.

As the three of us were maintaining small talk, I saw car lights appear on the ramp and figured Tammy was back with her high-maintenance sister. Bidding the old man a courteous adieu while walking backward and promising to come back one day (I never have), I desperately tried to focus my attention on Tammy and our new passenger without being rude to this apparition in the window. Oddly, he stayed at the door to his cozy little nest and never ventured outside to see who drove their car onto the ramp and parked next to one of the aircraft.

It was kinda weird being on the island/airport at 2 a.m. in the dead of winter, and I really wanted to get out of there since I figured if anyplace would go down, weather-wise, first, it would be that island.

Dan was helping to expedite the loading of Tammy's luggage adorned sister so we could beat the snow while Tammy's mom went on a cute little conversational thread with me.

I had never met Mrs. Weaver before, and I have to say she was exceptionally beautiful—like mother, like daughter—and very nice too. But as we briefly chatted—actually, it being more like her talking to me—she mentioned how crazy kids could be.

Really? I was twenty, what the hell did I know about kids? I could tell her that I'd bet her a million bucks that her capricious daughter wouldn't last a week in the dorm with Tammy (I think it was four days) and I also could have told her that I'd never let my two daughters fly on a night such as the one we were getting ready to fly into with two boys of whose flying credentials I had no idea, let alone their personal morals and mental stability. I mean seriously? What idiot boy would be out flying at night, on a very early Sunday morning, during a winter storm warning, just so he could garner a couple of hours of free flying time? Yes, I qualify as being the village idiot, but I knew that I was a somewhat sane idiot, and I was confident of my judgment and ability. But how on earth would Mrs. Weaver know of my character unless she was a lot more probing in questioning me, which she was not? To this day, I still find that odd.

So, after her highness's bags were stowed, the proverbial preflight walkaround was performed and the emotional mother-to-daughter goodbyes expressed, the pilots and passengers boarded the aircraft and we started the engine. After a short taxi and a little after an hour since our arrival, we departed into the same black void from which we came.

The ladies were all cozy in the backseats and happily chatted away while Dan and I quietly enjoyed our own personal thoughts as the lights of Boston, now on the right, easterly, side of us, came into view.

The flight back was more uneventful than the one "down" because the weather was the same and the lights of the mainland could be seen as soon as we got above a hundred feet or so while climbing and turning toward the mainland.

We landed sometime around 3 a.m. in seemingly the same conditions as when we left; it was as if time and the weather, had stood still. Dan and I escorted the girls to Tammy's room and, upon arrival, literally dropped all her sister's crap on the floor and quietly left. Dan headed to his room to get some more sleep, and I, instead of heading to my dorm room, headed back to the Chalet. I programmed the jukebox with a bunch of my favorite songs, poured myself a drink, started a wood fire in the huge fireplace that dominated one side of the bar's interior, and then lay down on an overstuffed couch that collected all the light and heat from that fire. I got into a cozy fetal position as the flames grew higher then proceeded to reminisce about what a weird night it had been while I waited for the morning, and the snow, to arrive.

Aircraft Down

Below is a true event that occurred on a flight to Tokyo on which I was the captain in early 2006. I've included the letters I received from a couple who were deeply affected by that "event." The personal letters I've included here are the nucleus around which this story is retold for posterity on these pages. They are the heart and soul of those directly involved and add a real world, personal touch to an accident that now-a-days is far removed and emotionally distant from my mind and soul. The writer of the first letter explains eloquently what I'm not able to do even as I type this. However, before reading the first letter, know, and I want to stress this, this story "is not about me and my F/O" and what we did....please, do NOT infer that. Anyone could have done what my F/O and I did on that day. What impressed me the most about this event was the absolute composure of the pilot of the aircraft that reported the accident; I doubt I could have had the same emotional coolness.

May 9, 2006

Dear Mr. Johnson,

I received your letter of 04/04/06 although it took it awhile to catch up with me. My aircraft registration is tied to my

Aniak address, as that's where I base my airplane most of the time. After the conclusion of the winter trapping season, I retreat to the Kenai Peninsula, where I spend the remainder of the year. My mail is forwarded to my Soldotna address. This year, due to Justin's accident, my wife and I have remained in Anchorage to assist in our son's care and our mail has piled up as a result.

I found your letter during a recent trip to Soldotna. I've waited till our next trip home to reply as my handwriting suffers the same as yours and I haven't had access to a computer in Anchorage.

Justin's injuries were quite severe but we are extremely fortunate to have him with us at all. Both of his ankles were shattered, as were his tibia and fibula of his right leg. His right hip socket was badly broken. His left upper arm was fractured in three places and his left shoulder was badly broken. He fractured his sternum although it has not caused him any discomfort. His left eye was badly injured, requiring surgery and a titanium plate to repair his eye socket. He had a cervical spine injury that only required stabilization with a cervical collar for 3 weeks, but no corrective surgery. There were numerous lacerations on his face and hands, which had to be sutured. He also suffered second and third degree burns. Skin grafting was required on his back, shoulder, and thigh, with other burns to his right ear and neck that seem to be healing without skin grafting.

We feel so fortunate that all his injuries will eventually heal. Considering the extent of his injuries, it's a miracle he escaped serious internal injuries, brain damage, spinal injury, etc. He lost the use of his bicep following the trauma to his left arm and shoulder due to nerve damage. He is just beginning to regain movement in that arm and has just regained some slight bicep function, which is very encouraging. The vision continues to improve in his injured eye. It will be at least 2 more months before he can begin bearing weight on his legs and almost that long for his shoulder and arm.

It will be a long recovery process but Justin is very competitive and highly self motivated. We are all optimistic he will be near 100 percent again.

I want to thank you for your kind words in the letter you wrote. I may have sounded composed on the radio, but as you can imagine, the turmoil just under the surface was nearly unbearable. I'm retired after a 24 year long career with the Alaska State Troopers. As a trooper, it was necessary to keep emotions from reaching the surface during a time of crisis. The more serious the crisis, the more important it became to maintain control. I have to admit, this one was a real test! No amount of training and experience could have prepared me for that night.

My son and I both had some guardian angels out there that night and you were the first. I can't possibly thank you enough for just being there and to have been monitoring 121.5. The fact that you were there, doing what you were doing, is the best example of a true professional in my view.

I normally have a list of local center frequencies at my finger-tips in case of an emergency. There's enough high altitude IFR traffic in the region to ensure someone within radio range will likely be on one of several Center frequencies. As a VFR pilot, I don't have those committed to memory. I had recently removed that list as Justin had been flying my airplane and didn't like the clutter on my instrument panel. Consequently I didn't have the Bethel, Sparrevohn, Iliamna, or Dillingham center frequencies available and had to rely on 121.5 as my only hope to find help for my son. Impending darkness limit-ed my ability to remain airborne for any length of time.

I don't know what we would have done without your help. Relaying my distress call and alerting Anchorage Center began the process that ultimately saved my son's life. He would not have survived through the night without rescue and medical attention. I could not have landed to help him without adding to the pile" and further complicating the problem. Leaving that crash site to go for help was undoubtedly the most diffi-cult choice I've ever had to make. I knew that if by some mira-cle he had survived the crash he would be badly injured and would be in desperate need of medical attention. I also real-ized he would require a lot more help than I could offer by myself. The Alaska Natl. Guard has several Rescue Squadrons in a high state of readiness and I believed Justin's only hope for survival would depend on getting those resources mobilized. Although it hurt me to have to leave him there alone, I know going for help was the right choice. My biggest fear was that I wouldn't be able to raise anyone on the radio. I thank God that you were there to hear my call for help.

The next few hours were the worst, not knowing if he was alive or dead. At our tiny trapping cabin I had a deep cycle battery and charger, plus a remote antenna for my satellite phone. I was able to have sat-phone communications through the night with family members and search & rescue personnel while awaiting word on the progress of rescue efforts. At around midnight our prayers were answered by news that Justin was alive and would be transported to Anchorage. He arrived at Providence Hospital shortly before 3:00 am on 03/22/06.

Justin has undergone seven major surgeries to repair broken bones plus skin grafts due to burns, but he will heal in due time. We thank the Lord for all the miracles that have fallen into place. The very first one was that you were there to hear my plea for assistance. For that fact I am eternally grateful and I can't thank you enough.

I am truly sorry to learn of the loss of your daughter. Even if only for a few hours, I can honestly say I understand the empty feeling such a loss can bring My heart goes out to you and your family. Your kind and compassionate words are an inspiration to us and I thank you for taking the time to write.

Ill enclose a newspaper article you may find of interest. Also the Providence Hospital provides a website on which patients and their families can post information.

Thank you again for all that you have done.

Sincerely,

May 9, 2006

Dear Mr. Johnson,

I hope you will indulge me. Although you wrote the letter to my husband Chuck and he has responded to your letter, I feel compelled to write you also. I do not have words to describe how excited I was when Chuck heard from you. There were numerous times that I wondered who the pilot was that answered Chuck's call for help. Chuck thought that it was a Fed-ex pilot, but he could not remember for certain. We were thinking of you while you were thinking of us.

It was important to me to have a connection with you because, aside from Chuck, you were the first link in the chain of events that ultimately saved our son's life. Again, I am a loss of words when I try to think of how I would describe to you my absolute unconditional love for my son and his importance in my life. He is, in his own right, an exceptional young man who is well loved and well thought of by many people. That this young man is my son seems incredible to me. I would love for his father, Chuck and me to take the credit for the man he is today, but he is his own person and deserves the credit for himself. For us to loose him would be an unbearable loss. So, thank-you, thank-you, thank-you a million times for being there that night, for monitoring that emergency frequency, for making those calls that Chuck asked you to make, and for caring enough to take the time to write a letter. Your letter renews my faith in mankind. It warms my heart to think of the truly good people, like you, that are out there in the world. The letter really meant a lot to both of us.

You mentioned families in your letter. Chuck and I have only one son, Justin. He does have a wife named Erika and they have been married five and one half years. We also have one daughter, Jessica, who is slightly younger than Justin. She too is married and has blessed us with two little grand daughters, ages four and two.

I am so sorry for the loss of your daughter. Although it was only a brief time that we thought we had indeed lost our son, the grief was nearly unbearable. I cannot imagine how people who loose a child endure that grief and come out on the other side of the darkness. But, look at you. You made it and are able to reach out to others in their time of sadness. You are truly an inspiration to us. There is a reason that God put you in our path and I do thank Him for that. Like Chuck said in his letter, many miracles occurred that night and I thank God for all of them, and especially for saving my son's life.

Chuck and Justin do enjoy the good relationship that they have with one another. They have lots of the same interests and participate in several activities together. Chuck is very grateful that he is able to have an active role in his son's life. I think their relationship with one another speaks well about both of them as men and I myself am very thankful for their relationship as well.

Thank-you again for your kindnesses and may God bless you and your family.

Warm regards,

The rest of the story….

On a March evening in 2006 my First Officer and I departed to Anchorage, AK for Tokyo. It was an odd time to depart for that destination then, and in fact in the 16 years since I'd began flying from Anchorage to Tokyo I'd never departed that late…maybe that was providence.

As you read above, as my F/O and I were nearing Bethel VOR, over Western Alaska, I heard a call on 121.5, which was tuned on the right VHF radio, asking for help. My F/O was flying this leg, but, he and I both heard the call.

I asked the pilot what help he needed and he said he needed to report the crash of an aircraft. I can't relay to you how calm and professional this gentleman was. In his words he said, "The aircraft is a red and white Super Cub. It is burning and there is no sign of a survivor." He then gave me some other information to include the LAT/LONG coordinates. I relayed all the pertinent information to Anchorage Center whereupon they immediately talked to the USAF.

The USAF eventually rescued the young man later that evening. He had actually crawled back to the aircraft after it was finished burning. He was thrown out of it upon crashing and cuddled next to the engine since it retained some latent heat and kept him somewhat warm as the freezing cold of the night tried to infiltrate his clothes.

I have kept in casual contact with the parents of Justin and am happy to report he has fully recovered from his injuries and added more children to his tribe. He and his dad are happily back to flying in the skies of Alaska together.

Finally...Oddly, my father, in the early 80s, was flying a FAA Convair 880 near the same area where I was flying in my MD-11, when he too heard an aircraft on 121.5 report an emergency. A Comanche pilot was flying with his family when his engine quit. He crash landed safely but was in the middle of nowhere, the wilderness and far from any village or town. My father and his crew orbited over the downed aircraft until a rescue was effected.

Phantom Fires

"Hey Jedi, you're from New Jersey, wanna' go back there on a vacation?" asked Don Janke, the Chief of Safety for the 184th TFG as he walked into the crew lounge.

"Uhhhh, what's the catch?" I asked as I quickly ate my lunch while between flights.

"A McGuire F-4 crashed in New Jersey and they are putting a team together for the investigation. They need a F-4 pilot for the accident board if you're interested. It's easy, it'll be like a vacation," said Don, with a straight face and no hint of sarcasm.

"No way!!!? Jeeezzz, I know some guys in that unit, was anyone hurt?!" I asked with concern, between bites of my burger.

"No, they both ejected and are fine. The aircraft was on fire. Should be an easy accident board to work on, since no one was hurt. Are you interested?" Don asked, a second time, and this time I could definitely tell he was putting the press on me to take the assignment.

Since it was the middle of summer and hotter than hell in Kansas, I thought a Jersey shore vacation would be nice, so I said with enthusiasm, "Yeah I'll go, this could be fun!"

The thought of going back to the Jersey shore during the summer and spending some time on the beach, bars, and water, all on Uncle Sam's dollar sounded too good to be true. Besides, I thought, I could spend some time with my parents.

So naive was I.

The next day I was on a commercial flight to Philadelphia, looking forward to relaxing at my parent's house on the shore but first I had to report to McGuire AFB in Central New Jersey and check into my quarters and then report to the board president to see what he wanted me to do.

Vacation my ass. If you've never been on an accident investigation board in the USAF, as I had never been prior to this "wonderful" event, it's not a picnic, nor a vacation. The final report for the accident is supposed to be published in 30 days…t h i r ty days. If an airliner crashes, those NTSB final reports can take weeks and months, if not years before they are published. But, the USAF? Nooooo, they want a report in 30 days (unless there are extenuating circumstances). That is not a long time when it comes to investigating why an aircraft crashed; to include all aspects of the accident from the crewmember(s),to life support, Air Traffic Control, maintenance, the aircraft, command and control, or any other possible factor(s) that could have influenced the aircraft and, or aircrew(s)' demise. It meant at least 16 hour days, 7 days a week, until the report was assembled and approved by the board president. It meant chasing down witnesses, some very weird and sketchy. It meant traipsing about the deep, dark woods, in my case the pine barrens of New Jersey, looking for "something", finding nothing, only to realize some "piney" (a person who loves to camp and go four wheeling in the pine barrens) has what you've been searching days for. It meant canvassing the many cranberry bogs surrounding or embedded with-in the pine barrens, looking for witnesses to the accident and then recording their testimony. It meant spending hours talking with all the other members and catching up on "where we are and where we have to go," and fighting with the board president who was bound and determined to find fault with the crew. It meant hanging with the aircraft, engine, and avionics representatives of the manufacturers of the aircraft and/or its component parts and watching them sift through the wreckage, trying to sort out the cause of the crash, and more importantly (to them anyway) their possible culpability.

The synopsis of the accident is as follows: The accident F-4 was number two in a four ship of Phantoms that were on the Warren Grove Bombing range, R 4001, which is in central New Jersey. The aircraft were flying in a pop pattern* dropping 25 pound BDU 33s, practice bombs, that simulate the same flight characteristics of real 500 pound bombs. As number two was at the apex of his pop and ready to roll in and drop his bomb, the pilot, the front-seater in the aircraft, noticed the fire light for the right engine was illuminated. He immediately leveled off and continued his left turn towards McGuire AFB which was approximately 20 nautical miles to the north. He reported on his radio he had a fire indication on his right engine and was heading for McGuire. The range control officer, some 3000 feet below observed smoke and flame coming from the Phantom and the lead Phantom, who had begun a hard left turn to rejoin on his wingman also noticed visible flames coming from the back of the terminal F-4. Both the range control officer and the lead F-4 were calling for the crew to eject, that they were on fire. Shortly after realizing they were indeed on fire, with flames seen in the rear view mirrors in both the rear and front cockpits of the stricken F-4, the crew ejected. They were both relatively unscathed during their ejections and consequent descents, but the Phantom made a smoking hole, 20 feet deep, in the thick of the pine barrens, initiating a sizable forest fire.

* (Pop pattern. The aircraft flies at low altitude, 100 to 500 feet above the ground, then as it approaches the preplanned target it climbs radically/rapidly up to a predetermined altitude, rolls either right or left while immediately reversing the climb to a preplanned dive angle and airspeed (usually 450 knots), drops the bomb(s), pulls up, and then drops back to low altitude and flies another pattern)

So that was the narrative upon which we, the accident board, were briefed. "We," the Accident Board were: a senior enlisted Life Support (PE, Personal Equipment) person; Flight Surgeon (aka doctor, MD, in the civilian world); me (Pilot member); a senior enlisted Maintenance (MX) person; and a few others of whom I can't recall their expertise and then of course there was the board president, a full Colonel who was from Shaw AFB and had been a F-15 pilot.

Upon being briefed of our duties and the expected timeline, the board president, Richard, then adjourned the meeting and thus we began our task…"Why did the Phantom catch fire and subsequently crash, and how could we prevent this from happening again?"

The good news is both pilots were alive and well. The front-seater, Joe, sustained very minor cuts and bruises in the 300 knot ejection and subsequent nylon (parachute) letdown into a thickly wooded area. The back-seater, Mike, who was also a pilot and not a WSO (Weapons System Operator. WSO's are specifically trained to fly in the back of the Phantom and to operate the various electronic systems installed there) was injured, but with relatively minor injuries; broken arm with face and head lacerations due to his helmet being lost in the ejection thusly exposing his head to various sized branches as he descended through the trees.

The bad news is the Phantom was horribly destroyed in the crash in the woods and literally left a smoking hole 20 feet deep. If I had not seen that proverbial smoking hole with my own eyes I'd not have believed how deep it was and how incredibly destroyed was the aircraft. Lord, there was crap all over the place. Upon seeing the absolute obliteration of the jet I would have bet anyone all of my money that there was no way in 30 days, or ever, we would have a final report on the cause of the fire. And, let's face it the jet crashed because the crew ejected; what started the massive fire that caused the ejection was the objective of the investigation.

So with the good news, bad news of the accident, did each of us on the board embark on our separate, but integrated, tasks to complete the report in that 30 day deadline.

The board president was not happy that two 1st Lts* were flying together, particularly since the Lt. in the back was not a dedicated WSO, but instead a pilot, who was trained to fly the Phantom (obviously from the front cockpit). The board president thought not having a WSO in the back may have contributed to the accident.

* (Lt, Lieutenant, in the USAF there are First and Second Lieutenants. The second Lt., 2nd Lt., is the most junior of the Officer ranks and the First Lieutenant, 1st Lt., is the second most junior; after the Lt ranks comes the Captain, Major, Lt. Colonel, and then "Bird," Full Colonel)

Another concern of the board president, and of the life support expert, was why the back-seater's helmet came off in the ejection. It was not supposed to.

My concern was what both pilots saw, with regards to the engine fire, and when, and how did thy react both as a crew and individually?

All three of the above unknowns would be answered with-in three weeks, though not without some infighting between the board president and myself as to the staffing of the aircraft.

As all of us on the board were involved in our individual tasks, about a week after the aircraft crashed the manufacturers representatives of the major components of the aircraft arrived. They immediately went to work scouring the broken and destroyed bits of Phantom, looking for a reason to the fire.

Of all the people involved in this accident investigation, without question the star of the show and the MVP was the General Electric (GE) Representative. GE was the manufacturer of the the J-79, the jet engine that powered the F-4E. This gentlemen was humble, quiet, of slight build and maybe 60 years old. He said he'd been investigating aircraft accidents for 30 years. The guy knew his shit. He talked to Joe (front-seater) and asked him what he saw and when, and what his reaction was to the engine fire. We determined, the GE rep, Joe (mishap pilot), and I that from the time the he saw the fire light to the time of ejection was approximately 30 seconds; the fire on the aircraft was that massive and it indicated that the fuel tanks on the F-4 had been breached and were dumping massive quantities of fuel into the fire. After the three of us had an extended conversation about the events leading up to the accident, the GE rep went on his own and started his physical and analytical examination of whatever aircraft and engine pieces had been brought to the nearby hanger and laid upon its floor. With-in a week of this man's preconceived (due to his 30 years worth of experience), determined, and detailed sleuthing and examination, he had the reason for the fire and the cascading of events that led to the ejection; I was totally blown away by this man's power of observation and corporate knowledge.

Though the GE rep would soon figure out the reason for the aircraft fire, the reason for the loss of Mike's helmet, which to me was not that big of a deal, became one of two cause celebres' of the board president.

The helmet issue was a pain the ass if only because we didn't have it to examine, initially, so as to determine the cause of its loss from Mike's head and no amount of walking through the woods brought us closer to finding it; though we did find some bits of wreckage from a F-105 that crashed many years earlier. On a tip from a cranberry farmer in the crash area an ad was placed in the local papers seeking help with locating the helmet. Shortly after the ad was published a secretary, as she identified herself and who lived near Philadelphia, called to report she knew about the helmet's whereabouts. Evidently this woman spent many of her weekends cruising through the pine barrens, camping out and socializing with others who did the same. I spent my younger days growing up on the fringes of those woods, camping out there myself, but, once the legend of the Jersey Devil (who supposedly called the Pine Barren's its home) was told to me I avoided those woods like the plague. After hearing of this lady's extra-curricular weekend activity I never realized the Pine Barrens was such a beehive of social activity. Go figure.

In the end, the life support expert, who personally spoke to this woman on the phone, asked her if we could get the helmet back, saying that it was the property of the US Government and it was needed for the investigation into the F-4 crash (an accident of which she was acutely aware). The woman agreed to meet, but she wanted to meet near the accident site, which we all thought was odd.

So, the PE man, the Flight Surgeon, and I all drove out to the accident site to meet this mystery lady. She was driving a jeep, which I thought was pretty cool; this is before Jeeps were in vogue. When the three of us met her she was wearing shorts with white socks and ankle high work type boots and a loosely fitting white tee shirt; she was relatively thin with short black hair in a bob (think Dorothy Hamill) and black rimmed glasses accentuating a kind of plain Jane look and reminded me of what a librarian might look like outside of work. Her personality was odd. She was sketchy to say the least in her mannerisms and didn't want to say where and how she came about to acquiring the helmet, which she refused to produce upon our first meeting. She reminded me of a female version of Anthony Perkins of Psycho fame (think The Bates Motel). When we first met, she didn't have the helmet, but agreed, and only if the Flight Surgeon was there, to meet again with the helmet. So, the next day the Flight Surgeon and the Life Support expert met her again, however the State Police, at the Flight Surgeon's request, were present at the next meeting. The Doc said she was even weirder on their next meeting and was definitely coming on to him. He declined her offer of a guided tour through the pine barrens after he asked her where she found the helmet.

As the helmet was being sought and then analyzed and the bits and pieces of the smashed aircraft being examined, the board president investigated the command and control structure of the unit. I too was busy in my area of expertise in the investigation and spoke to four pilots who were either involved in the accident or were witnesses.

First up were Joe and Mike, the crew members who occupied the front and back cockpits, respectively, of the crashed Phantom. I won't lie, I felt kinda odd talking to my peers about the accident. You could tell they were guarded when they spoke, no doubt wondering if this was some kind of modern day Air Force style Spanish Inquisition. From my end it was not. The jet caught on fire and they ejected; to me that was pretty much cut and dry. I was just wondering when they realized the jet was on fire, what they did when they realized it and what they did with regards to running checklists. I talked to them individually and together. I had no preconceived notion of culpability on their parts as to what caused anything, be it the fire, their ejection decision, nothing. I just wanted to know what they did, when and why they did whatever it is they may have done, and to get any take aways' that could possibly help others in the future who may be in the same situation.

I also talked to both the flight lead and the range control officer. The range control officer, Howie, an extremely experienced fighter pilot, only confirmed what the flight lead said; as soon as number two reported the fire and aborted his bombing pass, Howie looked with purpose at the F-4 as it passed above him and proceeded from his left to right, and he saw smoke and flames emanating from its aft area. Mark, the flight lead, another highly experienced fighter pilot, had a much closer view of the F-4 than Howie since he had rapidly rejoined on the boys as they headed for McGuire. Mark said by the time Joe and Mike ejected the flames had propagated forward and were with-in five feet of the rear cockpit.

The board president, a highly experienced fighter pilot himself, with extensive time in both the F-4 and F-15, was very good at corralling all of the accident board players and keeping us focused, on task, and on timeline, with-in the realms of what information we had at the time of our board meetings (which were almost everyday). He was not happy that a pilot was flying in the back of the accident Phantom and he asked me what I thought about that. I, personally, didn't have an issue with it. Mike, though a pilot and not a WSO, was fully capable of operating the systems located in the backseat of the Phantom and in backing-up Joe while they dropped bombs on the range. But, for some reason, and to this day it's still a mystery to me as to why, Richard felt that having Mike in the back cockpit, particularly since he was a 1st Lt, not an Instructor, inexperienced, and not a WSO was contributory to the accident. Since I was so junior myself, brand new Captain, but I was a fully qualified RTU Instructor in the Phantom, my thoughts on the topic of Mike being in the backseat didn't matter. Richard was dogged in his belief it was against the spirit of USAF regulations that Mike was flying in the backseat of the Phantom and nothing I said influenced him in the least; we were at loggerheads and would remain so until we parted at the end of the investigation.

The other bone of contention with Richard was that Mike's helmet was lost in the ejection; Joe's was not. In fact in most ejections the helmets are not lost off the heads of the pilots after they eject, so why was Mike's lost? Mike was under Richard's scrutiny and though I tried to deflect his angst against Mike, I wasn't making any progress, but then, I honestly don't think the board president thought highly of me either, so defending Mike only dug a deeper hole for me and possibly Mike.

To be honest though I didn't care what Richard thought of me. I was extremely respectful of his experience and rank in every way, but he was not my real boss, just for this accident board, and besides I was kinda of cocky and a wise ass back then. I mean, according to Don Janke this was supposed to be a vacation, not 16 hour days filled with unending minutiae. From the first brief of the accident I felt it was an open and shut case of a Phantom on fire, that there was nothing Joe and Mike could have done to prevent it and to land successfully once the fire started. Whether or not it was illegal (it was not) to have Mike in the back seat didn't mean Jack shit to the beginning, middle, or end of the accident; it happened and none of it was either of those guy's faults (Joe and Mike), no matter who was riding in the back seat. In fact, I'd had many non-WSOs fly in the back of my F-4 while I gave incentive rides to enlisted personnel or flew MX guys in my backseat to another Air Force base where one of my unit's Phantoms had landed due to an emergency/broken aircraft and needed a specialist in order to get it fixed.

Three weeks after we began our first accident board meeting, we had all the necessary reports from the aircraft/engine experts and from every pertinent player, eyewitness, or anyone else either directly or indirectly involved in the accident. It had taken three weeks worth of 16 hour work days, to get to the point where we could begin writing the final report; finally I could see a light at the end of a very dark tunnel and saw a South Jersey beach in my near future. We just had to get that report written and it took input, and debate, from everyone on the board in order to write it.

I can't say I added too much to the report, since the sequence of events that led to the crash were, as I said previously, pretty straight forward. I wish I could remember the finer points of the round robin discussions we had as the final report was being debated and the conclusions, causes, and recommendations being formulated, but, I can't. I do however remember a few salient points that will, in short order, be illuminated.

The accident occurred because the left engine, one of two in the F-4E, incurred a fatigue failure in the "pig's snout" in one of its diffusers. The pigs snout, as the GE rep. called it, sits just in front of the burner-can (also called a combustor) and directs highly pressurized atmospheric air, which enters the front of the jet engine, and is compressed by several stages of compressor blades, and then mixes that highly compressed and fast moving air with atomized jet fuel. This mix of air and fuel is ignited, upon start and continues to burn during engine operation. The fire is held in a "flame holder" just behind the pigs snout in the burner-can. The flame in the burner can must remain surrounded by cooling air that passes through the engine and which is not used in combustion. If the flame, fire, in the burner-can touches the liner in the burner-can it will cause the metal to melt; something like 50 percent of all the air entering a jet engine (pure turbojet), is used for cooling of the burner can(s) (most jet engines have many of these burner-cans, maybe 16, but newer jet engines have one, completely annular, located inside, in a circle, around the inside of the engine casing). The failure of the "pigs snout" caused the flame in the burner-can to deflect upwards, into the burner-can liner and then, after the burner-can melt through, the flame burned through the engine casing, which houses the compressor and stator blades, burner cans, and turbines and the shaft upon which the compressor and turbine blades are attached and rotate. This uncontained burner-can flame, which was now burning outside, and on top of the engine burned into the number six fuel cell located directly above it; at that point there was nothing that could have saved the Phantom. The fuel in the tank spilled into the engine bay of the left engine and, given that massive amounts of air flowed through the narrow confines of the engine bay, the fuel fed a very hot fire that rapidly burned into all the other fuel tanks in front of and behind it (the E model F-4 had seven fuel cells) as well as propagating into the narrow passageways that connected the right engine to the left. With so much jet fuel pouring into the left engine's bay, it was a fait accompli that the fire would make its way to the right engine. And, when it did, it illuminated the right engine fire light.

The left fire light may or may not have illuminated at some point. When the burner can flame burned through the engine casing, it burned through one of the engine's fire warning loops. It was postulated that the fire loop was burned through so fast, due to torch like temperatures emanating from the burned through engine casing, that the fire loop was not able to warn of the engine fire in the left engine (in the F-4, if a fire loop was burned through, and not just heated, it would not warn of a fire/overheat. Unfortunately, back then, a burned out loop would not trigger a warning to the crew; in newer jets that is not the case).

When Joe saw the fire light on the right engine, he said he brought the right engine to idle and turned immediately towards McGuire, where he and the jet were based. He told Mike to get the engine fire/ overheat checklist out and they intended to run it, but, he said Mark, his flight lead, had quickly joined up on his left side and was telling him to eject, they was on fire. In addition, the range control officer too was telling them to eject, and when he and Mike saw the flames on the outside of the aircraft through their mirrors, they agreed it was time to give the aircraft back to the taxpayers.

There was nothing the crew could do to prevent the demise of the aircraft. The catastrophic fuel leak was feeding an uncontrollable fire that was literally burning off the back of the aircraft and propagating forward at a rate that defied rational comprehension; it's a miracle that the aircraft didn't explode once the fuel cells began to dump their fuel into the left engine bay.

So the consequence of the failure of the "pig's snout" was a massive engine fire and subsequent ejection of the crew. The GE rep said that in most cases, 90 percent, an engine fire in one engine of a F-4 began to spread to the other, "good" engine. It's interesting to note, that when an engine fire is alerted to the crew via a fire or overheat warning light, they, the crew, immediately retard the throttle of the burning engine and usually shut it down if the fire light remains illuminated once the engine is pulled to idle. Shutting down/retarding the throttle of the "bad" engine slows the airflow in the engine bay of the bad engine, which creates a higher pressure of air in the malfunctioning engine's bay. Since the good engine is still running, with the consequence of higher velocity air moving through it, the difference in air pressure between the engine with the fire, and the one without, causes the flames to gravitate/spread through small gaps and openings between the two engines and into the still functioning "good" engine.

Adding more fuel to the fire, so to speak, is the fact that the USAF mandated pilots move the applicable engine throttle to cutoff in case of an engine fire/overheat, then turn off the associated engine master

switch. In both cases fuel valves that feed the engine are closed....
but....these valves are located in different places. The GE rep said
that for years he told the USAF they should shut the engine off with
the engine master switch first, then after the engine quits, move the
throttle to cutoff. He said there was a lot of jet fuel in the fuel line
between where the engine master switch closed the fuel valve (hence
stopping fuel from the header fuel tank) and where the engine's throttle cutoff valve was located (which was near where the fuel entered
the engine casing). The engine master switch fuel shutoff valve was
located more upstream, closer to the fuel tank, than the throttle cutoff
valve. Continuing, the GE rep said that shutting off the engine master
switch first allowed all fuel in the fuel line to the engine to be burned
by the engine, consequently removing as much flammable liquid as
possible from that engine and engine bay area, thusly reducing the
chances for a fire to spread to the other engine. The USAF would not
heed this man's recommendation, so, as he said, in almost every F-4
engine fire, whether the aircraft landed successfully or not, he saw
signs of the engine fire propagating to the other engine.

So to this GE rep, the unsung hero of this accident investigation,
who was able to determine through analyzing an obliterated aircraft
the causal factors for its demise, I pay homage. I hung with him as he
showed me the bits and pieces that led him through his analysis and
conclusions. Totally amazing stuff. The man has a gift. And, in addition to his ability at accident investigation he was also very humble.
He submitted his report to us without any fanfare, pomp, or circumstance. He simply did his job and left.

With the reason for the engine fire determined, it was still a question,
more out of curiosity to me than of any significance, given the reve-

lations of the GE rep... When did the engine fire light illuminate on the right engine? Noticing it sooner than Joe had, assuming it was illuminated before the crew noticed it, would not have saved the aircraft, but, I did wonder when did the right engine fire light illuminate and why didn't the USAF have a system in place on the Phantom that would alert the crew if a fire loop became inoperative, in the case of a rapid burn-through?

I did look at the time of day, sun angle, brightness, the pop pattern headings, etc at the time of the accident. It is entirely possible that given the stress of flying at low altitude in the pop pattern in a four ship on a small bombing range and trying. to maintain position within that formation while flying the proper ground track, airspeed, and keeping track of the target area may have taken so much of Joe's and Mike's concentration that they may not have noticed an illuminated fire light. Also, time of day issues, bright, high sun angle, and a flight path that would cause that sun. to shine directly on the warning lights may too, have delayed recognition of an illuminated fire warning light. But, once the crew was in a period of low stress, like apexing in the pop pattern (because they were looking at their altimeter for the pull-down altitude), did they notice the fire warning light. It was all conjecture on my part, except the issue of why the USAF never put a fire loop fail warning system in the aircraft in the first place or why was there no aural fire warning system, which other fighters of the era had.

The Life Support gentleman, once he got his hands on the helmet that was lost from from Mike's head in the ejection, was able to determine that the nape strap on the back of Mike's helmet was not adjusted properly. Being too loose, allowed the helmet to rotate back on Mike's head once the 300 knot wind buffeted it and which caused the helmet to fill with more air than it should and consequently caused so much stress on the other parts of the helmet, mask, chin strap, they couldn't withstand the tension and either broke or detached through brute force. Richard was quick to point the finger at Mike for the loose fitting helmet and put it in writing on the accident report.

As the accident report was being finalized it was tweaked a few times by additions and subtractions. Causes, factors, and recommendations were added, or deleted, depending upon Richard's gravel. When it came to recommendations the USAF may or may not act upon them. The Phantom was an aged warhorse by the time of this accident and was being rapidly replaced by the F-16, it was doubtful the USAF would spend any money modifying any aircraft based upon the recommendations to the board. My only input for the accident report was that the F-4 be fitted with an aural Fire/Overheat Warning system so in the event the crew was in a high stress, very busy period of operation, a woman's voice, warning of a fire or overheat, would most assuredly get their attention (back then, in the USAF, only men flew fighter aircraft). Little did I realize at the time of my input how prophetic and personal would be my recommendation.

Three years after that F-4E accident on Warren Grove Bombing Range, I found myself flying in the very same unit, 141st TFS, that lost the F-4. Two years earlier I had left my Active Duty orders in order to go into the airlines and then became a traditional Guardsmen, flying five or six sorties a month in the Phantom. It was a great best of both worlds life and I loved it.

Literally almost three years to the day after the above accident I was flying as number two in a four ship of F-4E Phantoms. My back-seater was a beautiful Flight Surgeon, Lois. I had flown with her quite a bit. She didn't spend much time at the unit, generally every UTA (Unit Training Assembly) and the odd day here and there because she was promised a flight in the Phantom; she loved to fly in the backseat and was always trying her best to be a productive part of the two "man" crew concept. In her civilian life she had a child, was a General Practitioner, MD, with a local practice and was married to an active duty USAF Captain who was in the military police. But, almost every time she came in she requested to fly.

Lois was not a qualified WSO, but she really tried hard to learn the position in the short amount of time she spent flying with us. Her main job was to give flight physicals to the boys (pilots) and Jesus God in Heaven, did they line up in order to get a physical from her....she was gorgeous. Trust me, not one swinging, errrrr, not one male pilot wasn't hoping that she would give a hernia/prostate check with their physical; its the only time we wished a Doc would give the cough test or bend us over. I am sure guys who didn't need a flight physical requested one when she was on duty during a UTA. (btw, she never did the hernia/prostate check...damn the bad luck)

I flew with Lois a lot and usually we would do lunch before or after the flights in which we flew together. I won't lie, she looked great in a flight suit and I secretly had a crush on her that was never gonna be admitted or discussed. She was inside and outside, a beautiful woman, mother, wife, and doctor and I greatly respected her.

The four ship Lois and I were flying in on the three year anniversary of Joe and Mike's accident was pretty involved. We took off, rendezvoused with a KC-135 over Pennsylvania, air-refueled, and then dropped down to low altitude and flew a low level around the beautiful PA countryside. The low level ended with us dropping bombs, practice 25 pounders, like what Joe and Mike dropped, on the Indian Town Gap bombing range.

The weather that day was positively spectacular! The sky was cloudless and the humidity low, so you could see for miles and miles; the kinda day that caused you to love being alive. Flying the low level was so much fun since the weather was so nice. We avoided gliders over some of the ridges in the wave like, low mountains of central PA and as we did so I talked to Lois about how to operate the Phantom's radar and APX system. She was always wanting to learn, to be better. I always thought she would have been an excellent fighter pilot.

After the four Phantoms dropped their six bombs (each), we flew back to McGuire in a loose route formation, with Lois and I to the left of lead and three and four on his (Frank's, the flight leader's name) right. We flew back in the low teens, altitude wise, since McGuire AFB wasn't that far away.

We got vectored by ATC some as we approached McGuire from the west and were then turned over to McGuire approach as we were given a descent below 10,000 feet. I was looking below Frank's Phantom as we passed almost directly over the airport and Frank was turning to the right to set up for a right downwind whereupon we would eventually come up initial for a right break to land on runway 24.

Just as Frank began the turn I heard a female voice say "Engine Fire." It wasn't a yell "FIRE!", just a kinda casual "Fire", but man even though she didn't yell, as maybe my ex wife would have, that calm female fire voice really got my attention. I knew it wasn't Lois saying that so I looked at my engine fire warning lights and sure enough the right engine fire light was illuminated. I about shit. I immediately told Frank I had a fire indication on the right engine and was taking the lead on the left and to chase me; he immediately roger'd me and then told number three he lead of his element and to make their own way back to the field.

I told Lois, right after telling Frank I had the lead on the left, to get the checklist open to the Engine Fire/Overheat pages. She said "ok."

As I maneuvered, without ATC instruction or vectors, for a modified straight-in to runway 24, I went through the procedures, from memory, for an engine fire warning light.

I pulled the right engine to idle, in fact both engines were at idle since I was rapidly descending to get down pattern altitude since we were still about 8,000 above the field which was just on my right side. At idle the fire light was still illuminated so I shut off the right engine's generator and then, remembering what the GE man told me years earlier, I shutoff the right engine's master switch (which was still not what the USAF F-4 procedures called for. We didn't put that in our recommendations on our Final Accident Report since Richard didn't think the USAF would ever agree with GE on their position). Once the engine quit, literally a couple of seconds after turning off the master switch, I pulled the right engine's throttle to the cut-off position. We were now single engine.

With Frank chasing me and telling me he saw no sign of a fire, I turned onto a short right base, while still descending. After the engine was shutdown the fire warning light went out. I tested the fire warning system and it tested good; since it tested "good" I had every confidence the fire loop in the right engine had not burned through and whatever fire had caused the light to illuminate was now extinguished. All we had to do was land.

I switched Frank and I to tower frequency as we turned on to a short final while still descending. I put the gear down and half flaps, since we were single engine. Tower cleared me to land, while telling Frank he was cleared for a closed pattern after he left me. It's funny, but I hadn't talked to Lois since I told her to get the engine fire overheat checklist open. I was so busy setting up for the pattern, approach, and landing and running through the emergency procedures I hadn't thought to see how she was doing. So, just I was flaring to land, Lois chimes in and said she had the engine fire checklist open.

I calmly said, "Lois, look outside."

"Oh," was her casual reply.

The landing was uneventful and we turned off at the end of the runway and shutdown, maintenance was already waiting with a tug.

I wrote the aircraft up as maintenance gave Lois and I ride back to the Operations building. Once inside the entire four ship flight was debriefed by Frank, to include the end of it, my aircraft getting an aural fire warning. I told Frank I didn't even know they had modified Phantoms with aural fire warnings, since the ones I flew while on active duty weren't so modified. He said, "Yeah, they started retro-fitting them as the aircraft went through heavy maintenance. They started about 3 years ago."

"Go figure," I thought. I never would have thought the USAF would have acted upon that recommendation, given the age of the jets.

Lois and I went to lunch after that flight and had a good laugh about how long it took her to get the checklist to the correct page. That was the last time I flew with, or saw her again, since I shortly thereafter transferred to a F-16 unit, 119th FIS, located at Atlantic City International Airport.

I know this was a long story but, I hope it was worth reading, if anything for the six degrees of separation between the accident in which I was a board member and the fact that a recommendation I made due to that Phantom accident actually, possibly, saved Lois and me from the same fate (MX said there was a fire in the engine, but shutting down the engine caused it to go out). How bazaar was that?

I actually did get to go to the beach after working 28 days straight on that accident board. Bloody hell that was not fun, educational, but not enjoyable.

Richard and I did not part as friends, since I felt he was too hard-over into trying to find some sort of fault with the crew, and he said I was too focused on wanting to go to the beach. Serendipitously, and thanks to Richard, I found out that there really is such a thing in the military known as AWOL. I did hang out at my parent's house on the shore, for a week without telling anyone after we finished the accident report. I needed to decompress. After seven luxurious days of beach and bar time, my boss called me up to inform me that being AWOL was still a punishable offense, though he was laughing when he said it. Evidently Richard called him to say the accident board had wrapped things up and that I may be heading to the beach for a few days instead of reporting back to my base immediately.

Joe, the front seater in that F-4 accident, has been flying with American Airlines since those days of his accident. He's now a senior Captain. To my knowledge he's never had another engine fire.

Mike eventually became a General in the New Jersey Air National Guard. He never elected to fly in the airlines, instead when the unit switched to KC-135s, he chose to fly them, while also moving up in rank.

Lois and I were pen pals for a few years after I left the unit. Her husband was promoted to Major and got assigned to the Pentagon. They moved to Maryland when he got his new assignment and they had another child. I am happy for her. She is still is one of the finest ladies I've ever known.

Small World

A few years after reaching puberty, I was flew a F-4 into Pensacola Naval Air Station. I was a 2nd Lt in the USAF at that time. I had just recently gotten into my first operational squadron when a backseater, WSO (Weapons System Operator) asked me if I would fly him to Pensacola so he could attend his nephew's Navy OCS graduation. Since I'd fly whenever and wherever anyone wanted to go in those days, I happily said yes. He said he'd pay for my room for the weekend.

We arrived on a chilly, blustery late Friday afternoon with heavy rain and gusty winds. The ceiling (the bottom of the clouds) was down to around 400 feet above the ground with a mile of visibility. Due to the low cloud height I was given a PAR (Precision Approach Radar, where-in a radar operator gives you precise radar vectors, both in the lateral and vertical dimensions, to the runway) in order to get below all the crappy weather upstairs. We broke out close to 400 feet above the ground, but the visibility was actually better than a mile because it had stopped raining. Tower said the wind was 15 knots with gusts to 25 from the south, which made it a direct crosswind. While strong crosswinds bother some pilots, due to turbulence and complicating the landing equation with regards to having to be aligned with the runway upon touchdown, in the Phantom, at least for me, that was not the case. That sucker was, and still is, other than the B-777 that I flew for eight years with my airline, the easiest aircraft I've ever landed, crosswind or not.

I loved flying the Phantom in the pattern, as long as the chute deployed on landing (which it did 98 percent of the time). The drogue chute really helped to scrub off the initial speed of the aircraft after touchdown, whereupon the anti skid brakes were then used to slow the aircraft to taxi speed. Even if the drogue chute didn't deploy, the steel brakes would still stop the aircraft, but if it was a shorter runway, 8000 feet or so (most USAF runways were 10,000 feet) the brakes may get hot, which necessitated the aircraft be parked in a remote area because hot brakes can cause a tire to explode, or at the very least cause a fuse plug to melt and rapidly deflate the tire.

Finally, as a last resort, if the Phantom (or many other USAF and Marine/Navy fighters) needed to be stopped in a real hurry the pilot could drop the tail hook and engage one of two steel cables strung across the runway, one at each end, near the beginning, or end, depending on the direction you are traveling. Navy and Marine bases had three cables, one at each end and one, a midfield cable, and as it implies, in the middle of the runway. Very rarely, and usually only in the event of an emergency, wet runway with no drogue chute for example, or a loss of brakes, did a USAF Phantom use the cable to stop. The Navy and Marine guys, on the other hand were very adept and not hesitant to use their tail hook to stop their fighter if the braking was sketchy after landing, even if they didn't plan on taking a cable; better safe than sorry.

So it was with no trepidation that I landed in blustery winds on a wet runway and stopped in about 6500 feet, thanks to my chute deploying and my wonderful anti-skid brakes. After clearing the runway tower asked me how the braking action was and I said, "If I can stop a F-4 in 6500 feet, it must be good!" I proudly exclaimed.

Once we got to the transient ramp and shutdown, I told my back-seater to take off and enjoy his weekend, I'd put the aircraft to bed. His nephew and family were waiting in base ops when we arrived so I was happy for him being reunited with seldom seen family.

As I put my trusty Phantom to bed, closed the canopies, repacked the chute, and got my bag from the travel pod, I heard the faint whine of a jet engine in the background.

Having no plan for the weekend, I gathered my B-4 (clothes) bag, and headed for the local Officer's Club. It was Friday night and I expected to party like a rock star, expecting an amazingly crowded and festive casual part of the O'Club. Boy, was I disappointed. When I walked into the casual bar there were at best 7 patrons haphazardly scattered about, one of them being the bartender. I was totally depressed. I had psyched myself up for a wild weekend of local Florida girls in the Officer's Club, hoping to meet their prince charming in a flight suit, instead I got 6 people, retiree's it appeared, and a bartender himself who was probably on Medicare…dang.

Feeling let down, but thinking maybe I could still salvage this Friday night, I walked up to the bar, bag in hand, and plopped down onto one of the seats in front of it. Since the bartender was busy doing nothing, he immediately asked me what I wanted to drink. I ordered my customary adult beverage and then proceeded to whine to the him about the lack of female prospects in the bar. He was sympathetic but, he said the O'club was not exactly the normal collection point of estrogen in the area, he said going to a bar off the base was a better bet. I had no wheels. That was not gonna happen, at least not tonight, maybe tomorrow.

Still licking my wounds, I talked to the bartender to get a better feel for what Pensacola was like, just in case I was going to return; not likely. About 30 minutes into my stay at the bar and on my second drink, I heard a loud, deepish voice announce from somewhere behind me, "WHERE IS THE F-4 PILOT WHO JUST FLEW IN HERE!"

It was a booming voice and one that could be heard even if your hearing aid was turned off.

Gulp.

Errrr, that would be me.

I looked back to see what megaphone this guy was using and it turned out he had none. It was a 5 foot 8 inch tall, 5 foot 8 inch wide (at the shoulders), built like a brick shit house marine, with the traditional flattop haircut and biceps of which Popeye would have been jealous.

I held my position at the bar, thinking if I remained still enough I would be invisible; if I'd had about 10 more drinks I would have been invisible, at least in my mind. I might add that I had a F-4 patch on each shoulder and I was wearing a green flight suit which gave hint to my USAF affiliation. (Navy and Marines wore tan, khaki in color, flight suits). Shit. There was nowhere to run and I could FEEL this dude's fire breathing as he got closer. The bartender remained in front of me and gave me bullseye (position) calls as this Marine walked closer and closer.

Finally, out of my right peripheral vision I saw movement. I dared not look left or right, instead I stared straight ahead at where the bartender had been standing. That chicken, the bartender, upon the Marine's close approach, retreated and went to another part of the bar to continue drying glasses that I have no doubt were already dry. Pussy. A USAF bartender would have maintained position, at the very least to eavesdrop on the conversation that was about to ensue.

Finally, I couldn't stand it anymore. The marine had literally leaned over the bar, looking at me and no doubt wanted to get my undivided attention. I reluctantly and against better judgment gave in to the not-so-subtle body language on the Marine's part and turned to face my nemesis.

As soon as we made eye contact he said, "Son, was that you who flew the F-4 in here about an hour ago and told tower that the braking action was good?" asked the blonde haired, I'm going to kick your ass Marine.

"Uhhhh yes sir, that would be me," I weakly announced.

"And why did you tell them the braking action was good?" was his next interrogatory.

"Well, if I can stop a Phantom in 6500 feet in a crosswind and on a wet runway, the braking action must be good," was my honest and matter of fact reply.

"Well SON (ya know his use of son, though maybe sounding fatherly, caused me actually feel, due to his condescending inflection, like he was saying asshole)..Son (asshole)...the next time you land at a Navy or Marine base, you do NOT report the braking action as "GOOD" if there is a crosswind or wet runway, and particularly if there is both.

I damn near went off the runway tonight in my A-4 because tower said a F-4 reported the braking action as good, therefore I didn't take an approach end cable. When I landed the crosswinds with the wet runway gave me the ride of my life and I had to take a midfield cable to get stopped and to keep from going off the runway. So, next time you land at a base other than your country club Air Force bases, the braking action is not good. Do we understand each other?"

"Yes Sir," I simply responded.

"Good. Learning has occurred. Enjoy your evening Lt."

"You too sir," I said.

At that last comment of mine he smartly about faced and exited the room, the mini tornado that preceded him also left with him.

As much as I thought that was the end of the story, and I must add that I don't think I ever landed at another Navy or Marine base after that, I never thought fate would show itself in me becoming aware of this grumpy Marine many, many years later.

In 2019 my oldest son was going through the Hornet (F-18) RAG at Miramar. VT 101 I think it's called. Yes, in deference to his old man's advice, and tears, he, my son, became a Marine; obviously intelligence is not inherited.

About midway through his Hornet training and during one of our semi-monthly conversations about how his flight raining was going, Kyle said he was really worried about an up and coming simulator session. He said the instructor was a retired Marine and known to be an asshole, with a high bust rate.

I said, "Kyle, Marine and asshole in the same breath is redundant, but moving on, I said well, just schmooze him during the brief, you're good at bullshit, lay it on him. You know, you know your shit and you fly well, just try and butter him up."

"Yeah, easy for you to say, you were a golden child in training, I suck," he retorted.

" Son, Jesus, you don't suck! You're far better than me! You got a F-18 out of flight school for Christ's sake. You are excellent, you will do well. You know your shit. Just be respectful, and do the best you can," I said. Adding I said, "Can you let me know how the simulator went when you finish on Friday?"

"You bet dad."

So Friday rolls around and I get a voice mail from Kyle; I was actually in Europe flying a trip with my airline when he called. I thought hell must have frozen over upon seeing the voicemail, because his generation NEVER leaves a voicemail. He simply said it was urgent that I call him after I listened to the voicemail.

When I got to Operations after blocking in, and while between flights, I called Kyle. He answered on the first ring.

"Dad, you are NOT going to believe this....I mean in a million, million years you will not believe what happened on my simulator today," said Kyle with enthusiasm.

"Whoa, cowboy, take it down a notch, your'e running at high PRF. What happened to cause you to actually leave me a voicemail?" I said casually.

"Well, you know that simulator I was worried about today?"

"Yeah," I said.

"Well, in the pre-brief the simulator instructor and I got to talking. I was asking him what he flew when he was on active duty. He was a Marine. He said F-4s and A-4s. Well I told him you flew F-4s too. I then asked him where he was based. He said a bunch of different bases, Cherry Point, Beaufort, etc...but for some reason I asked him if he ever flew an A-4 into Pensacola. He said many times. I then told him the story about the time you flew into Pensacola and got your ass chewed by a Marine A-4 pilot because you said the braking action was good when it wasn't."

Kyle then took a long pause..."Dad that simulator instructor was THAT A-4 driver. I meant the same guy that chewed you out. He said what I told him, what you told me, was exactly correct. He couldn't believe that he was giving a simulator to the son of a USAF Phantom pilot that pissed him off so many years earlier. He was laughing. It turned out to be the best simulator I've ever had in training so far."

What a small world it is.

Buzzing the Beach

In my years flying the F-4 it had become a tradition of mine to make an annual 4th of July pilgrimage to the womb of my aviation career. Southern New Jersey was the genesis of my wings, with Atlantic City International Airport (KACY) being the epicenter of where the seed germinated and began to grow with the taking of my first flying lesson when I was fifteen; my father was the instructor.

The trips back home never got old. I usually landed at Springfield ANG base, in Ohio, and refueled and then hauled ass to KACY since fuel was not a factor on such a short flight. In fact one time New York Center told me I had to slow it down to "sub light" speed as he termed it, in order for them to feed me into their traffic flow around Philadelphia and Eastern PA as we descended. I always loved working with the East Coast Controllers since they were generally always accommodating to my odd requests, at least odd for civilian pilots.

On this on particular trip back east I asked the controller, since it was clear, no clouds and with a million miles of visibility million, I asked the controller if I could fly directly to Cape May, New Jersey instead of heading to KACY, my destination. We were level at 19,000 feet, FL 190, when I asked. He said, "Approved as requested," so I turned my two ship about 45 degrees right and headed directly for the very southern tip of New Jersey, which was visible in the distance. We flew right over Philadelphia as we headed towards the cape and I remember looking down at the city, thinking that many of the people down there would be heading to the Jersey shore for the holiday weekend; it was Friday afternoon as we flew over the city's denizens. In addition to my request for the direction of flight I also asked for a descent below FL 190. This request too was immediately granted.

Once below 18,000 feet, I told the controller I was cancelling my IFR clearance. He bid us a happy 4th and we then switched to a squadron discrete UHF frequency in order to chat on the radio if we needed to. However, we didn't chat like ladies catching up on gossip when on that discrete frequency, it was more for inter-flight direction or information.

Now free of ATC (Air Traffic Control) and their direction I descended to 100 feet above the Delaware Bay and set 300 knots indicated airspeed (IAS) as our cruise speed. The Phantom, in mil power alone, and with one centerline tank will easily accelerate to 600 plus knots indicated, so, 300 was just like the lope of a horse.

Because hitting a civilian aircraft at such a low altitude and in an area frequented and populated with many general aviation aircraft was a real danger, we used our onboard radar for lookout. In addition to our radar, the Phantom also had an "all seeing" electronic device, APX 76, that would allow us to see the transponder "paint" ANY aircraft squawking a mode 3 transponder code, out to 200 miles. So on we cruised on the lookout for other aircraft, or boats (I didn't want to fly over any at such a low altitude) with my wingman, Aggie, wide to my right so he could maneuver at will without worry of us colliding if he, or I, had to maneuver so as to avoid the aforementioned nautical or aeronautical hazards.

Once I reached the very souther tip of New Jersey, I flew about a quarter of a mile, or sometimes closer, off the beach and began to follow it north. I knew banner aircraft flew close to the beach and were actually higher than I was flying, but much slower, like 55 MPH, so I was cognizant of their possible presence as my back seater and I sight see'd flying just off the beach. "Gino," the back seater, came from the Navy and he remarked he'd not flown that low over the water when flying Phantoms in the Navy; I wasn't sure if he said that because he was uncomfortable being that low and wanted me to climb, or just making a casual remark…I guess I should've asked him.

Northward we flew at an easy 300 knots, waving to people on boats, going past Wildwood, Stone Harbor, Avalon, Sea Isla City, and then Strathmere and further on passed by Ocean City and then Atlantic City. As we passed Brigantine, a city north of Atlantic City, I changed course just a tad and flew very low over Pullman Island. Pullman Island is a small uninhabited barrier island between Brigantine and Beach Haven and an island over which I used to buzz and terrorize the seagulls during my banner towing days in a Super Cub. Upon flying past Pullman Island I rapidly climbed to 2000 feet and called for Aggie to come in close to route position for our recovery to into KACY which was 15 miles to the west.

We had enough gas as we came up initial in fingertip formation to runway 13 to do a few "shine your ass" overheads. So just before touching down on the runway after coming up initial and out of the overhead, I rapidly increased power to military, retracted the gear and the flaps and accelerated in level flight at 50 feet or less and then quickly pulled up at the end of the runway, stroking afterburner as I did so. I'd fly a wicked tight closed pattern, pulling 5 gs or more, or to the on speed AOA limit, so as to arrive on downwind at 1700 feet as read on the altimeter. I'm pretty certain the locals didn't appreciate the sound of freedom generated by the Phantom's twin J-79s in full grunt.

My father was always at the airport, every year, watching my colleagues and I as we zoomed around the pattern. He loved it. He always wanted to fly fighters, but in WW2 but he flew transports instead and from the Army Air Corps he went into the airlines, so he lived vicariously through me. At this period of time in his life he was a Flight Operations Test Pilot with the FAA and had been so for the past 25 years. KACY was the FAA's Aviation Test and Experimental Facility, where all kinds of stuff related to general and commercial aviation was tested, conceived, validated, etc.

After landing and parking at the FAA ramp, my three colleagues and I headed for the local sports bar with my father acting as the chauffeur. The pub we went to was my father's favorite, Rugby Inn. I'd spent many an evening there while growing up, listening to my Dad's flying stories as I drank a coke and he his beer. We knew the owners, their wives and all of the bartenders. It was an extension of our home.

Since it was the 4th of July weekend and we were in our flight suits, we couldn't buy a drink if we wanted to. Most of the "local's" in the bar knew my dad and/or me, and two of the more longtime bartenders, Harry and Bruce, had watched me grow from being knee high to a grasshopper to flying with them (grasshoppers). A whiskey front was fully upon us in the bar that late afternoon as we related to the patrons of our military exploits or we listened to theirs (military or otherwise). Those are such lovely moments in life.

After maybe 30 minutes of being in Rugby Inn, and just as I was downing my libation of choice, an older gentleman smacked me hard on the back and said, in a very loud voice and while pointing to the TV above the bar, "There you are!! there you are!!! Kenny (my dad's name) Kenny!!! You kid is on TV!!!"

I immediately looked at the TV and sure enough, there, full framed, was my F-4 flying just above the water and just beyond the Wildwood beach; I mean that cameraman zoomed in so close to my aircraft I'm sure you could have seen me and Gino's smiling faces if our visor's were up. I about shit. It seems that WCAU TV had been doing a remote from the Wildwood Boardwalk in preparation for the weekend's festivities and they decided to include the military in their coverage...not that I hadn't made it easy for them.

After filming my aircraft, for all the world to see, some smoking hot "on the scene reporter" (lady, just to be clear) said something to the effect, "Well even the Air Force is out enjoying the beautiful weather."

Upon announcing my F-4 was on TV, and my Dad hearing this old timer's yelling of me and Gino being movie stars, I tried to quell the excitement as I didn't want any patrons of the bar associating me with that wild ass beach buzzing guy; scheeeshhh....I mean who would fly that low near a busy beach?? I was seriously worried that the FAA and then the military would get involved and I'd get my ass reamed by my Commander for flying so low, and near, the populated beaches. At worst I could lose my wings, at the least be grounded for a while. At any rate I didn't want my name highlighted or associated with the aircraft on TV.

Unfortunately, the more I tried to quell the pointing at the TV and announcing, "That's Kenny's son!!!" the more a chorus of merry-makers joined in and since they were getting drunker, the louder they became. The TV station continued to show the picture of the Phantom randomly that evening as they repeated certain segments of the broadcast.

After drinking for free for a couple of hours, my Dad took us to his house and the boys and I changed and headed to the shore to eat dinner and hit some beach bars.

At lunch the next day, now sober, with clear head and with much less fan fare and excitement, I talked to the guys about the TV video. We all agreed it could have highlighted us, but so far my father said the FAA hadn't received any complaints from anywhere/anyone on the shore, or anywhere that we flew while coming in to the airport. The FAA in Atlantic City will get calls from time to time from locals, reporting low flying aircraft, loud aircraft, or anything that someone thinks is dangerous or out of the ordinary with regards to aircraft. The local police too will get calls and then they report it to the FAA. But, as of Saturday afternoon, my father said all was quiet and no reports came in of low flying aircraft. To say the least, I was very relieved and could now enjoy the rest of the weekend.

On Monday morning the four of us in our two Phantoms blasted off runway 13 and began our trek west. I had decided, since it was a beautiful morning, to again fly low over the water, however this time much further from the beach as we flew from north to south. When we reached Cape May, I climbed to 16,500 feet and called Washington Center asking them for an IFR clearance to Springfield;

after a few minutes delay, Center got us into the system and gave us our clearance west.

The rest of the flight back to our home base was uneventful.

Monday night, after getting home from work, if you call flying an F-4 work, I got a call from my father. It went something like this:

Me: Hello.

Dad: OK what the hell did you guys do after leaving? What kind of bullshit stunt was that?

Me: What are talking about?

Dad: You know damn right well what I'm talking about! You buzzed the hell out of the beach in Sea Isle. We got a million calls from the locals and the police on this. Don't deny it wasn't you. You told me you were going back down the coast after leaving at low altitude, so don't deny it wasn't you guys. That was really stupid what you guys did, buzzing that beach and scaring the hell out of everyone. And flying so low!!

Me: Whoa…whoa, I don't know what you are going on about! I swear to God we didn't buzz any beach on the way back, we flew over the water. I have no idea what you are talking about.

Dad: Bullshit. I don't believe you. You know exactly what you did, you just had to shine your ass again, I mean Friday wasn't enough, you had to push it more. I'm telling you the FAA is investigating this beach buzzing over Sea Isle and they are going to prosecute you. Your military flying days are over you son of a bitch! This was way out of line…"click" sound of phone hanging up.

To say I was perplexed is an understatement. I was baffled beyond belief. I simply had no idea what he was talking about. I sat down and was retracing the flight in my head when the phone rang again. This time it was my brother-in-law, John, who just happened to be the head life guard for Sea Isle City Beach Patrol.

Me: Hello

John: You are a fucking asshole.

Me: Ok. I can be, what did I do now?

John: Don't bullshit me. Do you have any idea how badly you scared the shit out of the people on the beach today? People were ducking for cover thinking you were going to crash on the beach, your jet wash was kicking up sand and knocking over umbrellas. I mean kids were crying for Christ's sake. What the fuck did you have to do that for? It didn't impress me if you thought you were going to.

Me: John, I swear to god, I didn't do that. I swear. My father just called and gave me shit like you are, but I'm telling you, it wasn't my flight or my aircraft, it had to be someone else. We flew pretty far offshore.

John: Well just to let you know I called the police and gave them your name to give to the FAA. I hope they hang you....click.

Dumbfounded. An appropriate word after just talking to my father and John...if you could say I talked to them, more like a one way ass chewing.

I contemplated what my father and John had told me for the rest of the evening. I knew in my heart that my flight didn't buzz any beach, except Pullman Island on the Friday of our arrival, and unless seagulls suddenly evolved and and had the ability to use a phone, let alone talk, I wasn't worried about that coming back to haunt me. No, this was different. The anger of both my father and John was beyond belief. Whoever did that buzzing must have been low and fast, but who and what kind of aircraft did it?

In the days immediately following those angry phone calls I waited with some trepidation for a visit from my CO (Commanding Officer), or a call from the FAA, or some other higher up accusing me of buzzing Sea Isle Beach. But, none came. Ever. After a month the memory of the incident began to rapidly leave my conscience thoughts and died away, until 20 years later.....

20 years after being accused of buzzing Sea Isle City Beach in my Phantom, I was an MD-11 Captain and Instructor Pilot. On this gloriously sunny afternoon, just like the one in which I arrived in Atlantic City on that fateful 4th of July, I was flying to Seattle. In the right seat of the MD-11 was my student, a potential First Officer on the jet. This was his first flight on the aircraft after getting his type rating. He had a few more flights after this one before I would sign him off as being being fully qualified.

As we flew on to Seattle, about a three and a half hour flight in total, we occasionally chatted about our past military lives. This guy had been a Navy A-7/F-18 pilot and had been an instructor in the A-7 at Navy Lemoore at one point in his life.

Since I'd instructed in the F-4, he and I swapped stories of our respective military lives and recalled some of the more interesting events that came to mind as we taught our students, or flew in operational squadrons. So, it was somewhere on this flight west where I told this First Officer of that 4th of July where I was caught on camera and then of the fact that someone had buzzed Sea Isle City beach and I got blamed for it. As a point of note, I rarely told anyone that story since it really didn't seem that epic, or worth telling.

Upon hearing of the Sea Isle City buzz job, the F/O looked me square in the eye and said, "I know who did that."

"No, way I responded!!!" being totally shocked. "I've been wondering all of these years who and what did that. My father never believed me when I said I didn't do it."

"The scoop is this. The guy was an A-7 pilot and instructor in the sister squadron. His family had a summer house in Sea Isle and he flew into to Willow Grove NAS to spend an extended weekend with his family in Sea Isle. He left Monday morning, just like you did, but an hour later. He flew VFR from Willow Grove to the shore where-upon he buzzed the shit out of the beach because all his family was there and some old friends from school. He did three passes and from you said and what I was told after he lost his wings, they were some seriously low passes. He was so low his exhaust was kicking up sand and I heard, literally mothers and kids were crying. They thought he was crashing. Lifeguards jumped from their chairs. It was ugly dude."

"Wow…wow…wow," that's crazy I stated. "What the hell was he thinking? I mean didn't he think anyone would get upset? What happened to him?" I then asked.

"After he buzzed the beach the FAA was called. They looked at the time the beach was buzzed and then saw his aircraft's radar return on the recording of the radar scope that covers that area. They were able to then follow the raw radar return to when he picked up an IFR clearance and began squawking a discrete ATC code. It was then that they had him identified and the Navy was informed of this guys beach buzzing. He was grounded upon landing at his refueling stop and never flew in the Navy again; they pulled his wings."

"Dude," I replied, "Ya know what is a shame? My father died a few years ago believing that I lied and did that buzz job. I really wish he was alive right now so I could clear that up with him. It's the only thing in my flying career of which he was ashamed. He would just not believe that I was telling the truth."

Vampire Pilot

After the Second World War, Germany was divided into sections which were controlled/occupied by the allied nations. Northwest Germany, about 30 percent of the entire country, was controlled by the UK immediately following the end of hostilities.

During this post war period of time the RAF and British Army held regular, joint exercises amongst either each other or with the other allied forces.

During one such exercise an RAF Vampire (type of early jet fighter) was flying over the northern plains of Deutschland. The pilot in it was desperately looking for any recognizable landmark that would help him to determine where he was so he could continue on his assigned low level. Like a pig in space, he flew brazenly and blithely over the featureless and flat terrain, mostly farmland, his visibility hindered somewhat by a thick haze. But, though he knew not where he was, he was making good time getting "somewhere" since he was flying at full power, which in a Vampire was around 400 knots indicated air speed. Looking down at his navigation map, which was on his thigh, he took a longer than normal glance at it since he was trying to figure out where he was. He was supposed to locate a certain regiment of the British Army, with whom he was to coordinate a simulated attack. Sensing "something" was amiss, our intrepid fighter pilot looked up from his map just in time to see a rather large tree directly in front of him. Impact was certain, but he pulled back on his flight control stick anyway, while also ducking down, in order to try and minimize the full effect of the very large tree's branches on his rather stout Vampire. This tree, by the way, just happened to be the only tree with-in many miles of his still unknown position.

After the collision, and with branches adorning his Vampire, as if it was camouflaged, the pilot rapidly climbed to altitude, and now using his electronic navigation radio, he headed directly for his RAF base and landed without incident. It should be noted that the aircraft maintainers on the flight ramp were laughing hysterically at this seemingly well camouflaged, but lightly damaged Vampire as it taxied to its assigned parking spot.

Reporting to the assistant base commander, because the base commander was back in the UK, the mishap Vampire pilot was scolded by his superior for his stupidity in hitting the tree. After his ass chewing he was ordered, for his punishment, to join other ill mannered RAF personnel, those who had gotten on the bad side of their MFWIC (Muther Fu&ker Whose In Charge, pronounced "miffwick") and were told they had to visit the local infirmary at the end of the work week.

So, Friday morning at 9 AM a truckload of RAF personnel boarded a truck, including our Vampire pilot, for the short ride to the local village in order to visit the hospital there and spread cheer amongst their fellow British, army and RAF, compatriots who were hospitalized for various reasons.

Those that were sent to the hospital were not in the least bothered by this seemingly onerous duty. Though their superiors felt it was an appropriate punishment for their misdeeds, sending them on this goodwill tour of the hospital, what they didn't realize was that the village was having an Oktoberfest party starting that Friday afternoon, and since the boys would already be in town, they would get a head start on the festivities when compared to the others on base and away from the town.

Our Vampire pilot was the lone RAF pilot, well, for that matter the only pilot in the group and he peeled off from the rest of the lads as he made his way from room to room. He spoke briefly with the sick and injured in each room, attempting to give them an encouraging word. Sympathy and good will was not his forte as he struggled to find the appropriate words of cheer as he saw the men in various conditions of disrepair and disease. Quite simply, he thought, most the boys didn't seem that bad or worse for wear.

As two o'clock rolled around and having spread as much cheer as he could muster, the Vampire pilot headed for the nearest hospital exit, in order to be the first to get a pint at the Oktoberfest party. As he rapidly approached the only exit in sight, he chanced to glance into a room as he was running by. The sight of the patient in the room caused him to immediately slide to a stop. In fact he coasted a few feet beyond the doorway to the room and had to backtrack in order to enter it.

Entering the room, he saw, by far, the most injured man he had seen that day as he had roamed the hospital. This patient's head, except for one eye, his nose and his mouth, was bandaged while his entire left arm was in a cast and held above his side by a wire. One leg, too, was bandaged heavily and there were other lessor cuts and scrapes adorning his other leg and arm.

"Bloody hell mate!" Exclaimed the Vampire pilot as he entered the room, "What in the hell happened to you?"

Taking a draw from the fag (cigarette), which was in his right hand, the patient responded dryly…"Well, I'm an artillery observer in the regiment, right. And I was taking a break from our war game exercise on Thursday, smoking a fag under the only tree in Northern Germany, and some bloody RAF pilot flew through the tree and knocked it on me."

Near Death Experiences

I've never taken a survey of those with whom I've flown over the past 45 years, since I began flying, about how many near death experiences they've had, but, I suspect some have had many close calls (with regards to dying in an aircraft accident) while others very few. I'm sure the nature of the flying has more to do with the number of near deaths than the ability of the pilot: crop dusting, airborne fire fighting, fighter pilot, bush pilot, et al. If you combine the two aspects, inadequate pilot and hazardous flying, I suspect natural, Darwinian, processes take over to weed out the inept.

At one point in my life, I was one of the inept and it nearly cost me my life. But, before I tattle of my near death experience while still young, let me elucidate on a few close call episodes that occurred because I did survive my Darwinian moment.

There is a saying that what doesn't kill you, makes you stronger. This can apply to almost every walk in life, but, I think we could substitute "smarter" with stronger in the case of lessons's learned while enjoying a flying career. I definitely have had my defining, learning mistakes while flying, however the more notable, more dramatic moments came while flying in the military. Although, many of my fleeting moments of "learning" were due less to errors on mine, or anyone else's fault, but had more to do with the nature of military flying and the more inherent dangers in that occupation.

Flying F-4s and F-16s in the USAF has caused me, without question, more near death experiences than any other position I have ever held while flying. Oddly though, and quite simply, most of the "close calls" while flying in the USAF were so fleeting they were forgotten almost as soon as they happened. Near mid air collisions, while involved in multi bogey air to air battles top the list for the most close calls. However, three notable near death experiences have occurred while I was flying the F-4, two of them while flying low levels and all three involving another aircraft.

The first near tragic collision with another jet so low to the ground occurred over the skies of Colorado while I was a student in the F-4 and flying on the second to last flight in my F-4 training. I was number two in a flight of four Phantoms. We were bombing an airfield at a bombing range in Colorado and were ingressing to the target at low altitude. At some point numbers three and four Phantoms were to drag, slow down, and get separation from my element, the leading element. At the IP, Initial Point, where the final attack run is to begin, we were to speed up to 540 knots ground speed. Which is what my lead did, at the IP, he increased speed to 540 knots ground speed. Numbers three and four, though initially well behind us, sped up to 540 knots well before the IP. The difference in speeds between the leading and trailing Phantoms caused the trailing F-4s to get too close to the lead element, thusly creating a potential conflict with the aircraft over the target area since time deconfliction was being used to separate the Phantoms in their attacks. As expected, though I didn't know numbers three and four were so close behind, when I performed my "pop" (You go rapidly up, from being at low altitude to a few thousand feet so as to acquire the target visually and then you rapidly reverse your climb and descend in a preplanned dive angle in order to bomb the target; in this case we were using 20 degree dives) and rolled in to bomb the target, the number three Phantom and I, who were attacking the same target, passed exactly over each other and headed in exactly opposite directions. I saw him just as I dropped my bombs, 6, 500 lb Mk 82 inert (concrete filled) bombs; he said he passed under me by 50 feet, though I'd swear it was less. How he missed my bombs as they fell I have no idea. He and I both drank heavily at the bar that night.

The second "I should've died" event happened on what should have been a very benign lost wingman demo. I was training a new Phantom pilot and I was in the backseat of his aircraft, in the seat normally occupied by the Weapons System Operator (WSO). In most of their training student pilot's fly with a student WSO, but there are some phases of F-4 training when an Instructor Pilot (IP) flies in the back-seat of the F-4 for training and safety reasons. I can almost guarantee you if a student backseater had been with the student pilot on this flight, four people might have died that day.

We were number four in a flight of four and we were flying at 300 knots indicated airspeed and about 15,000 feet MSL. We were on the right side of number three, who was on the right side of number one, with number two F-4 on the left side of number one. We were in fingertip, close formation, where only ten feet, or less, of separation is normal between the aircraft. In this exercise, lost wingman demo, lead calls "Lost Wingmen Demo Now!" or some radio call like that.

What is supposed to happen is for number four, and number two, to simultaneously turn away, not rapidly per se', from number one (in four's case, turn away from number three) and establish a 30 degree heading change and maintain the change for something like fifteen seconds. Number three turns away from number one, after watching number four turn away and ensuring there is a safe separation, and turns fifteen degrees away and holds that heading change for fifteen seconds whereupon two, three and four are supposed to return back to the heading lead was flying; good luck with that was always my thought if I had to do that in real life in the clouds (I never did). The purpose of the exercise was to show the students how much separation you get with the heading changes.

On this flight, and why I'll never ever know, since I never asked the pilot flying the aircraft in the number three position (he was an Instructor Pilot) why he did what he did, but...when lead, number one, call for the "Lost Wingmen Demo Now!" number three rolled rapidly right, like 80 degrees of bank, and turned rapidly into my aircraft. Even though the fronseater, student, in my aircraft was operating the controls, flying, when I saw the extremely rapid roll of number three begin, I slammed the stick forward which caused our aircraft to experience about 3 negatives G's and caused us to immediately descend so as to avoid number three as he turned rapidly right, just above us.

"WTF" I thought to myself as I saw three peel off to the right, and over, us and then, recovering his senses, roll out and began to rejoin on lead. Four people almost died. There is just no way you can train for that sort of near miss. Number three and I never did discuss why he did what he did.

The third more memorable close call occurred as I was going through USAF F-4 Fighter Weapons School. It was in fact my last flight in the program and it damn near ended three lives; mine, my backseater's, and an A-10 pilot's (life). The brief encounter with fate occurred as I was leading a four ship of Phantoms in a spread, tactical formation, flying at 480 knots, and passing over a relatively low, in height, line of mountains called The Belted Mountains. My four ship was ingressing to a target in Gold Flat, a dry lake bed, which was on the west side of the range and an A-10, unbeknownst to me, was heading east, leaving the same target area. I had picked a notch, an area in one of the mountains where a ridge took a sharp dip, to fly through and at an altitude of maybe 50 feet above the mountain pass, or notch, and nearly inverted I was "pulling down" down so as to try and conform my flight path to match that of the mountain's and not fly too high above the terrain. Unfortunately the A-10 had picked the same notch to fly through, though he was on a reciprocal heading and flying upright. I passed right over the guy (no women in A-10s back then) by maybe 25 feet. He was looking up at me. I could clearly see him and the inside of his cockpit, not to mention his whole aircraft, up close and personal. "Son of a bitch that was close!!!" I quietly screamed to myself as we exited the pass on the west side.

Changing gears here, well before the USAF experiences however, another, and in my opinion much closer near death experience (if you can define them by degrees of "closeness") occurred that, to this day, I can see in my mind and recall as vividly as the moment it happened.

I was beginning my third season of banner towing with Paramount Air Service and this was my second summer as Chief Pilot at their satellite Bader Field Operation. Quite honestly I'm fluffing myself up when I say Chief Pilot, since I was the only pilot towing banners regularly out of Bader. Our main operation was in Cape May, where we had six to eight aircraft towing down there. My operation was small beans, but I was the boss, with two smart ass banner kids under my charge and I really enjoyed my summer job; after my first tow that season however, I seriously rethought about embarking on an aviation career.

My father began training me to fly when I was fifteen. He was one of two instructors who taught me while I was in high school and both continued to teach me until I got my Commercial License shortly after graduating (high school).

My father was my biggest hero in the aviation realm. As I approached the time required to get my commercial rating, 250 hours, he insisted I learn aerobatics. It was not required by the FAA at that time, nor is it now, but, the Old Man was old school, having learned to fly in 1940 and he wanted me to learn to do spins, wicked steep, full power on, departure stalls, loops, rolls, etc.

He did not teach me, however, those aforementioned maneuvers. He got his friend Jack, the previously alluded to Instructor, to instruct me. Jack owned a beautiful 1947, 8A Luscombe. It was a single engine, 65 horsepower, all metal beauty in which I had soloed shortly after my first solo and in which I had the pleasure to fly from Marathon, in Florida Keys, to New Jersey while still in high school. I was intimately familiar with this aircraft and adored it.

Over a period of a week, and just before I took my Commercial Flight Test with the FAA, Jack and I "went up" and performed more spins, stalls, loops, and rolls than I care to remember; unlike my father, who was the "good cop" of an Instructor, Jack was the "bad cop" and could be a real asshole in the cockpit. Fear, sarcasm, and ridicule were his "motivational" tools, man that son of a bitch and I argued at times, but, no matter what we always kissed and made up by the end of the flight. What can I say? He was Italian and passionate. I knew his style of teaching was the only way he knew how to instruct and he always kept saying that what he was teaching me may someday save my life.

So, let's return to that previously mentioned third season of banner towing at Bader Field. I would usually arrive home from college in mid to late May. As soon as I got home I immediately began working at the airport, getting ready for the first weekend of towing by sprucing up the office, checking on what banners may need to be assembled for the first tows of the season and making sure my aircraft was ship shape. Usually, the Friday before Memorial Day Weekend was when I had my first tows of the summer.

My landing currency when I began that first tow of the season was always marginal and I was usually rusty when it came to hands on flying ability. While in college, 3 takeoffs and landings every 90 days (The FAA minimum currency requirement), was always just met. I didn't have the money to rent an aircraft while at college and my school was seven hours from my parent's house. If I did go home I could have used one of the flying club aircraft to which I had access in order to stay more proficient, but I enjoyed my freedom while at college, so I only went home during the mandatory school breaks.

When the Friday of the Memorial Day weekend came round I had the banner kids, John and Jeff, set up the first banner to be towed. We had five banners to tow that Friday of the season opener and I was ready to fly! Lord I missed flying that Super Cub, N6897B, when I was in college. It was my third season towing with her and I knew all of her quirks and idiosyncrasies.

It was a gloriously beautiful late morning when I took off on runway one six, 16, the shortest of the three runways and closest to where my aircraft was tied down. After liftoff I immediately turned left and climbed to eight hundred feet and began a wide left turn so as to then head back towards the airfield, which was surrounded on three sides by water.

The banners I picked up were laid out into the prevailing wind, with the tail of the banner being furthest up wind with a long tow row rope attached to the front end of the banner. One end of the tow rope was attached to a very strong fiberglass bar, about 6 feet in length, onto which the first letter (of a possible 36) was connected (obviously in series, with each letter being attached to the other). This long rope, maybe 100 feet in length, had a loop on the "other" end. This loop was draped between two poles that stood about ten feet apart and about five feet above the ground. I had a long, maybe 12 feet, metal pole that was mounted under my aircraft. The front end of the pole was attached to three metal braces that apexed between the front wheels, and under the aircraft, but not so low as to touch the ground. The front end of this pole could move left and right and up and down, IE. It could swivel while still being firmly attached to the metal braces/rods that secured it to the aircraft. The aft end of the pole went all the way back towards the tailwheel, but, was still in front of it by about a foot. The tail end of the pole had a little metal hook, not unlike a fishing hook, but one that could could be released to snap back. Also, the pole was held "up," retracted position, against the bottom of the aircraft by a wire that I controlled in the cockpit. Thusly, once I was airborne I released the pole, since it was in the up in position, and let it drop below the aircraft. Due to air loads against it, the pole would slightly drag back, but still, was down far enough below the aircraft so that when I swooped down and put the pole on my aircraft between the two poles holding the loop of rope, the little hook at the end of pole on my aircraft would snag the tow rope as soon as I flew between the "pots" (poles where the tow rope was strung).

To those that have never seen a banner pick-up, it may seem dramatic, and, I suppose, to some degree it is and it's certainly not something you see everyday and the dramatic change in the aircraft's flight path as it picks up a banner is noteworthy. My personal technique for picking up a banner was to descend somewhat gradually from 800' MSL (Mean Sea Level) while I flew precisely in line with the banner's that were laid on the ground and with the intention of having the pole hanging underneath my aircraft pass between the two poles between which the banner tow rope was strung. It was my intent to have at least 100 mph indicated air speed when I passed between the pick-up poles. As soon as I passed between the "pots" (pick-up poles), I added full power on the aircraft's engine and began a very rapid climb, with the nose of the aircraft going up to 40 or 50 degrees of pitch. As I passed between the pots I would look out the left side of my aircraft and down, and try to see (I usually could) if my pick-up pole had snagged the tow rope (The window that was normally there had been long since removed). Shortly after reaching 40 to 50 degrees of pitch, the tug of the banner would naturally lower the aircraft's nose and the airspeed would dramatically decrease from 100 mph to maybe 50 MPH. But, as fast as the airspeed decreased the nose was lowering faster and at some altitude above the ground, generally around 250 to 300 feet, I stopped allowing the aircraft's nose to lower and held a slight positive pitch. With the pick-up complete, I then held a slow climb to a thousand feet while also turning left so as to stay away from Bader Field's runways. I would continue the left turn until north of the airport and clear of its traffic pattern. From that point I would turn to read the banner, in other words I'd turn sharply while looking back at the banner, so as to read what it said. I had a paper in the cockpit that stated what each banner said and where it was to be towed. So, once I read the banner I knew where it was supposed to go and I'd adjust my route of flight to fly over the beaches the customer desired. Some customers might only want the Atlantic City Beaches, while others wanted from Ocean City to Atlantic City, and Brigantine Beach too. The shortest tow took 20 minutes from pick-up to drop-off, and the longest, Barnagate Light to Cape May, 2 hours.

I did not, and actually still don't, think banner towing was/is dangerous, per se'. Yes there are dangerous aspects of it, the pick-up for example, but for the most part I thought it was pretty benign.

And therein lies the rub for me on this first banner tow of my third season of aerial advertising, the pick-up.

As I came through the pots that morning I was carrying a little extra airspeed, 110 mph verses 100. Because I had this excess speed I pulled up more steeply than normal. As I normally do I looked over the left side, and down, to see if the I had snagged the tow rope; I had. But, and here's where I became hyper vigilant of the flight environment around me, and where everything started to occur in slow motion.

First, after looking to see if I had snagged the tow rope, I looked forward. I felt the tug of the banner, but for some reason I didn't lower the nose as rapidly as I normally did. Rusty flying skills perhaps?

Shortly after sensing the airspeed decrease, I noticed the left wing start to drop. This was odd I thought, why is my left wing dropping? It never did that before. I added right aileron to stop the left roll. The left roll increased more rapidly with the addition of right aileron and then all hell broke loose.

The nose dropped extremely rapidly and precipitously, even though I had been holding the stick back, and the aircraft continued to roll uncontrollably left. It was when the nose dropped and rolled that I actually pulled the throttle to idle, momentarily, and simultaneously shoved the stick forward, briefly increasing the nose down pitch; at that point all I could see was the ground and water, and I had a fleeting thought then, that when I crashed I didn't want it to be in the water but on land.

I can tell you, to this day, I remember absolutely, vividly, this entire event and in the same slow motion temporal distortion (as a USAF flight shrink likes to call it) in which I perceived it happening. In actuality, after talking to the banner kids it took all of a few seconds for this event to unfold and then finish.

After I had shoved the control stick forward, the left roll stopped and I immediately added full power on the engine. I was now pointed extremely nose low, how steeply nose low I don't know, nor can I tell you how high I was, but I did notice I was now headed exactly 180 degrees out from my initial run-in heading and I could see the banner kids standing by the trailer that held the rest of the day's banners.

In a tempo that I have no idea how I knew to balance, speed of pull verses pulling to rapidly and stalling again, I began to pull the control stick aft so as to try and avoid from hitting the ground. By the grace of God I did, avoid the ground, and I still had the banner attached. The banner kids said, later, I recovered maybe 50 to 30 feet above the ground.

Recovering from the near crash, I towed the banner on its normal tow. It was an easy Atlantic City only run and I was dropping the banner on the field twenty minutes after that unusual pick-up.

Instead of picking up another banner right away, as I normally would, I landed. I taxied onto the grass from where I normally picked up my banners and shutdown. My legs were shaking uncontrollably. I literally could not stop them, I had gotten an adrenaline overdose…I almost died in that banner pick-up and I was extremely aware of my near death experience. It all happened so fast, but yet so slow in my mind. I have revisited that near death experience in my life more than any other aviation faux pas I have committed so far.

The banner kids came rushing up to the right side of the aircraft, which was normally wide open for the most part, and they begged me to "do that again," they said it looked so neat. I could hardly talk. I literally just sat in the aircraft and tried to put together the events that caused me to stall and spin at such a low altitude. All I could think of was that I just didn't let the nose lower fast enough after feeling the tug of the banner and held too high of an angle of attack as the airspeed decreased; it's the only thing that makes sense.

What amazes me to this day, was my perception, or lack thereof, in my conscious brain that I was stalling, but, the fact that my subconscious knew. My instincts, once I stalled, took over to rectify the situation. Everything I did once the aircraft stalled and rolled was by automatic response to the elements as they occurred. I can honestly say, I didn't think as the left roll was happening and while the nose dropped that I was stalling and I must reduce the power because I thought the torque of the engine was exacerbating the left roll. Every action I took to keep from crashing came out of automatic response.

Yes, all, the steps I took to recover from that totally inept flying, the initial part of the banner pick-up, were instinctual and I give Jack the credit for beating into me the automatic responses I needed in order to recover from a stall and spin. That week of aerobatic flying, and then my own practicing after I got my commercial, ingrained a set of automatic responses in my conscious and subconscious that were utilized when I stalled and spun accidentally.

Though I never had another banner pick-up that was near as dramatic, I can tell you that the next summer, before my first banner pick-up of the season, I took off in 6897B and practiced stalls, steep turns and basically got my banner towing skills back.

Also, it is interesting to note that the airfield manager saw me do that stall and spin. After my flying was done for the day he walked up to me and told me what an asshole I was and that he could smell death.

"I smell death on you, you're gonna die. You're a smart ass (I could be) and its only matter of time before you crash and die while towing banners out of this field."

Wow. I love you too Mr Argus. In a way maybe his prediction was motivation for me to mind my P's and Qs and not grace him him with his prediction. I can certainly tell you that I got more serious about my faith that day and I took all flying training that I received after that near death experience with the belief that it might one day save my life.

Bob Grace

Robert Grace did something only Tex Johnston before him, as far as I know, has done—he barrel rolled a four-engine airliner. But, before I tell you of that amazing daredevil act, I must briefly illuminate the man in more detail.

Robert, Bob, was an extremely humble man (he is now deceased) who lived in the shadow of his good friend Bernie Hughes. Mr Grace was my neighbor and a colleague of my fathers. All three men, Bob, Bernie, and my father were Flight Operations Test Pilots with the FAA at its National Aviation Facilities Experimental Center (now called FAA William Hughes Technical Center).

Bob was extremely laid-back and modest, yet my father said he was one of the best stick-and-rudder pilots with whom he ever flew; coming from my father that was a great and very rare compliment.

Mr. Grace started his career flying P-51s in World War II and then, after the war, came back to New Jersey and flew a variety of fighter aircraft in the Garden State's Air National Guard Units: P-51, then F-84 (both models), F-100 (both models), and then the ultimate testosterone producer (in men, no women fighter pilots during those days) the Republic F-105 Thunderchief.

Bob was hired by the FAA in the early 60s. While flying full-time with the FAA, he also continued to fly part-time in the locally based Air National Guard Unit where he flew whatever fighter jet they operated at the time (every few years or so, they would reassign the unit based at Atlantic City Airport a different type of fighter).

One day a whiskey front (impromptu alcohol fueled party) happened to blow into my backyard, and I couldn't have been happier as that was the day a whole flock of eagles landed in my backyard to exchange flying tales, big and small, while refueling on scotch, bourbon or beer. As the sun faded emotional spirits soared as the liquid spirits, acting like jet fuel, propelled these jet jockeys into the stratosphere of story-telling heaven. So may aircraft where whirling about in their stories I didn't know which group of men to stand next to and eaves drop. Being in my early teens, I felt gifted by God as these amazing aviators told their tales. I had so many wonderful witnesses around me revealing secrets to a world that only God and the angels were privy.

I remember this one particular backyard soirée because Mr. Grace was party to an interesting tale that I will never forget. Bernie Hughes, the originator of the story had flown P-47s in the war and who, like Bob, flew all the same fighters in the same Air National Guard Units. Mr. Hughes recanted the story, no doubt to quell my incessant badgering of the pilots for flying stories.

After Mr. Hughes took a nip of his Scotch he began to tell of the day that Bob Grace almost had to bail out of an F-84 whose engine had flamed out as they were returning from a mission flown off the New Jersey coast. Continuing his narrative and his nipping, Bernie said that as they neared Atlantic City and while still above 10,000 feet Mr. Grace's engine quit for no apparent reason. Bob immediately set up a glide and headed toward the Atlantic City Airport, which is actually ten miles northwest of the city. As the F-84 rapidly lost altitude, F-84s do not glide well, Bob had diverted most of his attention to trying to start the F-84's only engine. Down Bob descended, and, as Bernie told the story, he flew alongside Bob trying to keep him abreast of their position and more importantly of their altitude since Bob was so intent on getting the jet's engine running. Bernie was afraid Bob would lose track of his height above the ground and might possibly get too low to bail out should the engine not start at a reasonably high enough altitude, so that's why Bernie maintained a close watch on both their altitudes.

Bernie said to Bob, as they went through 3000 feet, "Ya know, Bob, you may have to jump out of that thing."

Bob did not respond.

From three, to two, to finally one thousand feet, Bernie was calling out altitudes and telling Bob to get out of the jet…still no word from Bob.

Finally passing one thousand feet Bob told Bernie he got the engine running and was waiting for it to spool up to speed so he could develop usable thrust and climb. At 500 feet Bob's descent stopped and he climbed to 1,500 feet and landed straight in on runway 31, now only a few miles straight ahead.

Concluding the story, Bernie said to Bob, "Ya know, Bob, I've never told you this before but you are my hero for going so low to save that jet. I would've punched out much sooner!"

For Bernie to say that Bob was his hero was a big deal for Bernie, because quite simply, Bernie had a really big ego and my father always thought Bernie's biggest hero was Bernie himself.

As my father and I listened to the end of Bernie's short story Bob chimed in, "Bernie, to this day, I have never told anyone this, but do you know why I never ejected that day?"

Bernie, in a look of surprise as he added more jet fuel to his gas tank said, "I assumed you wanted to save the jet."

"No, that's not why. To be honest, I didn't care about the jet. No, the real reason I stayed so long in the cockpit was because I had never armed the ejection seat prior to getting in the jet so I couldn't have ejected if I wanted to . . . so let me tell you, I had a lot of personal motivation to get that engine started."

And with that Bob took a sip of his scotch and gave a quick wink to me while my dad and Bernie belly laughed and I vowed to myself that if I ever flew fighters I would always arm my ejection seat.

While that heretofore untold story is cute, it is just a lead-up to one of the coolest thing's I've ever heard a pilot do—maybe not the smartest, but what Bob did in the early 1980s in a Convair 880 rivals the acclaim that Tex Johnston gets for rolling a Boeing Dash 80 (B-707 prototype) over Lake Washington in 1955.

The magnum opus of Bob's flying career, and an event any pilot would relish to claim as an accomplished feat (but without the scrutiny of the FAA), came in the summer of 1980. In my heart it remains the gutsiest move of any pilot I have ever known to have done, even to include Maverick's infamous spilt S in the movie Top Gun.

On a sultry August day, Nan 42, a FAA owned CV-880 was being flown by Captain Bob Grace, Captain Jess Terry, and Flight Engineer Louie DeStefano (no relation to Jack in another story) to Oklahoma City, Oklahoma. The aircraft had been purchased by the Navy and was being delivered by those guys to its new owners.

As my father drove with Bob to work that day, my dad said, "Bob, you don't have a hair on your ass if you don't do something special as you depart."

Bob, like an eternal young boy in spirit, assured my father that he had "something special" in mind.

Taking off on runway 13 and trailing the signature black smoke emanating from its four CJ805 General Electric jet engines, Bob flew the aircraft out past Atlantic City, about ten miles to the southeast, and then turned around to come inbound on runway 31. Heading in the opposite direction from which the aircraft departed, it was now flying at 1,500 feet and 250 knots.

Just to be clear, Bob was actually in the right seat, not in the left.

My father and all the flight test pilots loved the CV-880. It was an old jet by then but it was like the fighter jet of four-engine jets, so said my father. It was fast, at least for a four-engine transport jet and had an aura and mystique that few big jets of that day carried. That particular aircraft had flown practically around the world testing this or that thing that the FAA and ICAO wanted tested.

So, as Nan 42 powered to the northwest in a stately fashion all the flight test pilots that weren't flying that day and other interested FAA employees were either on the ramp or on the roof of the massive flight ops hangar, watching the flyby and paying silent tribute.

As the sleek four engined airliner reached midfield, its nose began to rise, along with the whole aircraft, at first through ten, then twenty degrees of pitch and as the aircraft climbed more black smoke squirted out the back as power increased to support the rather rapid climb. Then the aircraft began a right roll and climbed some more and rolled even more until it was soon upside down. Once upside down the nose fell slightly, the black smoke lessened, and the aircraft continued to roll and the nose fell some more and Nan 42 rolled some more. Shortly after beginning the pull-up the big aircraft was at now in level flight at 1,500 feet, heading 310 degree, and near 250 knots after having done a barrel roll.

Louie DeStefano told me later that it was about as perfect a barrel roll as could have been flown. He said he was looking at his flight engineer's instrument panel, which faces away from the front of the aircraft, and as he looked he noticed a slight increase in "seat-of-the-pants pressure," G force. But, what really caught his attention was the change in the light pattern on his panel. When he looked forward he about threw up because they were completely upside down and upon seeing that they were inverted he got instant vertigo. Seeing they were upside down, his first reaction was to grab his coffee and pencils which were sitting on his flight engineer's table. In his words, he was, "Amazed that the pencils never moved and my coffee remained level in its cup, never spilling."

After that grand event, to the shock and awe of the observers below, Nan 42 continued on to Oklahoma City. Jess Terry, the other captain, not being privy to Bob's mischievous intentions, was not a happy camper that they just rolled a FAA owned CV-880 above a FAA owned airport and test center. He was sure repercussions were soon to follow; it took Bob two years to get his flying privileges reinstated.

With a much smaller crowd of spectators observing Bob, but with no less the same swashbuckling swagger, Bob did something that I've not heard done since Tex Johnston's infamous maneuver. He may have had to do the tap dance of his life in front of his bosses and the higher-ups to get his flying privileges reinstated but in my humble opinion it was worth it.

Bob really was an amazingly wonderful and understated mentor for me. My father told me more of his stories than he himself did. Whenever I asked him what it was like flying all the fighters he flew and when I asked him of his P-51 days in World War Two he would just shrug his shoulders and say, "I did what I did because I love my country and I love flying."

In my senior year of college Bob walked across the lawn that separated our two houses and came to see me while I was home for Christmas break. He asked me what my career aspirations were after college. He knew I was flying then and I talked at various times of trying to become an airline pilot. Before Bob's visit that day my father tried many times to steer me in other directions, not the airlines, for reasons I will never know. But Bob, Mr. Grace, on that cold December day gave me a gift that I truly feel was heaven sent: He said, "Roger, go into the military, go fly fighters first. You can always get in the airlines after serving your time, or better yet, join the Air National Guard and then you can do both."

I followed his advice and oh what a blessed change it made in my life.

Mr Grace I cannot thank you enough for your wisdom, your advice, your service in the war, and above all your friendship. I have no doubt the angels are learning a thing or two about how to fly from you in heaven, where you belong, and where you spent most of your living years.

Washington Center

It was the late 80s and I had left the active duty Air Force and joined the NJANG (New Jersey Air National Guard). I had gotten an airline job about a year before and was enjoying the best of both aviation worlds…flying fighters in the military and flying in the airlines; it just didn't get any better.

But, as anyone who loves their job knows, no matter how wonderful you have it in life there are just some days when your life sucks. And I don't care how hard you try to change the course of that day, most times you just seem to make things worse. Those are the days you need to just say "What the fuck", let go and just accept the fact that that day will suck.

That day for me began on a Saturday in late February. I was at one of my very first guard Unit Training Assemblies, UTA, where most of the part-time guard people show up for their once a month weekends to do whatever job it is they do in the guard. Now, since pilots in the guard have to fly a certain amount of sorties (flights) per month to maintain currency in various areas of their expertise (Flight lead, bombing quals, Maverick, Pave spike, etc), we pilots actually came in to the unit more than just one weekend a month. In fact I was coming in maybe 6 to 9 days a month since I loved flying the F-4E.

The weather on the east coast had been abysmal in the preceding two months and we had not flown much as a unit. The Commander was getting desperate to "launch the fleet" in order to get the sortie count up and to help the crews maintain currency in whatever areas they needed to maintain it. So, being desperate for his crews to fly, and even though the weather was forecast with low ceilings, heavy rain, and thunderstorms the word went out to launch the fleet.

I was given the task of leading a four ship of Phantoms to Bloodsworth Bombing Range which was located in the Chesapeake Bay Area, the northern area of it. It was a Class B range, meaning there was no actual range control officer on the bombing range controlling you. Approaching the range the flight lead would call the range control officer, who was seated somewhere (other than on the range) and tell him/her that their flight was requesting permission onto the range. Once on the range the flight lead executed the briefed mission objectives.

Getting onto the range was going to be a problem, let alone getting to it. The weather at McGuire was 500 overcast and a mile in rain and mist and it was due to remain like that all day. In fact the whole northeast was covered with wave after wave of drenching rain bands. The only way to get a four ship off a wet runway that day was to take off in 20 second radar trail spacing and fly in a nonstandard formation. ATC calls it a nonstandard formation if one, or more aircraft in a flight of two or more aircraft are outside of 1 mile separation between each other.

We NEVER, I mean never, did radar trail departure out of McGuire. I was told by another pilot in the unit Washington Center would not accept non-standard formations into their airspace on bad weather days. The controllers were too busy and the airspace was too crowded for them to have to deal with fighters that were strung out with maybe between 6 to 8 miles between the first and last fighter

So, it came as a complete shock to me when the Supervisor of Flying, SOF, told me my formation was going to have to do a radar trail departure. I asked him if Washington Center knew we were going to do this and he said he didn't know. So I asked if someone was going to tell them and he said probably not, just do it he said.

So my four ship is lined up on runway 24 at McGuire and its raining like a cow pissing on a flat rock. We do the proverbial 80 percent RPM run-up check, I get a thumbs up from the boys and wave to number two as I release brakes and light all four zones of the J-79's afterburner. It's chilly, the acceleration is brisk and I liftoff in maybe 3500 feet.

In twenty second intervals two, three and four do the same.

Then the fun begins.

In a radar trail departure, as the name implies, the radar of the F-4 is used to maintain a position behind the preceding aircraft. Aircraft number two in the formation follows me (the Lead, number one), three follows two and four follows three. It literally can be that easy and the radar in the Phantom was actually very reliable The spacing between the aircraft is two to three miles and they all fly at the exact same altitude and speed as lead. The distance between the lead Phantom and number four, as previously mentioned, is maybe between 6 and 9 miles. With that spread out spacing, you can probably understand why ATC does not like controlling non-standard formations in a densely packed ATC environment when you have all sorts of airliners, General Aviation and corporate aircraft on IFR (Instrument Flight Rule) clearances.

After my number four gets airborne, he calls "four is airborne" on the radio to let me know we are all flying. McGuire approach clears us to climb to four thousand feet and to turn left to a 210 degree heading. Now mind you, all of the F-4s are on the same ATC frequency and we can all hear the same radio calls. So I acknowledge the new heading of 210 degrees and turn to it and level off at 4000 feet.

This is where it all goes to shit.

Number two calls "gadget bent" as soon as I turn to 210 degrees. Gadget Bent means his radar is not working. Number three says on the radio that number two is diverging from my heading so number three picks up a heading that is between 210 and 240 degree respectively, instead of the fact that he should be turning to 210. Number four has no idea who to follow since he sees three aircraft all going in different directions, but he rightly turns to 210 to follow me.

McGuire Departure control is shitting gold bricks because they thought they had only one flight of Phantoms to control and suddenly they've got a fluer de lis of 4 Phantoms heading in different directions in their rather confined area of control. What a shit show.

Immediately I recognized the impossibility of getting our four ship in any sort of recognizable and orderly formation before getting into Washington Center's airspace so I told McGuire, didn't ask, but told them that we are all going to head to Coyle VOR and enter a hold.

Coyle was only ten miles away and well with-in McGuire's airspace. I told the guys to hold on the 180 degree radial inbound at 500 foot intervals down from 4000 feet...hence I was holding at 4000 feet MSL, two at 3500, feet, etc. McGuire radar, I found out later, was relieved that I had taken control to rectify what could have been a pathetically chaotic situation and contain it to a very manageable level.

And that is what we did. It actually worked out exceedingly well that all four of us were able to so expeditiously get organized and situated in the holding pattern. The clouds were ridiculously thick and it was raining so hard I gave up all hope of getting visual rejoins while we held. So while we settled in the hold over Coyle, I talked with my backseater about our next steps to land safely and without pissing off any more ATC controllers.

While I didn't think of a plan B before we took off, since I really thought we'd not have an issue with the radar trail, my backseater and I thought of the easiest approach to salvaging this flight. I told the boys, and McGuire Approach, that we would do ILS approaches until whatever fuel level you/we felt comfortable with and then land. So from a bombing ride to an instrument sortie, cest la vie. Before breaking up for individual approaches I did re-brief the boys the same info we were briefed in the morning's mass brief that Patuxent River NAS was the alternate and that 5,500 lbs of fuel was the no shit bingo fuel in order to get there.

I was the first aircraft McGuire pulled out of the hold and was given vectors for the ILS to runway 24. The weather remained the same as previously discussed. I did a touch and go and went back into the radar pattern for another approach. To be honest the F-4 was a great instrument platform and relatively easy to fly on instruments, though it did have a fairly high approach speed (about 165 knots).

Our fuel load that day was the "normal" 16,000 lbs; 12,000 pounds of internal and a 4,000 pound centerline external tank. If you wanted to "skyhook," hold at minimal fuel consumption and airspeed, 16,000 pounds will get you maybe two hours of holding??? I'm guessing because I never tried to do it nor ever wanted to. The aircraft would burn about 6000 to 7000 pounds an hour in cruise, at altitude, so you can do the math, but down low maneuvering for approaches it may use a bit less since you were flying slower; but 6000 pounds per hour always seemed to be the normal fuel flow when just cruising about, either high or low.

The biggest issue that day, while doing our approaches was the landing roll. The F-4 had good brakes and anti-skid, but, since it landed so fast, and with a wet runway, it needed the drag chute to deploy upon landing in order to stop us on the 10,000 foot runway. If the chute didn't deploy you had to drop the hook and take the departure end cable, or go around and take the approach end cable after doing another approach. My backseater checked the landing performance charts as we did our patterns and 13,000 feet was required to stop (again it was a 10,000 foot runway) if we didn't get a drag chute, or we'd have to take a cable.

As the boys in my four ship were doing their approaches I decided to full stop on my third approach. Still, the weather was abysmal, pouring rain and one mile visibility. The ILS was easy enough and I touched down about 1500 feet down the runway. After touching down I pulled the drag chute release handle and felt no tug of deceleration. The backseater said the chute plopped onto the runway and never deployed. Shit. If I dropped the hook and took the departure end cable it'd take 30 minutes, at least to get me out of the cable, reset it, and then have a clear runway for any other aircraft that wanted to land. So, knowing this, I went around and told McGuire approach I was going to once again enter hold at Coyle so they could recover the my wingman.

I entered the hold and immediately my backseater and I went into the "What if mode:" What if we get too low on gas and they haven't recovered all the jets?; What if another F-4 closes the runway?; What if weather closes the airport?

So as we held and waited for the other jets to land, my backseater talked to the McGuire weather shop on the radio to find out what the weather was like at the surrounding bases. The next closest base for us to go into was Atlantic City since F-106's flew from there and they had arresting cables. Unfortunately they were well below minimums, approaching WOXO (W-indefinate ceiling, O-zero height, X- obscured visibility, O- zero visibility...in Heavy Rain (RA +). Dover AFB, was about 35 miles south of us but pretty much the same as McGuire and they didn't have cables on the runway, they were in the overruns, which meant going off the runway to stop in a cable; not something I wanted to do. Every other airport around us, Philadelphia, everywhere with-in reason, was being pummeled by wave after wave of heavy rain with embedded thunderstorms. The one good news is since the Phantom was built like a "brick shithouse" (my father's saying that has stuck with me forever) and had such a high wing loading, the turbulence we were constantly experiencing was generally light and was never as bad as it would be with airliners or other, more lightly, wing loaded aircraft.

I was watching our fuel reserves closely as we waited to recover at McGuire. After a few minutes of holding I told McGuire approach we had about 20 more minutes of fuel before we would have to divert to Patuxent River. They just said "Roger." After a few more turns in holding I asked again, "How are we doing on recovering those aircraft?"

"Well there is just one more aircraft of your flight to recover, but another two ship of F-4s is coming in from the whiskey areas and they said they are minimum fuel. We are going to recover them before you."

"Roger that, just be advised they we can hold for another 15 minutes and then we will have to divert."

"Roger," was their standard reply.

And so it was...10 more minutes.."Roger"....5 minutes...."Roger"....

OK..."McGuire, Shogun One declaring emergency fuel, we are diverting to Patuxent River. We are squawking 7700 and climbing to 31,000 feet and proceeding directly to PAX River."

"NO!! Shogun One maintain 4000 feet and contact Washington Center on XXX.X frequency"

"Washington Center, this is Shogun One starting a climb to flight level three one zero, emergency aircraft. We are proceeding direct to PAX River. Please inform them we will be taking an approach end cable."

"Shogun One level off at 8000 feet. We will get you into Atlantic City"

"Negative, Atlantic City is well below minimums, we can't get in there, we're climbing and proceeding directly to Patuxent."

"Ok Shogun, how about Dover or Philaelphia?" said Center, almost in desperation.

"I have told you what I am going to do and what I need. I have to take a cable due to stopping distance on a wet runway, PAX river has the closest, available runway with a cable. We have a radar and instruments to avoid aircraft in front of us as we head south if we need to."

I was turned over to two more Washington Center Controllers after the initial one. The second controller was whining like the first and recommending I go to Philadelphia which was like McGuire, heavy rain, and had no cables. Finally the third controller asked me what I needed and said she would help me. I reiterated what I had told the previous two controllers.

PAX River was 140 miles away once we began, in earnest, our divert and climb. I did what I told Washington I was going to do. We climbed to 31,000 feet (never did get out of the clouds) and at 45 miles from Patuxent I pulled the power to idle and we did a idle descent, vectored approach from Washington until they turned us over to PAX River Approach whereupon we received a PAR (Precision Approach Radar) to runway 14 and took an approach end cable. From 31,000 feet until landing we never leveled off, only changed our descent angle once we began the PAR. We "trapped" with 1,000 lbs of gas…roughly ten minutes if the fuel gauges were accurate. I can't tell you how much a sigh of relief my backseater and I felt upon engaging that cable and stopping.

After getting out of the cable and taxing in to park, Patuxent ground control said it will probably come as no surprise to you that Washington Center wants to talk to you. They gave me their number.

After getting into base ops where we coordinated a "gas and go" in order to get back to McGuire, I called Washington Center, collect. I told the operator that this was a collect call and she said what is the name of the caller. I said "Shogun One." You could tell she was perplexed by the name, so she asked me again and again I said, "Shogun One." There was no way I was going to give Washington Center my real name. Still perplexed by my name, but not questioning me again, but with a certain amount of stuttering, she informed the Washington Center Watch Supervisor, who answered the call, that a "Shogun One was calling collect, will you accept the call?"

He then replied, "I will only accept the call if he gives me his real name."

To which I replied, "Look, I didn't want to talk to you in the first place, you asked me to call, I can hang up now, but you're not getting my name." It must be said that back in this day cell phones did not exist and calling collect was not unusual. With that said, when the operator asked the party that was being called if they would accept a collect call, and all three people: the caller, the operator and the receiving caller, were all able to hear and talk to each other.

With my threat of hanging up the controller resigned himself that I would not divulge my name and said he'd accept the call.

""Shogun One do you have any idea the mess you created when you decided to divert through such a heavily traveled airspace such as you did today. Jesus you created a headache for my controllers!" He exclaimed with certain contained rage.

"Well if you think it was bad for your guys on the ground, image the crap I was eating trying to figure out where in the hell to land without giving the aircraft back to the taxpayers destroyed. If ya'll want to be pissed at someone, be angry at McGuire approach since I was giving them a running dialogue as to when we needed to divert and what I needed to do if we did so and they just kept blowing me off."

To which Washington Center responded," Well we will talk to them since we had no idea you were telling them what you would have to do, but I have to ask, why didn't land at Dover, Philly or Atlantic City. We couldn't understand what your problem was." He was much more calm now.

Since I was now chilling myself, since this guy got off his high horse, I said, "Look I tried to tell the first controller what the problem was, but to be honest, my backseater and I had no idea idea, due to how strong the headwind was once we began to climb, if we could make it to PAX River. Also, we were looking at and using our radar and APX systems and we could see ALL of the mode three aircraft and my backseater was continuously checking for deconfliction from what we thought were threat aircraft. We didn't climb blindly. Do you have any idea how crappy the weather was? We climbed purposefully through an embedded thunderstorm thinking traffic would be deviating around it. We simply could not land at any of the airports you mentioned due to wet runways and no cables. Atlantic City was WOXOF, I'm not sure if we could've gotten in there."

"Ok, ok…I get it. I guess maybe in the future there needs to be better coordination with your base on what your divert fields are if someone has to divert, just so we can brief our guys in the event of an emergency. Well, I hope your return flight to McGuire is better. And oh by the way, another one of your boys is going to be joining you, he's diverting now, I gotta go…."

My backseater and I never waited for our squadron mate. We were fueled, received a replacement drag chute, curtesy of the Navy, and departed just as the other diverting F-4 was taxing in; it was a very quick turn indeed.

The weather returning was no better upon arrival, and I have to say, I was glad I was not flying the next day as the weather system was forecast to remain through the weekend.

After getting into the squadron building I had another storm to deal with, the Group Commander who asked me to report to him in his office. He was pissed.

"Do you know Washington Center was really upset with your divert today?" He scolded me. "What the hell is up with what you did?"

Remember, I was new to this unit and it was the guard, which had some good commanders and some bad.

I said," Well, every morning you give a mass brief and in it you give a divert field and the no shit bingo to get there. So I took it that bingo for gospel. If you didn't mean to use that as a no shit divert fuel, maybe you should tell us. But, in my defense I did tell McGuire approach how much time I had left to hold before I had to divert and they kept blowing me off. Should I have just taken the departure end cable after my chute failure and closed the runway and had at least three aircraft divert, or just have one divert? You tell me what you want, I'm open for suggestions" I was not trying to be a wiseass.

"Well you're not instructing in the weapons school anymore and you're not in the wide open spaces of the Wild West, around here we don't just divert, we coordinate with ATC, don't do what you did today ever again.....dismissed."

The drive home through the countryside and then the drinks that occurred at the Rugby Inn with my dad that evening were the best part of my day. Sometimes, you just can't win.

The Light

It's amazing to me how many times in life I find I realize something is "wrong," without truly understanding initially what is wrong…just that something is amiss. I don't think I'm "special" in this power of observation, since mothers seem to have the supernatural ability to know when their kids are up to no good when there is absolutely no indication that indeed they are up to no good.

I don't know what it was that caused me to think that the very small light about 5 miles ahead of me was "not right," but I did. I was in the left seat of a MD-11 and was on final approach to land on runway 36 Center at Memphis International Airport, in Tennessee. The night was dark (no moon) but clear, calm winds, beautiful. The weather conditions were the perfect way to finish a ten day trip with a student.

My student was the First Officer. We were finishing up his MD-11 training. We had just flown over to Asia with a few stops here and there in some of the major Asian cities and now here we were on his last flight as a student, arriving from Osaka, Japan; about a 12 hour flight. The kid, all the first Officers seemed like kids to me, flew well and unless he totally buffooned his last landing he was going to pass with flying colors.

Approach Control past us on to tower at around 7 miles on final. The hour of our arrival was a busy time for the Memphis Air Traffic Controllers. Most of the evening arrivals converged on Memphis between 10pm and 1 am. That's about 150 aircraft arriving in 3 hours, 50 an hour, and really the most concentrated arrival time was between 1030 PM and 1230 AM. I say this because most of the airline traffic was arriving, not departing. There were some departures before midnight, Northwest and Delta mostly, and then the occasional cargo flight being flown with one of the supplemental cargo companies flying for who knows whom and to who knows where.

Just as I checked in with tower, one of those supplemental cargo aircraft checked in too and said they were holding short of runway 36 center; we had just hit five miles to go and given our weight, heavy, and the abnormally high approach speed of the MD-11 at that weight meant tower couldn't let the aircraft depart, not enough separation. So, tower told the aircraft holding short that they could expect to depart after the landing traffic on five mile final.

When I heard tower tell the aircraft holding at the approach end of our runway to hold short, by instinct I looked to see if I could see the aircraft. Who knows why we pilots do stuff like that. I mean really? At five miles, and a dark night, why would I care to see if I could see the aircraft? I certainly didn't recognize the call sign of the company. I was, however curious as to what type of aircraft it was, so maybe that piqued my interest, all I know is, at five miles I looked intently to where I thought the aircraft might appear and that's when I saw "the light."

I roger'ed tower when they told me we were cleared to land, repeated the cleared to land runway, and then I said to the F/O, "Does it appear that there's a strange light coming from that aircraft holding short?"

The F/O, I have no doubt, could really have given a shit what kind of lights that aircraft was displaying as all he wanted to do was land safely so he didn't have to fly with "this pain in the ass instructor" (me) anymore. So, his answer was, "No." Yes, his answer was that succinct.

I continued with my PM, Pilot Monitoring duties, as we continued on towards the landing. But, I was still glancing up at that aircraft holding short. Something was just not right with the lights it was displaying. The light I was looking at was white and it flickered a bit. It wasn't a wingtip strobe, it wasn't a rotating beacon, so I thought the pilots had left a runway turnoff light on as they held short; maybe they forgot to turn it off.

Closer still we approached, at 500 feet above the ground the ground proximity warning system dutifully announced, "Five Hundred."

To which I confirmed we were cleared to land on runway 36 Center and the F/O replied "Landing."

Ok, the F/O was flying a flawless visual approach, backed up by the ILS and the auto throttles were controlling the speed perfectly, as they usually did. Gear was down and locked, spoilers were armed, flaps at 35. We had already done the before landing checklist above 1000 feet AGL, but I always did my own, silent, before landing checklist once, twice, sometimes three times before landing, whether I was flying or PM, Pilot Monitoring.

So I did my OCD (Obsessive Compulsive Disorder) before landing checklist/scan after the five hundred foot call by the ground prox.

system, and then I went back to it…that damn light. What the hell was it? It just wasn't right.

We were closer still and it was brighter still, and it was bugging the shit out of me. I'd never seen a light like that on any aircraft. In fact, besides the rotating beacon, I really didn't see any other lights on that aircraft. It wasn't that well lit up to be honest, had no "logo" light shinning on the tail and I could barely make out the wingtip naviga-tion light, but, there was that one light. That odd bright light, which I could now see was about mid fuselage, near where the wing was, if not on the wing itself.

As we approached 100 feet above the runway the F/O had the approach wired. I had no doubt about his ability to land on this looming 10,000 foot long runway, since he'd been doing it on every landing since we'd departed Memphis over a week ago. So, after confirming the runway was clear of other aircraft, vehicles and just before the ground prox. system announced 100 feet I took one last look for the light on the aircraft holding short.

It was on fire. The light was a fire. I about crapped. The right engine had a fire sprouting out of the top of it, like a tassel, maybe about 4 feet high, starting as a narrow flame from where it came out of the engine, but fanning out as it increased in height above the engine.

Now that is something you don't see everyday! I was wearing my head-set and even though the F/O had begun his flare, I told tower that the aircraft holding in position to takeoff on runway 36 center had a fire emanating from its right engine. I knew by telling tower the aircraft holding short would also hear the radio call and hopefully react… and they did. About as casually as you can say "Rumple stilt skin" the aircraft holding short said they "had a problem" and needed to return back to their ramp. I mean they said "we have a problem and need to return to the ramp," in such a calm and measured tone of voice, you'd have thought this was a "routine" fire; maybe it was for them.

As I write this I am still amazed at the pilot's calm voice in announcing they had a "problem." For all I know maybe there was pure hell in that cockpit after I announced they had a fire and the F/O looked back over his shoulder and saw that big flame, but, in "Chuck Yeager" style the radio call needs to be calm and collected, irregardless of what hell may actually be occurring in the cockpit. Of any of that, I'll never know.

But, what I do know is I now know what that light was. I know the crew was safe and I know what type of aircraft it was: a CV-640.

I slept well that night.

My Finest Flight

Like many people, there are various times where my present day life briefly intersects and reacts, in a providential way, to certain events or moments from my obscure past. Jobs, friends, adventures, etc…many times certain experiences from my past share six degrees, more or less, of separation and commonality with those of my present. It's not deja vu per se, more a commingling of the past with the present producing a lovely montage of images, from both past and present, and consequently some wonderful heartwarming feelings.

I started flying at the age of 15, my dad giving me my initial instruction; that was 48 years ago as of this writing. Since those early, tentative forays out of the nest from which I learned to fly, I've since flown around the world, many times, over many years, and in all kinds of aircraft. My longest flight has been from Shenzhen, China to Memphis, TN, a flight of 15 hours and 30 minutes, block to block, in a B-777. My shortest flight was a 10 minute repositioning flight, in a MD-11, from Oakland, CA to San Francisco; we never even raised the gear. While I've enjoyed so many of the flights I've flown over my years aloft and in so many different aircraft, without question the finest flight I've flown, so far, is also the shortest; even shorter than the MD-11 flight just mentioned, and in the least sophisticated and technologically advanced aircraft I've ever flown.

In 1969, when I was 11 years old, my father took me to an air show at McGuire AFB in New Jersey. It was my first airshow. While going there with my father may not seem too earth shatteringly special, particularly since he was a career, professional aviator, what was special is how I got there.

The very short story is McGuire was having huge airshow and the Thunderbirds were the star attraction. Flying the Phantom, those magnificent men in their flying machines certainly raised the bar at that time with regards to noise, aerial maneuvers, and "daring do"; it was always a treat to watch the Phantom perform.

My father, in 1969, was a Flight Operations Test Pilot with the FAA. He was based at Atlantic City International Airport, which at that time wasn't so international, but it was the headquarters of the FAA's National Aviation Facilities Experimental Center, NAFEC for short. I could write a book on all that they did there, but suffice it to say my father and his colleagues over the years have test flown, developed, and been involved with more "things" aviation...LORAN, OMEGA, GPS, TCAS, Approach Lights, Autoland, Windshear, etc, etc, etc... than you can shake a stick at.

I was always begging the old man to take me flying. Every time he flew a work related flight on the weekend, and when I was not in school, I asked him if I could go flying with him, ninety nine, point nine percent of the time his answer was no. So, it was with unbeliev-able excitement and anticipation and shock, that he asked me if I wanted to go to the air show at McGuire AFB with he and some of his colleagues. He asked me about a month before the actual event and I swear to god time slowed, agonizingly so, as I waited for the Saturday of the event. As I just said, while going to an air show with a bunch of pilots may not seem like such a big deal, how we got there however, was...in a DC-3. But then, adding even more diversity to this aviation themed day was that the flight coming back from McGuire to Atlantic City was to be flown on a Gulfstream 1. I just couldn't believe my luck.

The FAA does not allow relatives to fly, willie nilly, on their aircraft, it's against the rules, well at least back then it was. So, simply put, my dad asked his boss if I could go on the flights and Dutch Osterhaut, said boss, said yes, but, my Dad had to keep it on the QT.

On THAT Saturday, the day so etched in my synapses, I was smuggled out of the FAA's Operations building and surrounded by my dad's colleagues. They quickly ushered me to a DC-3 that was conveniently parked right in front of the Ops building and sat me down in one of the seats in the back.

I swear to you words cannot describe what it was like for me to fly in that DC-3 with my Dad as the pilot. Heaven may have the words, but down here on Earth none exist. My Dad started his airline career on DC-3s and flew many many hours in the Pacific in WW 2 on that venerable old bird. He loved that aircraft and I loved him because every time I was immersed in the world of aviation with him I could see the true man, the spirit which lived in him, come shinning out. If ever a man loved flying, it was my father, and his passion infected me with every flight we flew together.

The 20 minute flight to McGuire was not long enough, it seemed like 5 (minutes).

After deplaning, another FAA crew flew the DC-3 back from whence we came.

We then walked over to a FAA Gulfstream 1 that was mingled in with an assortment of other aircraft, either military or civilian which were being used as static displays for the masses to inspect and gawk over.

There were folding chairs arranged in a circle off to the side of the forward entry stairs to the aircraft and that's where my dad and his colleagues spent the day. While sitting, or standing, the men would answer questions the airshow's spectators might throw at them. But, the real treat for the public was to climb the ladder and enter the cockpit. Seeing a cockpit, the business end of an aircraft, with all its lights, dials, displays and what not, was always the best treat when going to an airshow, other than watching the aerial acrobatics of the aircraft of course. I am truly amazed not one of my dad's colleagues had a beer on that hot August day. Technically they weren't allowed, but I thought one of them may try since it was so hot. But, they were on duty and two of them had to fly the G-1 back to Atlantic City.

What was so cool for me that day was in hanging around the guys and being able to go in and out of the G-1 as if I flew it there. I was "behind the ropes" and was one of the boys. Kids my age would come up to me and say why are you allowed behind the ropes and I'd say because my dad was one of the pilots and I flew in with him.

Then the Phantoms flew and though I didn't know it, one day too I'd be flying in the likes of them. The sights, the noise, the aerial acrobatics, sensory overload. I couldn't believe what those jets and the fighter pilots in them could do while flying so close together, with the solo Thunderbird (The F-4E Thunderbirds flew with only one solo) highlighting the more radical performance capabilities of the Phantom.

My father's favorite performer at that air show was Bob Hoover and his Aero Commander. Truly, my father said, that man is one of history's most skilled aviators, a humble man, whose flying ability matched that of an angel. I didn't know enough about pilots to disagree with him then, but now 48 years after earning wings of my own, I still can't disagree with my Dad. Seeing Mr Hoover, the gentleman that he was, maneuver, dead stick, that Aero Commander through his routine was truly one of my more memorable moments at that, or any other, airshow where he performed.

The Thunderbirds land, all is quiet, and the crowds start to thin. Stragglers appear, asking to go into the cockpit as the boys fold up shop and take the chairs into the aircraft. We are one of the few aircraft leaving the static display line that late afternoon, so there was quite a bit of attention on us as we boarded the aircraft and my dad and his colleague started the engines. Oh my Lord, again, another unbelievable rush of aviation dopamine in my heart and head; I was addicted.

Given that the G-1 was quite a bit faster than the DC-3, the flight home was even more expeditious than the one up, which was a bummer because if we could have flown another 5 hours I'd have been a happy camper.

After sequestering me out of the aircraft and into the operations building, my father and I then headed to his favorite watering hole whereupon more aviation themed conversation raged with me as the talk show host.

In 2007 that flight to McGuire occurred 38 years earlier. In the summer of 2007 my youngest son was 11 years old and had never been to an airshow.

By the grace of God in the summer of 2007 a very dear friend and colleague let me borrow his 90 horsepower Piper Cub Special for a month. That was such a wonderful month of flying with my youngest son flying as my copilot. On most of those flights we floated amongst the clouds, chased flocks of birds over the Mississippi river, explored oxbows long since abandoned by the river's flow or examined from treetop level the deeply green and richly forested areas of Western Tennessee that give mother nature her breath.

But, the best was yet to come.

As that month with the Cub neared the end another wonderful friend and colleague of mine asked if I wanted to fly that Cub, with my son, into Millington Naval Air Station and sit static display for the upcoming Air Show. (My friend was the coordinator for the civilian static displays that year). They were hosting not only the Blue Angels but, also the Canadian Snowbirds, plus a multitude of other amazingly gifted aviators. My friend said he wanted us to fly in on Saturday Morning, adding that we were to be the last aircraft to arrive before they closed the airport to transient and non airshow performing aircraft for the weekend.

Austin knew about the airshow and in fact he and I were going to drive up to Millington on Saturday and see it. But, oh my!!! What a blessing from both of my friends for the gift of being able to use the Cub in the first place and then for the wonderful opportunity to actually fly into and participate in the airshow with my son.

The morning of the flight into Millington dawned clear and cool as my son and I pulled the Cub out of a hanger at Charles Baker Airport. As the crow flies the distance between Charles Baker and Millington might be all of five miles, but, oh that five miles represented 38 years worth of a rush of memories. Wonderful aviation infused memories of my father, his wonderfully talented and colorful colleagues, the aircraft they flew, and the sights and sounds of flying into and being at the airshow. All those memories were now mixing with the present, juxtaposing me, my father and my son. Such a beautiful quilt of images and feelings layered upon each other, or side by side, emulsified in a mix of the old and the new, being savored with each breath and with each newly formed visual rendition as the day unfolded.

With the Cub prepped to fly, I called Millington Tower and told them I'd be departing Charles Baker in about five minutes and to look for me coming from the south. The tower controller said to land on runway 4 and to look for a green light for landing clearance (The Cub didn't have any radios or navigation equipment).

With Austin in the back, and with a smile so broad upon his face he looked like a smile emoji, I hand propped the engine. She started on the first swing of the prop blade. She always did. I then jumped in and we taxied to the approach end of Charlie Baker's runway and after a quick three sixty of the aircraft to check for traffic while also checking the mags, we departed heading north.

The flight to Millington was so surreal its hard to describe. We departed at 7 AM, since they wanted to close the airport early and were waiting for us in that little' ole Cub to arrive. The sky was clear which allowed radiation fog to blanket many low lying patches on the multitude fields and streams that surrounded the two airports. Misty white blankets, curtesy of mother nature, neatly tucked in horses and cows to their velvety green sheets of grass with birds overflying the white, highlighting their crossing.

The smoothness of the air manifested the magic of the flight, as if mother nature herself was paving the way for us through the atmosphere, through time, which was rich in a tapestry of colors. The golden rays of a newly risen sun were illuminating the greens of chlorophyll infused trees that dappled the farm fields below. In addition, brightly colored, or dull in sheen farm houses and their outlaying buildings were scattered all around us, while corn fields, which ranged outward from the farm houses, communicated their readiness for harvesting as their dark green corn stalks became festooned with yellowish tassels. Small roadways, like capillaries running through the body that was the earth below, sported the occasional lone vehicle as it drove in seclusion immersed in the still of the morning, being observed by only my son, me, and the birds.

While the visual input to my heart and head was prominent that morning, and most welcome, the sound as we flew, which could have been offensive, was much less of a nuisance than it could have been. My son and I wore earmuffs, and though designed to mute the sound of a shotgun blast, worked well at quieting the engine's roar and that of the air rushing by. This muted roar was actually kind of narcotic and somewhat soothing as we serenely cruised above a world that looked as if Thomas Kincade had painted it.

All too soon the magical world in which we had been immersed came to an end when I saw Millington Naval Air Station straight ahead and noticed a green light from the tower. I looked back at Austin as we began our shallow descent to the runway and pointed to it. Still smiling as I signaled the runway's approach, Austin gave me a thumbs up.

Not having radios I turned off the active runway and taxied to where I thought the air show administrators wanted me to park. As Austin and I entered the main ramp all eyes were on us, from other pilots and early rising spectators, as we were marshaled to an area where all the smaller general aviation aircraft were parked. We felt like we were rock stars, arriving at the last minute, with swagger and an attitude. We shut down once near the other aircraft and then pushed and pulled the cub to its resting place for the next two days.

I'll never, ever forget the magic of that oh so short flight, but one that was oh so steeped with nostalgia. That flight was one where I flew as both a father and a son, with a son, as the past and the present merged on that day, that time, that flight. I saw my father flying the DC-3 that morning, just as my son saw me flying a taildragger (albeit much smaller than a DC-3). We were flying to a big airshow, where high performance fighter aircraft celebrated power, agility, and speed and where other equally talented airshow pilots were to demonstrate their skill and daring. Seeing my son smiling continuously and looking in awe as the Blue Angels performed their death defying maneuvers that day is etched in my heart and reminded me of me as I watched the Thunderbirds roar. Each of those flights, in 1969 and then in 2007, forms a readily accessible memory as one the finest father/son bonding moments I've ever had with me being the connection between my father and the grandson he never got to meet.

Kite Wars

Right after we took off, I relinquished the flight controls to Austin and let him fly. He is as natural a pilot as was his late grandfather and he immediately began banking to and fro above the well-watered forests near the airfield from which we just departed. Millions upon millions of dark-green, chlorophyll intoxicated leaves emerged from the branches of a slightly less number of trees; there was no question that spring was in full bloom.

As I let my youngest son explore the boundaries of his nascent aviator's skills over the seemingly impenetrable carpet of green below, I gazed upon the distant horizon. The day's dry air offered unlimited in-flight visibility, and as my eyes looked far ahead, my heart contradicted their gaze as it searched far in my past, reminding me of the significance of this flight.

I had begun to experience déjà vu from the moment I woke up that morning and prepared to leave for the airport with my very enthusiastic son. Once airborne and as my heart retraced my life's steps in getting to this euphoric moment, I suddenly realized that it had been thirty-four years since I first took flying lessons from my father. Now, here I was with my wonderful child, sharing an experience that I felt so privileged to have made into a career.

I don't know how old I was when the tradition of my father giving me an airplane ride on or near my birthday began, but somewhere in my distant youth, that tradition ignited. As the days to those wonderful, annual moments of flight approached, I was tortured by time. I swear the tick of the clock drastically slowed as the days remaining waned toward the flight. But when the aircraft's engine started, a quantum reversal in the space-time continuum always seemed to occur, as it felt to me that no sooner had the wheels left the ground on takeoff than we were touching down before I could fully grasp the surreal experience of the actual ascent. Those youthful flights were usually an hour in length, and though my dad never failed to take me, there was one caveat to the whole experience... I had to ask him to take me flying as he never, ever, extended the offer.

My dad was big on the desire theme of life: "Desire and attitude. Buck, desire, and attitude—that will take you far." He used to say that unrelenting desire is what made a successful career.

So, in the month of May, as my fiftieth birthday rapidly approached, my eleven-year-old son asked me if I would take him for a ride in a friend's Super Cub. Although Austin had previously been on many flights, and in a multitude of different aircraft, that was the first time he had ever asked me for an airplane ride. There was no delay in my saying yes, as that was about as good as it could get for me with regard to receiving a birthday gift—sharing the magic of flight with my own child. Could this be the beginning of me passing the torch to my son?

The morning of the flight with Austin dawned clear and chilly as a moisture-laden weather system had moved through the area the previous day, taking very grayish, heavy, and low lying clouds with it. The passing cold front left the Earth unclothed, causing the trees to shiver with each gently blowing breeze.

My son's excitement was contagious and had fully infected me by the time we started up and taxied. As we made our way to the grass strip's only runway, I told Austin, via the intercom, when I flew as a teenager many times I pretended to be a fighter pilot preparing to go into battle while taxing my mount for takeoff.

The previous night's deposit of dew upon the grass runway's blades gave obvious hint to the left-right deviations of our takeoff roll as the history of our passing was temporarily impressed upon the turf. Though not extreme, the miscues of my feet upon the rudder pedals alluded to my lack of currency in this type of aircraft. It had been thirty years since I last flew a Super Cub with any regularity before recently being reunited with that same make and model aircraft owned by a friend and colleague, who so graciously allowed me to borrow it for this flight.

The low angle of the sun above the horizon, the sound of the engine, and the chill of the air rushing in and around the open cockpit reminded me of one particular day, many years ago, when a fellow banner tow pilot and I departed in our banner-towing Cubs with aerial battle a certainty...

Kite Wars

Flashback to late May, 1977. I was only nineteen years old and beginning my first season of aerial advertising (banner towing) with

Paramount Air Service, located at Cape May County Airport, in Rio Grande, New Jersey.

It was a typically busy midmorning at the airport as I gassed up my clipped-wing cub, nicknamed the Silver Slipper, in preparation for the day's towing. My buddy, Jeff, also being assigned a clipped-wing cub for the day's flying, pulled up next to me on the flight line and waited to do the same with his aircraft. As the new guys that summer, we were the last to be able to get our aircraft fuel so that we could snatch banners from the grass and earn some beach, bar, and babe money.

I finished feeding my beast and was attaching three grappling hooks while Jeff took his turn fueling his ride when the owner of the business, Mr. Andre Tomalino, drove up, rather rapidly, and waddled over to Jeff and me. He had a pensive look on his face as he usually did when something was pissing him off. He shepherded Jeff and I together, and in a very bold and outspoken manner told us that we, "the company," had lost a banner over Diamond Beach (it's a beach on Wildwood Crest, in Southern Wildwood) due to a kite (kite string will cut through a banner's tow rope like a hot knife through butter). Mr. Tomalino told us that the banner pilot who reported the loss said there were a lot of kites near/over Diamond Beach. He then told us, since we hadn't yet started towing, to go scout out the situation and, if we had to, "take them out."

I asked Mr. Tomalino, "When you say 'take them out,' what exactly do you mean...?"

At that seemingly stupid question—at least I gauged it was stupid due to the immediately quizzical look and then subsequent frown upon Andre's face—he said, "I don't care if you have to shoot them down,

I don't want any more of my banners being lost due to those kids and their kites."

Well, you don't have to tell two nineteen-year-old college kids full of piss, vinegar, and hormones, twice that they have creative license in taking down those "sons of bitches communist kids' kites." In no time, Jeff and I neared Diamond Beach, the southern-most beach on Wildwood Island, from where most of the day's banners start their northbound run headed up said island or beyond, depending upon how far north the advertiser wanted his particular banner towed. Since the airspace above Diamond Beach was so pivotal to Paramount's towing operation, it had to be held at all costs, and nothing less than unconditional surrender by the enemy would suffice!

Because Jeff was older than me by a year, and was the finest natural pilot I have ever known (other than my father), I deferred the lead to him and flew about fifty yards off, and slightly behind, his left wing.

I have to admit a certain adrenaline rush as we alighted from the runway bound for certain battle. As I usually did when flying my banner aircraft, I imagined that I was flying some sort of World War I or II fighter aircraft, and today, Jeff and I were flying Sopwith Camels and heading toward Richthofen's Flying Circus... I make no excuses for my vivid daydreaming, it made life that much more colorful.

As we approached the beach from the northwest at 500 feet above the ground, I was amazed at the enemy's numbers. In my rather imaginative mind back then (and no, I didn't do drugs), I envisioned that the kites were barrage balloons and needed to be taken out, but with so many, it was intuitively obvious that we had our work cut out for us.

At this point, I must say that I never gave thought to any possible ramifications for this up-and-coming duel—not in regard to the FAA and its regulations, any local laws/regulations forbidding kite killing, or to the possibility of injury to those flying the kites, neither the tethered ones nor those powered by their Lycoming engines. (The term kite is often given to the type of aircraft that Jeff and I were flying because they are built with a light metal frame and covered in fabric.) Though I can't fully speak for Jeff, as we never really talked about our personal feelings after this event, I think I can safely say that we just never gave it a second thought. Our boss had told us to go take out the kites, and that's what we were going to do. Andre's immediate wrath was far more real than the FAA's, and I go back again to the aforementioned, "We were nineteen-year-old college kids" phrase. In addition, I think I might have rationalized that I was under the "corporate veil" or some idealistic college bullshit such as that and could not be legally prosecuted for my actions.

To digress a bit, the reason the kites were a factor that day, versus most other days, was due to the rather strong wind from the northwest. A cold front had come through, and with it, the winds shifted from an onshore sea breeze to an offshore blow. In the limited time I had been towing, I was told that this would happen periodically, the kites being "blown" out to sea, and to avoid the kite string that tethered these seemingly innocuous vehicles of flight. I don't really understand the aerodynamics of it, but the string from a kite stays relatively low over the ground, and then as it nears the spot over where the kite is flying, it rises dramatically upward; it's not linear at all. As you tow a banner down the beach and are crabbed into the wind, your banner is driven out to sea. Invariably, if you are not careful, the kite string comes between the banner and the aircraft and, as the twine runs its course across the tow rope, slices it, and the banner drops to the sea. When the kites are few and sporadic, avoiding them is usually not a big deal and easily done. But that day...whoa...it was like revenge of "The Kite Kids from Hell." There was no way to really avoid them without flying too far offshore or avoiding the beach altogether, leaving the advertisers feeling as though they weren't getting their money's worth.

So, there we were, Jeff and I, and I had no idea how to "down a kite." I threw out my grappling hook with the intention of snagging one, and then I watched, mesmerized, as Jeff just literally smashed into one with his propeller. Hmmmm, I never thought of being that straightforward, but I have to say that made short work of the kite. Now mind you, all the kites back then were the standard box kite, the plastic bat-wing style, or the traditional triangular-paper-and-wood one that defines our thoughts of what a kite looks like. After Jeff's initial smashing success, I tried to drag one from the sky and failed miserably. Meanwhile, Jeff had quickly spun around and taken out another. In no time, he was going to be an ace.

Ya know, his aggressiveness was actually surprising to me, because on the ground I swear this guy was one of the most laid-back and nonthreatening individuals I've ever known. But Lord, put him in an aircraft and, jeez, he turned into a killing machine!

As I watched "Baron von Richthofen" go for his third kill, I was startled when I accidentally slammed into a kite myself. I hadn't seen it because this one was flying much higher than the others, and I had been "hawking the fight" while Jeff waded right in amongst the pesky critters.

As the Baron took out his third kite, I decided to fly over the beach to see what kind of miscreants had decided to invade Diamond Beach and challenge Andre's air supremacy. I was amazed as I zoomed over the beach to see all the kids below—well, those actually flying kites— desperately reeling in their weapons! One kid had a trailer that he towed on his bike, and on it was a drum/spool type thing that appeared to hold all his kite string, which he could wind in with bicycle pedals, literally a winch type of setup. I looked to see where his twine headed so I could locate his kite, and quite literally you could see it—the kite—descend as it was being pedaled in. With such a setup, I knew this kid was a true professional, and I had to tip my hat to him! And though I knew he would be back one day to do certain harm to our banners, I just couldn't take out his kite. I had looked into the enemy's eyes, albeit from a few hundred feet up, and decided to be chivalrous and grant him a reprieve.

After what I was assumed was Jeff's fifth kill, the skies were quickly clearing of the vermin and Jeff and I headed back to the airport, feeling totally victorious—with Jeff unofficially crowned as ace of the base. We taxied up to our operations area on the ramp without any fanfare and with no sign of our Italian leader. Thusly we began, again, our day of gassing up and rearming for banner towing.

The rest of the day was pretty routine and though there were a few kites flying off some of the other beaches, it was light resistance at best and not very well organized. We had broken the back of the enemy and once again Paramount Air Service had air superiority over the South Jersey beaches; life was good.

Until the day I towed my last banner and left for the USAF, four years or so later, I never again saw that many kites in one place. Their first attempt, the Communist Kite Kids of Wildwood, was their last...their limited numbers disappeared into the many numbers of law-abiding beachgoers and "Shoo Bees" of the shore.

The story doesn't end there though since there was a revenge of sorts by the kite kids. One day, as I was heading to Ocean City with a banner in tow, and while still over the back bays off Sea Isle, Jeff came zooming by me and did a barrel roll, pulling nothing but a tow rope. It seems he had lost his vigilance while towing a banner off Sea Isle, and a kite got it. Chalk one up for the kids. I'd lay money down that it was that bugger with the little trailer and big spool of twine. Ultimately, in my four years of flying for Paramount, I never lost a banner to a kite...mercy has its rewards.

Jack

We all know that one person in our life, from our past, who was larger than life. A character whose personality was so immensely powerful, in a positive way, that not one person who was in their immediate area, whether engaged with them or not, wasn't touched in some profound way just by their mere presence. A person whose eyes were like torches on a rainy, dismal, fog cloaked night and whose bright eyes beamed wonder as they told story after story, tale after tale. Those eyes acting like a cinema projector radiating stories and adventures upon your heart and soul with the added treat of overly dramatic body language adding even more detail.

There was not a day in my life that was not brightened by the presence of Jack, even on the days when I royally pissed him off (I could do that to adults back then).

Jack was an overweight, short on stature (5 foot 6 inches) giant whose personality could overcome, overwhelm, and win the hearts of even the most reticent of humans. His beer belly ruled his midriff in the same manner that his big, deeply blue eyes and double chin ruled his very bald head.

His eyes. He wore very thick glasses that furthermore accentuated his already earth-like (blue oceans as seen from space) all seeing orbs. I'll never forget the beauty of his eyes as he told me his stories, watching them open, or close, or shift with each exciting change in whatever human interest or aviation tale he was bringing to life.

To totally describe Jack in this blog would bore you, though I could try and emulate Dr Frankenstein, who brought an eclectic assortment of human parts to life, by using a vast array and assortment of words to try and bring the essence of Jack back from the grave. To that end however, his spirit would still be absent from that verbal sort of conjuring. But, Oh how I wish I could have a prayer answered and have God allow him to come back into my life again. Jack was magic to me, answered prayer not prayed for but, brought to me at a time in my life when depression ruled and where I lived with serious doubt that I would age past my teens for any number of reasons.

Jack was blue collar raised in South Jersey and spent his late teens and early twenties as a crew chief in the Navy. He was exceedingly intelligent and also gifted with a tourettes type wit, all too spontaneous, that could get him in trouble with his superiors and yet could literally charm the pants off the ladies.

After the Navy he began working at the FAA, initially as a mechanic and then as a dispatcher for the multitude of flight test aircraft located at the FAA's National Aviation Facilities Experimental Center (NAFEC) at Atlantic City International Airport, in Pomona, New Jersey. It was in that position where he and my father, one of the FAA's Flight Operations Test Pilots, befriended each other; I'm pretty certain their mutual love of beer was the lubricating agent for that lifelong friendship.

And with that short introduction of Jack, I met him in the summer of 1974. I came back from riding my dirt-bike in the rather extensive collection of woods a few miles from my house and while I was putting my motorcycle in the garage I encountered my future mentor. He and my dad had gone fishing on my Dad's boat and they were savoring the taste of Budweiser while lying about the fish they had caught, using the shadows of the garage to avoid the penetrating effects of a hot late afternoon sun.

Jack affronted me with his first spoken words and I thought, what a jerk! But, then knowing he'd caught me off guard, as he judged from the sneer on my face, he began to belly laugh, which caused my old man to laugh and then cascaded onto me. I never looked back after that initial meeting…he and I were friends for life.

I didn't know it then, but my father had an ulterior motive in bringing Jack into my pathetic life back then. He wanted him to teach me how to fly. Even though the old man would solo me, he knew, my dad that is, if he and I flew together too much we'd butt heads so he figured Jack would be a better match for my laconic and cynical personality. My father was very wise.

Jack and I first flew together in August of 1974, he called the night prior to our flight to tell me he was picking me up the next day, early and we were going to fly to Cape May Airport. My dad had been teaching me to fly and indeed soloed me in Jack's amazingly beat-up but-still-able-to fly Cessna 150; this aircraft, 11Z, was the definition of a rudimentary flying machine. But, still I loved climbing into her because I knew that vehicle of flight was my doorway to heaven, if only for a short time, since it was my temporary escape from the hell on earth that was my home life back then.

At the secluded little grass airport that cradled Jack's two aircraft, we arrived early the next morning. I automatically began untying 11Z, the 150 Cessna I'd been flying in with my dad, and releasing her from her bonds when Jack said, "No, no, no, we're flying the Luscombe to Cape May, not the one fifty."

Wow, what a treat. Jack's Luscombe was a 1947, 8A, all metal, model and she was b e a u t i f u l. I mean she was polished and shiny and pristine, as if just off the assembly line, though to me human hands didn't make her, off duty angels did.

She had to be hand propped though, so Jack taught me the ways of propping an aircraft without getting killed by a spinning propellor, which would bode me well, this training, for a future summer job when I was in college.

But, in terms of rudimentary, she had no internal generator supplying her electrical needs for the radio, transponder and lights. Nope, I was back to my newspaper bicycle days, relating to the equivalent of a small spinning generator mounted between the aircraft's wheels and being spun when the aircraft's propellor was spinning: To be clear, the Luscombe was a tailwheel aircraft with all of 65 horses powering her locomotion. I did ponder, before take-off, if those few ponies could get us elevated to any degree given Jack's aforementioned girth.

The flight to Cape May was wonderfully enchanting because the sights and sounds were so mesmerizing to such a neophyte as myself. As we serenely cruised only a thousand feet over the heads of people, birds and other animals, I thought to myself how liberating it was to fly and I wondered how anyone could ever tire of being airborne.

After Jack finished his meeting in Cape May and upon getting ready to fly back to Knocky's airport, from where we came, Jack said he wanted to teach me to fly his Luscombe. With those words I thought he meant on the way back to Knocky's. Nope, he was going to teach me how to fly her in the pattern at Cape May Airport with the intention of having me solo her there; though he kept the solo part out of the conversation until he was actually going to let me (solo). I guess he was afraid he'd spook me if he told me beforehand.

For the next 30 to 45 minutes or so Jack and I did pattern after pattern, touch and go after touch and go on runway 19 at Cape May, this being done after we did a couple of stalls so I could see how she "spoke", through vibrations in her airframe, the aircraft that is, before she stopped flying...otherwise known as stalling. Unlike my father, Jack was not a kind instructor and in fact at times his instruction was boldly ruthless. He may have been jovial as hell when gravity kept his feet to the ground, but when levitating, he could be an asshole. With that attitude I elucidated honesty on a level I'd never known before; Jack didn't mince words. When he said I was flying like crap and not paying attention, he was correct and I put my tail between my legs. When he praised me for a good flying performance a halo appeared over my head. My father was always nice, always calming, always supportive when instructing me, even when I know I totally screwed up. The problem is at times when my father said I was doing good I really wasn't sure if I was, because I always seemed to do good. Holy crap with Jack, no free passes baby, if I did a poor pattern there was no, "Oh son that was good, but I'm sure you can do better," gibberish. No, with Jack it was, "What the fuck was that??!! Are you trying to kill me? I don't want to die with you, I can do that myself, get your head out of your ass and concentrate." Seriously I thought I'd turn to jello with his harshness, but then the Jersey in me kicked in and said, "I'm gonna prove to his sorry ass I can fly this aircraft!"

And that's what happened. After about 45 minutes of "lovely" training, Jack asked me to pull off the runway after a full stop landing whereupon he climbed out of the little Luscombe. I think the aircraft immediately grew 5 inches in height once he deplaned and gave an audible "ahhhhh.."

With Jack watching by the runway, I did three patterns, two touch and goes and a full-stop on the last pattern in order to pick up the aircraft's owner. Jack said I had a smile on my face that beamed when he opened the door to get in. I've never stopped smiling from that day on in fact.

Words cannot convey the confidence Jack afforded me by being who he was on that day and soloing the timid, pip squeak little boy I was then. I stood up to the giant's well-intentioned manner of authoritative and at times draconian instructional technique and soloed a tailwheel aircraft, a most beautiful one at that, in less than an hour of instruction and with maybe 40 hours in my logbook…my confidence level in life due to the gift of Jack's time and aircraft created a positive ripple effect in every area of my life, and which continues to this day. That day with Jack was just the beginning of some amazing adventures with him.

I had to pass my FAA written test before I could take my practical flight test with a FAA Examiner. I was not a studious person back in my teens. I was in the bottom ten percent of my high school graduating class that made the upper ninety percent possible. I don't think I was stupid then, though maybe I was. No matter what, I hated high school with a passion, including the school work associated with it, so my effort at academics did not include effort. This intro to my academic abilities in high school leads me to the fact that I had to actually study to pass my FAA written. It was the first real serious test of my ability to actually learn, and Jack was my teacher.

Jack was very avant garde when I was sixteen since he said he could relate to my hating high school and the academics associated with it. His answer to my worry about my ability to pass the FAA Test was to take me to the "Landing Strip" in the evenings after we went flying together, or when I just saw him in order for him to teach me the stuff a private pilot needs to know. The Landing Strip was what the last word of the name of the establishment implies, a strip joint. Yes, I was sixteen, but that didn't stop Jack from smuggling me into the dark and seedy interior of that "fine" establishment. There were many nights when Jack brought me home, on a school night mind you, at 12 or 1 o'clock and I was drunk. My dad was an alcoholic, Jack was probably close, I guess they were mentoring me in other areas as well.

The best part of the Landing Strip was "Upside Down Norma." Probably my second real crush on an older woman, and the first woman I ever saw with breast implants. Jack illuminated that fact to me since he used her breasts as a teaching device. You see when Norma was upside down, the silicone in her lovely shaped beauties did not drop near as much as the other ladies who had real breasts, hence the reason she could go upside down without blocking her vision. The other large chested babes, well, you get the idea, it wasn't pretty. No, upside-down Norma had a lock on the pole gymnastics. Jack would call her over to us and she was definitely a bit older than the other ladies who "danced," but she was always so sweet to me and very attractive, despite her advancing years.

I hold those times at the Landing Strip with Jack as wonderful bonding times, though my mother hated him for exposing me to what she called the dark and seedy side of life; and for allowing me to get drunk on a regular basis at sixteen, and on school nights. My mother did extract a sort of revenge on me though in that she never let me stay home from school while I was horribly hung over. No matter how much I begged her to let me stay home from school on days in which I was hungover she stood firm and never let me. Ever. She would literally pull me off my bed at 6 AM in order to get me out the door for school on time. It was a great way to keep me sober.

The flying life with Jack was adventure after adventure. The most notable flight we had, well flights, because it was a bunch, was from Marathon in the Florida Keys to New Jersey. I attended summer camp in the Keys during my high school years and in the summer before my senior year Jack flew down to pick me up from the camp. Now, ya gotta picture this, most of the kids who attended that camp came from very wealthy families, mine being the exception. After my three weeks at Sea Camp (it's still in operation) in July/August of 1975 the head of the camp drove me to Marathon Airport in order for me to catch my "flight" home. I have no doubt this guy had seen some seriously nice aircraft fly into Marathon to pick up some of the more affluent of camp attendees. So imagine this guy, as we walk into the lobby of the FBO (Fixed Base Operations), and he's looking for some pilot in a tie and possibly a uniform, or a rich, well dressed dad who was an owner/operator of some nice twin-engine Cessna or Beechcraft. As we walk towards the doors that lead to the flight line Jack walks up to me, beer belly draped by a white, over-hanging, non-tucked in tee shirt, ball cap that looked like he used it to wipe the oil off his hands, thick glasses, jeans with holes (he was ahead of his time and a trend setter) and sneakers. He walks authoritatively up to me and says. "Hey Shitbird! Are you ready to go?" Shitbird was Jack's term of endearment for me.

I thought the camp counselor was gonna drop dead. He said, after Jack introduced himself, "Who is that?"

I responded casually and with an air aristocracy, "Oh, Jack? He's my pilot."

With jaw dropped, and after Jack grabbed my duffle bag of clothes to take to the aircraft, Mr. Camp Counselor said, "Where's your aircraft? Which one are you flying back to New Jersey?" He said this after walking up to the door that led to the flightline.

"Oh it's that beautiful blue one sitting on the ramp right there," said I, pointing and still keeping up with the posh talk, type attitude.

"All I see is some small thing, with its tail on the ground."

"Yup, that's her, such a beautiful aircraft. You wanna go for a ride before we depart. I can take you up?"

He left skid marks in his exit.

Jack was a funny guy, a very funny guy, but he was not exactly polished which I think kept him from being more successful at the FAA and maybe in other ventures as well. His mouth could be very crude, and his personality was so gregarious and loud at times. I am convinced since he wasn't exactly a snappy dresser either, his beer belly sometimes peeking from below a non-tucked in tee shirt, that even before he spoke most had formed a negative opinion of him. But, those that knew "him," his heart, loved him.

That trip from Florida to New Jersey in that beautiful Luscombe is still one of the high points in my flying life. We never climbed above 500 feet for the whole trip back except, maybe to join the traffic pattern altitude at some of the airports we landed in order to refuel or spend the night.

Some of the more notable things we saw and did on that trip was for us to make a faux approach and simulated wave off on a carrier that was docked in Charleston Harbor. It caused workman on the deck to scatter…needless to say Jack got a letter from the FAA for that. We had a helicopter chase us as we passed through Myrtle Beach AFB's control zone, we were about 15 feet above the water and just over the waves of the beach, but the runway at that AFB butts up to the beach. Jack thought buzzing the nudists multiple times over some obscure Cape Hatteras Beach was fun, me thinks they did not think it so; finally we had an A-4 fly along-side us as we passed by NAS Oceana. We were just off the beach and over the water at about 100 feet when I looked to my right and saw this A-4 with flaps, gear, and hook down at some crazy high angle of attack as it slowly passed us on the right, the fighter pilot in it waving as he did! I mean how cool is that???

That trip from Florida was actually a celebration present from Jack to me since before leaving for camp I had passed both my FAA written and practical flying test. I left for my Florida camp as a certified private pilot and felt on top of the world.

Before that lovely Luscombe trip however, there was some light to moderate turbulence encountered in Jack's and my relationship. The first bump occurred when I flew a trip with Jack in a Bonanza. We were coming back from Alabama, we had flown down much earlier in the morning, and heading to Blairstown Airport in New Jersey. Jack wanted me to use a sectional to navigate to Blairstown. I did, but, what angered him was that I used some very obvious landmarks to get me there…like following the Delaware River. Jack said that the great thing about aircraft is that they can go above the earth and in straight lines, unlike cars which must follow a road. I was intransigent in my belief I did nothing wrong and Jack was also intransigent in his belief that I had flown too much on the East Coast and was too used to having a huge ocean or river too help in map reading, or lack thereof in finding a destination. We had a seriously loud argument after we landed at Blairstown about my reluctance to fly as a crow flew, a straight line to the destination.

So, in order to alleviate his anger, one day, not that long after the aforementioned argument, Jack calls me up, now mind you, I'm still sixteen and working towards getting my private pilot's license, and says we were going to fly to Youngstown, Ohio in a friend's Mooney Mk 20 C. I was all for that and we cruised at a serene 12,500 feet enroute to Youngstown. A notable event occurred on that flight when four F-105 aircraft passed very and I mean very close on our left side, as they turned to the left to go behind us. They were banking hard left, almost 90 degrees, having come from our 10 o'clock position—to this day I wonder if they even saw us; seeing four Thuds that close and loud was impressive.

Once on the ground in Youngstown, Jack parked the Mooney and said that 11Z, the C-150 I'd been training in, was parked a bit further down the flight line and he said for me to go open her up and air her out. He said she'd been sitting there for a few days. So, I casually walked to 11Z as Jack, with a shit ass eating grin on his face taxied by in the Mooney and waved. WTF ? (What The Frig) I was so perplexed. So, I got to 11Z opened her up and on the pilot's seat, left seat, was an envelope with my name on it and a couple of sectionals were sitting below the envelope. Another WTF.

As I opened the envelope, I looked up to see Jack taking off. Now ya gotta remember this is before the days of cell phones, ATMs, etc... life was crude then by today's standards. And by the way, I had maybe twenty dollars in my pocket with no credit card, cash card, nothing except my FAA medical certificate; I didn't even have a driver's license since you had to be 17 to get a driver's license in New Jersey. The envelope was one of Jack's "lovely" communiques that said: "Since you insist on flying by either ocean or river, now that you are ensconced in the mid-west, you must use your skill and cunning and navigate to the Reading, PA airport. I will be happily waiting for your arrival. Good luck. Oh, by the way, I'll give you a clue on how to get there, head south easterly Shitbird."

"Asshole," I thought.

So, right. The prudent thing would have been to get the sectionals Jack left in the aircraft, go into the FBO and do some map preparation and line drawing on the map to convert true course to magnetic course and heading (East is least, west is best for variation...blah, blah, blah) and maybe get the weather, which since I had just flown from that direction, I knew was it clear. But, did I do that? Noooooooo, I just circled Reading Airport on the sectional and took off with the thought of what my father had always told me about the Allegheny mountains, those in Pennsylvania, that they run in waves with their longitudinal axis oriented northeast and southwest. Why I remembered this as I took off and headed to where I thought Reading was I don't know, but, irregardless, I took up a heading after taking off that I thought would get me to my destination.

Look, I'll admit, I was a bit scared. I had no ocean on the left or right of me and no river on either side either. I was taking off from the innards of America but, I did know if I headed on an east by southeast heading I'd hit the Atlantic Ocean eventually. However, I wanted to prove to Jack I could meet his challenge; Shitbird or not, I was gonna get to Reading and I wasn't going to miss it either to the north of south. And just to be clear, 11Z had no, none, nada, zip navigation gear of any kind installed in her. Flying from A to B was accomplished by "dead reckoning," in other words looking at a map and flying to your destination.

After about forty-five minutes of flying at 100 mph I felt like I was pretty much on course, not that I had actually drawn a line on a map that I could relate to as being on course. Nonetheless, I thought I had all the landmarks below me figured out, until, suddenly I saw a power plant out the window to my left, that I couldn't find on the sectional. Then in a cascade effect everything on the map and then everything on the ground around me looked different from what I had been relating to on the sectional. In short order major doubt about my position rushed into my head like water rushing from a burst dam. So overwhelming was my concern for 'being lost" that, like a very quick reacting laxative, I immediately had to take a bowel movement and I mean immediately. I was suddenly "prairie dogging it," if you know what I mean. I was closing down on my sphincter muscle with all my strength since I really didn't want to crap my pants enroute to Reading—Jack and my father would never let me live that down. Now, the newest of emergencies was not finding my exact position, but finding an airport.

By the grace of God, just as I began my visual search for any airport, out the left side and just past that unknown power plant I saw a small airport, with an east west running runway, approximately 3000 feet in length. I tuned to the normal, universal Unicom radio frequency and made a hard left turn, overflew the airport, saw which way the wind favored for landing and landed without further ado. I was damn near flying into the ramp I taxied so fast, still maintaining a firm clasp on the 'ole sphincter muscle. I parked and shutdown in one fluid motion, jumped out of the aircraft and walked, ran, hobbled, to the FBO building. I was so close now. I flew into the building with abandon and to the surprise of an older gentlemen sitting behind a counter. I squeaked out in pain, "Where's your bathroom??"

Smiling, he pointed to my right and said down the hall.

I barely made it to the toilet before the sphincter protested and relaxed its grip, by then though it was bombs away since I was now over the target. I must have sat on the throne for 20 minutes, the gentleman at the counter making a house call to see if I was OK.

I actually had the presence of mind to bring reading material in the toilet with me, the sectional that I was using for navigation. During my "personal space time" I poured over the map, trying to figure out where I was. In the end I did find the airport where I suspected I had landed, and after talking to the very kind man, the only person in fact in the FBO building, he confirmed that the airport I showed him on the sectional was where I landed. I felt so relieved at this confirmation and in the fact I had lightened the payload of the aircraft by a few pounds; to this day I could not tell you what airport it was where I made that emergency landing.

Once airborne I was a lot more relaxed than when I took off from Youngstown. I began map reading and landmark locating as soon as I was airborne after that physiological break. I made it to Reading with total confidence without following a river, a road, or relying upon anything other than going map to ground, ground to map, with regards to referencing landmarks between the real world and the sectional. I was proud to tell Jack, upon seeing him after I landed that I flew as direct a route as a crow would fly. He had made his point.

Jack could be an asshole at times, but he was a well-intentioned one.

The next fair amount of turbulence I experienced with him, and one in which he really yelled at me, was a thunderstorm encounter, well, near encounter.

One early afternoon I rode my bike to Knocky's, where Jack normally kept his aircraft, took off in 11Z and flew to Woodbine Airport for some landing practice and general air work in preparation for my private pilot's license. I still had about nine months to go until I was seventeen and could get my license. I really was just having fun puttering around the South Jersey skies killing time flying until my birthday and that magic 17 number came up. Like a little boy playing in the sand with his toy trucks and oblivious to the world around him, so too did I play around Woodbine Airport. As I did touch and goes on the same runway upon which I soloed, I suddenly became aware of an infiltration of towering cumulonimbus clouds, their numbers and size became so overwhelming I couldn't help but notice them. I quickly scanned the sky in the direction of Knocky's as I did another touch and go and figured I'd better get my butt home before it was impossible to get there due to those obnoxious, windblown giants.

With my epiphany about the consequences of the interlopers, I immediately left the security of my playground. I stayed low, eight hundred feet or so, and in clear air and deviated at will around the massive, white, and ever-bulging cloud bases looking for a way to the sanctity of Knocky's. But with every turn I encountered a dead end of bubbling and menacing-looking clouds full of energy and enthusiasm and with torrents of rain pouring forth from their bases, drenching the land below. Again, and again, and again I turned this way or that, every avenue of escape being thwarted by grand canyons of clouds rising 30,000 to 40,000 feet above me. The massing was seemingly complete, and when I saw lightning burst forth from a rather low-hanging bit of cloud, maybe two miles in the distance, I put my tail between my legs and high-tailed it for the security of Woodbine Airport. This sanctuary was still remarkably free of the weather, though it was starting to encroach there too as I landed. Once on the ground I taxied to one of the aircraft ramps and shutdown. There was a payphone near one of the buildings and I used it to call my dad who was at work.

The old man wasn't flying that day, thank the Lord, he was in the weather shop and I had to be transferred to their number after calling flight ops.

When my dad wasn't flying, he liked to go up to the weather office and help the guys. He knew the weather better than Mother Nature and I held his weather wisdom in as high regard as his flying ability. Anyway, when he answered I told him what the situation was, about as fast as light goes from the Earth to the moon. He asked me to slow down to sub-light speed in my conversation, after telling him about three times and getting a pregnant pause in return— he laughed! He thought it was great that I was getting this experience! When I told him about the lightning he thought that was even better and said at least I was getting some good weather experience in preparation for my pilot's license.

With an internal sigh of relief, I asked him what I should do. He said he'd check the weather radar and then call me back.

About twenty minutes after calling my dad, the pay phone rang and I ran to answer it. The reassuring voice of my father told me that there should be a break in the cells (storm cells) long enough for me to fly "home" in about thirty minutes or so. He said he'd call me when he wanted me to take off.

I waited. I wandered around the ramp a bit, inspecting the many single engine airplanes parked there. After my nervous meandering and looking at my watch enough times to never allow a pot to boil, I ended up back at my trusty old steed and waited for the phone to ring. It wasn't long.

After the Brrrrring! of the phone and my answering it, my dad said the coast was temporarily clear, and he estimated I had a twenty-minute window to get my keister back to Knocky's before another set of storms would block the way. With no time to spare, I started up and took off.

Actually, the weather almost looked worse this time, once I began to head toward home, because the smaller "puffy" cumulus clouds were now a lot bigger. But I could see that there was a break in the line of weather in the direction in which I was headed. I could see lightning off my left side, all of my left, northwest through southwest, major league lightning at that, about ten miles away at its closest, but with my little engine that could at almost full bore, there was no way those tempests were going to catch me. On my right, the storms that I saw earlier were almost over the beach and no doubt the cooler, more stable sea air was taking the rage out of them and calming them down.

With clouds to left and right, I continued home at 100 mph, 800 feet above the ground as my heart raced at a million beats per minute. Once I saw the beautiful grass of my aerodrome from about five miles out did my heartbeat begin to slow since I knew I would make it to a landing. On my taxi back to parking I briefly reflected upon the flight home and how it really was a bit anticlimactic, save for the incredible display of lightning.

After landing and tying the aircraft down I had another tempest, of the human kind, with which to deal—Jack.

Oh Em Gee (OMG) Jack was mad. He came storming (no pun intended!) up to me and asked me what in the hell I was doing flying HIS aircraft in weather like this and with only a student pilot's license. I had no answer other than it seemed like a nice afternoon to go flying and I got caught down in Woodbine. My dad had called Jack to tell him what had happened. There was no appeasing his anger, and after getting my butt chewed out for the better part of ten minutes, I hopped on my ten-speed bike and rode home bewildered— not so much by the weather, but by the contrast in emotions between my dad and Jack; hell they were both bipolar, and I wasn't sure which one was more whacko. The greatest generation types sure had some anger management issues.

That night, after my ass chewing, my father had me go with him to the local pub and there we met Jack. I am sure they both conspired to have me there with them so we could have a more sane discussion about what happened that day. I figured I was going to get another dose of Jack's anger, but instead he was very happy and in short order he and my dad were slapping me on my back saying what a great experience I had gotten that day.

At some point during that surreal evening I stood back from the bar and thanked God for such an eclectic mix of aviation mentors.

In the late summer of 1975, just after Jack and I had flown from Marathon, Florida in his Luscombe, I asked him if I could fly his aircraft up to New Bedford Massachusetts so I could spend a few days with a smoking hot girl I had met and dated while in Sea Camp. Anne Watson was the girl and she and I had been constant pen pals since my return to Jersey with the occasional phone call thrown in. Jack said he wouldn't let me fly his Luscombe up there alone, however he would let me fly him up there and he'd fly the aircraft back and pick me up a few days later. I was elated and on a Friday afternoon we departed for New Bedford with one fuel stop in Connecticut.

After arriving Anne and her mother were waiting in the local FBO's lobby. I asked Anne if she wanted to go for a flight since Jack actually suggested it as we taxied in. Quite enthusiastically she said yes and with her mother's approval I ushered her out to the aircraft. Once I got Anne to the Luscombe I knew why Jack wanted me to give her a flight—he wanted to strap her in so he could check out her physical dimensions, such was Jack.

I flew Anne over the local area, and particularly her home which was only a few miles away in Nonquitt; everyone loves to see their house and neighborhood from the air.

After the flight and before I left to spend the weekend at Anne's house Jack called me over to him as he stood by his aircraft. I was quizzical, since I had already profusely thanked him for letting me fly up there and for his time and for letting me use his aircraft. So, I walked cautiously up to him not knowing what to expect. He said with a frown, "Shitbird, haven't Upside Down Norma and I taught you anything?"

I was perplexed, deeply perplexed. I had no clue what he meant and I didn't know how to respond so I just blurted out, "What are you talking about?"

"Her tits."

I was utterly dumbfounded. There was not one time in my life where my father ever made a comment about the physical nature of any girl I dated. Now, here was Jack, a supposed adult to whom I am to look up to making a rather crude comment about a girl that I really liked.

"Anne's breasts or Upside Down Norma's?" I asked, truly not understanding what the hell Jack was getting at.

"She has no tits. Yeah, she's very pretty, and has a nice ass, but no tits. Son, ya gotta go for the girl with jugs. I thought if you learned anything while watching Norma it was that. I need to educate you when you get back. Now have a good time and I'll see you in four days."

"Yes sir," I said, totally amazed at the conversation we just had.

Anne asked me what Jack wanted when I got back to the FBO lobby and I said he wanted to tell me how pretty you were—she blushed—if only she really knew.

At one point in my senior year of high school I began dating a girl from my senior class. My father had just recently joined an FAA Flying Club so I had access to a few Piper Aircraft during this period of time in my life. One day after school I took this young lady for a flight. It was around 4PM in the afternoon when we took off. I decided, on a whim, to buzz the high school athletic fields. Now mind you the high school was situated in a heavily populated suburb and there was a lot of activity going on in the school yard then. Screaming down from a 1000 feet I flew maybe, 50 feet, over the green grass of the baseball, football, and field hockey playing areas. I did one pass and then headed back to the Atlantic City Airport and landed.

Jack met me at the aircraft after I landed. He was driving an FAA airport vehicle and he was mad. He told me to take the girl home and that he wanted to take me flying. I asked him what his problem was and he said he'd tell me in due time. So, I took my girlfriend home and met him at the airport. It was late in the spring and it didn't get dark until later in the evening.

We actually met at Knocky's and he said get into the Luscombe; he'd already prepped it for flight. We took off and he said to fly over the marshes which were a buffer between the barrier islands of New Jersey and the mainland. The marshes had many creeks, narrow and wide, that intermingled, separated, and then reengaged within the marshland's confines. I was directed to fly over a fairly large bay and then drop down to low altitude. Jack didn't define what low altitude was so I went down to about 100 feet. He also said to head south and then directed me to follow a rather large, wide, creek that was pretty much in the middle of the marshland.

At what I thought was a comfortable altitude, I began to follow the serpentine nature of the creek. As I banked left and right following the curves of the creek Jack began to push on the stick and he forced me to fly lower. I began to fight him and was pulling back. He got extremely stern with me and said I better not let go of the control stick. We were slowly going lower and lower with each mile of creek followed, to the point we were barely 20 feet above the water. At 20 feet he let off on the forward pressure and instead used his booming voice to cause me to fly low. However, if I did climb a bit he began again with putting forward pressure on the control stick. At that point I was gripping it as if my life depended upon it, which, in my thoughts it did since I thought we'd crash into the water. We were flying about 100 MPH and with each turn and bank as the creek did its twists and turns Jack told me to be smoother on the flight controls. My dad said the same when he was teaching me to fly. Consequently, in between fighting Jack against his forward push of the control stick I was also verbally fighting him on my left and right banks of the aircraft because I thought I was being smooth in my maneuvering and he said I wasn't. I was pissed, he was pissed, it was not a fun flight. I thought the man had lost it. I mean I really did.

We fought like this until the creek divided into a couple of tributaries that went in somewhat opposite directions. Jack said to follow the left tributary and climb which I did without hesitation. We flew north, at 1000 feet, and followed the beaches of each respective barrier island until we got to the northern tip of Ocean City whereupon we headed back to Knocky's and I landed without anymore comment from Attilla the Hun.

From Knocky's Jack asked me to follow him for a "debrief."

"Crap," I thought to myself, here comes another ass chewing.

We wound up at the "Landing Strip" where my cougar crush, Upside Down Norma, was hanging out that evening. At this time in my life I was 18 and allowed into the establishment without help from Jack. Once I my eyes got accustomed to the dark I could discern Norma on center stage, her breasts still defying gravity. Jack handed me a beer when I saddled up next to him since we took separate cars and he beat me to the establishment.

"So Shitbird, have you had enough of low altitude flying?" He asked with a smile on his face.

"Jack, what is your issue? I mean you scared the hell out of me today. I thought you had a death wish," I said with excitement and amazement.

"No, I don't, but you do. Do you know how many pilots have died buzzing? You don't have the skill or judgment at this point in your life to fly as low as you did over your high school today. That was dangerous and I hope I taught you a lesson. I know, I know, we flew very low all the way from Marathon to New Jersey, but I know what I'm doing and I was with you when you flew. You don't have that judgment yet. So, Shitbird, take it easy. Let your dad and me teach you. OK?"

"Yes sir," I responded with a sigh, as I glanced a look at Norma's inverted breasts, remembering what Jack said to me in Massachusetts. "How the hell did you know I buzzed the high school so low?" I asked with genuine surprise.

"I was driving down Route 9 (It borders the school grounds) and passing by the high school when you flew right over me. I knew, I mean I knew it was you. You were so low I recognized the aircraft's numbers. You really are a Shitbird. No one with registration numbers that big on their aircraft would fly that low over people. I was going to the airport to pick something up and thought I'd scare the crap out of you. Do you know you could get your license suspended, or revoked for dangerous flying like I saw you doing? If you really want a career in aviation you gotta do better in the future kid."

"Yes sir," I answered as Upside Down Norma rolled upright, landed, and walked off the dance floor, throwing me a smile as she left.

After my instrument phase of flying where Jack taught me the ins and outs of flying in the weather and on instruments we began the road to my Commercial Pilot's License. My father wanted me to learn aerobatics before I got my Commercial License which requires 250 hours in your flight log and another written test.

Yes, there was more of "Upside Down Norma" as Jack helped me study for the written test. By then I was able to drive myself to the "Landing Strip" so I might have one alcoholic drink, much less than when I was a hostage to Jack's driving. Besides, I was a bit older and wiser and not wanting to get a DWI or that dreaded hangover.

The flying required for the Commercial is, as you would suspect, more involved than that required for a Private Pilot's License, so when he could Jack taught me the required maneuvers and I performed the cross country flying by myself. My father insisted that I learn some basic aerobatic flying before I took my Commercial Flight Test and there again Jack was my instructor. Unlike some other phases of flight training, he was never, ever draconian or harsh when teaching me to do loops, aileron/barrel rolls, or spins—and Lord did we spin. We started out with one turn, and then two, and finally we got to where we were doing five and six turns. He wanted me to be to be completely comfortable with spinning and to recognize the instant an aircraft was about to enter a spin and how to immediately prevent it, with minimum altitude loss. His wisdom in teaching me this was heaven sent as three years from then his instruction saved my life.

Another moment of sheer terror when flying with Jack was when he taught me stalls in a Bonanza. He was borrowing the high-performance aircraft from a friend and it was the same one we once flew to Alabama. Out of the blue he called me up and said let's go do some stalls. I was thinking, "What's the big deal, I've stalled a bunch of other aircraft, what's so important about stalling this one?" No matter he said, let's go. We had climbed to about 3,000 feet above Wildwood, New Jersey, slightly over the marshes and near where I flew low with him a year before. He says, "OK, dirty the aircraft up, and configure it as if you were about to land and then bring the nose up as if to extend a glide like you were low on a visual glide path to a runway, but don't add power." I did as he said and I got the aircraft in the buffet, since it was just starting to stall. As soon as the aircraft started to stall Jack told me to recover. I immediately added all 285 horses of power and instantly the aircraft rolled over going inverted and the nose dropped dramatically. I about crapped. Jack was with me on the controls as soon as we began to roll and helped me to recover right side up without exceeding the aircraft's gear, flap, and G limits. He said I looked white as a ghost after we got back to straight and level flight.

His point was to show me that with that kind of torque, 285 horses, recovering from a stall with the Bonanza was different than with an aircraft with 65 or 100 horsepower which I'd been used to flying. The rudder had to be used with more authority and you had to be slower when feeding in the power, particularly if you were right on the verge of the stall or even stalled. Even the Piper 180 which I flew a lot, the FAA Flying Club Aircraft, was much more docile than that Bonanza. To this day that lesson of Jack's in the Bonanza is ingrained in my synapses though I've never flown a single engine propellor aircraft with that much horsepower again.

As usual, Jack's style of instruction was so "in your face', so brutal, yet so well meaning and to the point. He taught me much in our earthly debriefs of our flights together in whatever venue they took place. He was never harsh while teaching me on the ground but always enlightening with a fatherly kind of wisdom and love. Jack's bipolar nature in the air verses on the ground always kept me on my toes.

Without question the greatest moment of Jack's and my flying life together came when I was towing banners out of Cape May County Airport, in Rio Grande, New Jersey. It was doing my first season of banner towing and after my freshmen year in college. It was a hot August day and the boys, two other banner pilots, and I had gathered at the windsock of the airport which was in the center of the triangular arranged 3 runways. We had finished banner towing for the afternoon and were just BS'ing about the usual stuff when a FAA Convair 580 landed on runway 19. The runway was 5000 feet long and the aircraft went past us in its landing roll. It then taxied onto the rather large ramp that was just to the south of another east/west runway. The boys and I stood by the windsock, incredulous, as if a UFO had just landed. We then saw the left forward door and airstairs open and then descend to touch the ground. Two "aliens," one rotund, the other of a slighter build, descended the airstairs and walked towards us. We stared at these aberrations like deer looking in the headlights of a car, as these men walked across the runway and kept heading for us. I was wondering if we had violated some FAA Regulation that day and were in trouble. Soon enough though, I saw the two men were my dad and Jack.

They walked up to us and asked what we were doing. I said we had finished towing for the day and were just talking. With that my dad asked us, all three of us, if we wanted to go for a ride in the 580. I couldn't believe it. In all the years I begged my old man if I could fly with him 99 percent of the time he said no and now he's landing a 580 where I'm towing banners and asks me if I want to go flying?? Words couldn't express my shock and elation.

Walking with my father and Jack, we all climb aboard the 580 with Jack in the right seat and my dad the left and we took-off. Once airborne my dad asks me if I want to fly. Are you kidding? Again, another heart stopping moment which I never thought I'd experience with my dad, or Jack. Fly a 580? Hell, I'd never flown a twin-engine anything at this point and my old man is wanting to know if I wanted to fly a big 580 Convair.

Of course I said yes. With my heart beating a million times a minute Jack climbed out of the right seat and I replaced him. Jack moved to the jumpseat which was between and slightly behind my father and I. My dad had leveled the aircraft off at 2500 feet and had flown to the east of the airport over the marshes and then headed on a wide down-wind for runway 19. He handed the controls to me once I got squared away in the seat, the height and fore/aft distance I was guessing at, since I'd never flown this aircraft. I don't remember the numbers, airspeed, I was supposed to fly as the old man talked me through it all. All I needed to do was manipulate the control yoke and rudders he said and he'd control the throttles. We did a wide pattern to runway 19 whereupon I performed probably the most horrible approach anyone has ever performed in an aircraft with the exception of crashing; my lord the flight controls on that beast were heavy!! We actually did a touch and go with my father seriously over-powering me on the controls almost constantly. After gear and flaps up my dad let one of the other guys fly. We stayed in the pattern until all three of us banner pilots did one touch and go whereupon we landed.

After deplaning my colleagues and I profusely thanked my father and Jack for their courage and hospitality in letting us each get a pattern in that most powerful of twin-engine turbine aircraft.

To this day that spontaneous act of kindness shown to me and my fellow banner pilots has never been rivaled, particularly since it was such a big aircraft for my father and Jack to have just dropped in to the airport to just say hello.

However, another much earlier example of Jack's good nature and generosity was the time I introduced him to a fellow colleague, Jeff, with whom we both had started our first summer of banner towing while I was home from college (Jeff was not one of the other banner pilots on the day we flew the 580). One of the most interesting moments of both Jack's, Jeff's, and mine friendship was when Jeff met my dad and Jack. The two (Jack and my father) had already had a few beers when the four of us met at the Rugby Inn.

As the "Hi, ya doin's" were expressed, Jack in his typical very forthright manner said to Jeff and very loudly I might add, "I know you from somewhere!"

Jeff said, rather sheepishly, "Yeah, I remember you too. I was the guy who borrowed your Luscombe."

Jack's eyes got real big, his arms starting flapping and then he said, even louder this time, "Yeah that's it! Borrowed it my ass, you stole it!"

The rest of the story is this: Jeff was a lineman at the Ocean City Airport and he loved Jack's Luscombe, so when Jeff got off work one day, he literally untied the aircraft, hand propped it by himself (just like Jack did), and flew it around (he had never flown a Luscombe before this flight); it would not be the last time he took the aircraft for a spin. Every time he landed he parked it in the same tie-down spot and filled it up with fuel equal to what he had used. It took a while, but Jack began noting certain subtle differences in his aircraft when he went to fly it and eventually caught Jeff in the act of tying it down after a flight. Jack was absolutely furious. Jeff said the eruption of Mt. Vesuvius when it covered Pompeii was probably a mere burp compared to Jack's emotional display that day. But Jack's temper quickly died down, and once composed he said to Jeff, "Give me one good reason as to why I shouldn't call the cops and have you arrested!"

Jeff simply said, "I think your airplane is the neatest one on the airport and the only one I wanted to fly."

Jack was so taken aback by his answer that they both got in the Luscombe and Jack gave Jeff a proper checkout. Jack said that Jeff was one of the most naturally gifted pilots with whom he had ever flown.

Needless to say, Jack and Jeff had a lot catching up to do that evening and it was so wonderful to step back listen to and watch Jack and Jeff catch up on life and to listen to Jack bring his stories to life.

After college and upon entering the USAF I left home and was stationed out west, flying F-4s. Jack had taken me as far, instructional wise, as he could when I got my Commercial license. I had decided in my senior year of college I wanted to let the military train me further so I joined.

On occasion I was allowed to fly an F-4 back east and of course I headed to Atlantic City Airport, my aviation roots and from where I first began to fly with Jack and my father. Jack would always have a follow-me truck lead me (and my wingman if I had one) to a parking spot on the FAA ramp the wands in the hands of the marshaller being beer bottles—so Jack'esque. My father would be in the Ops building when I arrived in that wonderful Phantom, but Jack, no, he was right there on the ramp greeting me handing me and the lads I was with a beer upon deplaning.

After my last visit in the F-4 in 1987 Jack wrote me the most wonderful of letters. In the letter he told me how much of a wise ass he thought I was when he first met me and how he figured I would fail miserably in life but how much he saw himself in me and wanted to help me become a pilot. He said he was so proud of me when I came to visit in the Phantom and that I had exceeded all of his expectations (and mine!!). He said he considered me a son and that if I ever needed anything, with-in his ability he would be there for me. I had tears streaming from my eyes by the time I finished that letter and yes, he ended it by calling me a Shitbird.

Five years after reading his words and while only in his early 40s Jack had a severe stroke. I was flying F-16s and airliners then and he was such a proud peacock when I went into a pub with him wearing my flight suit after a Viper flight at the local airport. I was devastated. I remember his last words to me in the hospital since he was actually very alert for my visit. From his hospital bed he looked at me and said, "Do you have Jesus?"

I was incredulous. I mean, do you have Jesus? Are you kidding me? This kind of talk coming from a man who, when I was 16, took me regularly to a strip joint, fed me beer (school night or not) and had me analyze Upside Down Norma's" breast implants and body in general?

Maybe at some point after his and mine regular socializing he received an epiphany from God himself and had re-converged with a faith he so long ago had abandoned, I don't know. Or, maybe when in the presence of death an angel comes to visit offering you a last chance of salvation. I don't know what caused Jack to mention the Christian faith to me but on his death bed he floored me with his question.

"Yes, my dear Jack, I have Jesus," I said solemnly, "It was Jesus, you, and my dad that blessed me with my aviation career."

Jack passed away the next day.

So many lives did he and I live together, all of it being centered around aircraft. The hot summer nights I spent with him watching Upside Down Norma as he taught me aviation academics or told me some esoteric and funny as hell story. His love of women's breasts is still etched in my head. His edification of flying smoothly, or at low altitude, and to think well ahead of the aircraft have permanently shaped my flying. His teaching me aerobatics that one day would save my life and cause me to have no fear when flying military aircraft. Or, the time the water pump on my car broke causing my car to overheat on the way to my banner towing job. I called Jack and he came out and helped me take out the broken water pump and put in a new one, all the while my car was parked on the side the road. Jack taught me so much my own father was incapable of. He supplemented some of life's instructions that my father was too narcissistic or drunk to convey. I loved Jack for what he will always be to me, a gift from God, prozac in the form of a man who came to me when I needed someone like him the most; Jack saved me from myself. I know one day he, Upside Down Norma, and I will be hugging each other in heaven and Jack will be making the angels laugh with his stories. No doubt though, he will still be calling me Shitbird.

Last Flight

The morning sky was cloudless and dark blue and the air cool, as I began untying Nine Seven Bravo (henceforth to be written 97B) in preparation for our flight to Cape May County Airport.

The length of the days was waning on this, the second week of September, slowly giving way to the coming equinox that marked the beginning of autumn. As it does every year, Labor Day sounded the unofficial end to summer a week ago. This seasonal passing of Labor Day weekend acts as a broom, "shushing" the tourists, en masse, back to the innards of America and back to their winter homes, from whence they came, and come, each and every summer.

This annual end-of-summer departure of the masses also brought an end to another season of banner towing. "Aerial advertising," as it is more eloquently called by people more refined than myself, is a summers-only business along the South Jersey shore. Paramount Air Service, which is located at Cape May County Airport in Cape May, New Jersey, owns eight aerial advertising, "banner towing," aircraft. Seven of these aircraft plied their trade towing banners out of Cape May from May to early September. The eighth aircraft, 97B, flew out of Bader Field, a small airport about thirty miles north of Cape May and at the back door to Atlantic City.

I had been towing banners in 97B for most of the past four summers while on summer break from college, but the flight today was to be my last in her, at least for the foreseeable future. I had graduated from college in May, and I was to start Officer's Candidate School in late September with USAF pilot training to follow. On that morning, I was going to fly 97B to Cape May where she was to roost until next summer's towing season, a routine to which she had been relegated for the past few years. So, like a connoisseur of fine food who chews each morsel more than the old wives' tale allotted twenty-first times, to savor each delicious bite, I too, as a connoisseur of the sky, intended to absorb and relish as much of this flight as I could.

Nine Seven Bravo, 97B. Those two numbers and that single letter are indelibly etched upon my heart. That simple combination of human symbolism and communication represent the name, the "N" numbers, to be more specific, of the "lady" with whom I had a love affair. She was a 1956, orange and white, Piper Super Cub. Her official name was 6897B, so dedicated by the FAA bureaucrats, but to me she was simply 97B. We had a relationship that lasted for four years and almost 750 hours. In that time, I went from crawling to walking in as far as gaining "seat of the pants" flying experience. She taught me so much and gave so much and, and with the exception of gas and oil, expected nothing in return. I am sure that she had seen more glorious days. In her prime, she may have crop-dusted or flown in the bush, or maybe she lived in the lap of luxury, sheltered in some cozy hangar, flown only on Sundays. But, now she was semiretired flying four months out of the year towing "Eat at Joe's" signs or some reasonable facsimile thereof; like a once-proud cutting horse, she was now relegated to pulling the equivalent of a plow. In spite of her years, to me, she was beautiful. Time and the elements had taken away her physical attractiveness, at least to the casual observer, however, as dull as she was in sheen, underneath, she still had spirit and I always thought she looked like a high-spirited World War II fighter aircraft.

No doubt that given her age, 97B had seen many a cocky young knight with swagger and a cocky attitude, jump into her cockpit and then get humbled in her hands. But once the young would-be master of the skies realized that he didn't know it all did she begin to teach. That's how it was with me. I knew all her idiosyncrasies, and she accepted mine. We were a singular machine once I got settled into her cockpit. My arms and legs, acting as neurons melded into her flight controls when we took flight, neither one of us separate from the other. I was the biological part of a living entity, part metal, part flesh—neither one of us capable of flight without the other.

And so it was, on this beautiful morning, that I found myself untying 97B in preparation for our last flight together.

The aroma of freshly ground coffee tantalized my nose as I performed my walk around. The source of this gloriously earthen smell, Ireland's Coffee, was right across the street from the airport and near the ramp. I had been smelling it for the past three years, and I never tired of its scent. It reminded me of my days as a very young kid, going to the A&P food store with my mom and burying my head in the burlap bags of coffee that sat at the end of each checkout counter. Also, because I smelled the coffee from Ireland's it meant that the winds were light, an unusual thing during the warm days on the shore, considering there was an almost constant sea breeze. Finally, the smell, particularly that day, brought back three years' worth of memories, happy memories, of Atlantic City Airport and banner towing and of 97B . . . the womb from whence I began my aviation career.

Once all the preflight rituals were accomplished, I started 97B's engine and we taxied to the active runway. I always thought of her as a P-51 Mustang, although the only similarity, albeit a weak one, was that they are both tail-draggers. My mom always said I had an active imagination, so where the truth ended my delusional thinking took over. I imagined I was getting ready for the dawn patrol and my "Mustang" and I were the leaders of the pack. As we taxied to the runway the morning sun would glint off the propeller and create a stroboscopic effect that, along with the rumble of the Lycoming engine, would seduce me into believing that I was more than I really was.

In reality, 97B was not a Mustang and I knew it. The instrument panel was about as rudimentary as you could get. It had indicators for airspeed, oil pressure and temperature, altitude, vertical speed, rpm, and finally turn and slip . . . luxury for Jimmy Doolittle maybe—but in today's world, definitely spartan. She had a split door on the right side that allowed me to fly with the right window, the top half of the door, folded out and up and against the bottom of the wing. The lower half of the door could be left down during flight. So, in essence, my entire right side, from the top of my head to my knee was easily exposed to the elements; and if you had a fear of heights, well, definitely not a good way to fly. The view, however, was fabulous! In the three years that I flew her, I always flew with both halves fully open . . . thank God for seat belts. On my left side, the Plexiglas windshield folded back to where it blended into what should have been a side window. That window, though, for at least a good two to three feet, was not there. Somewhere during her years of towing, the left side window was removed to afford better downward visibility. (When I went in for a banner pickup, I usually stuck my head out the left side, where the window had been, to look straight down and see if I caught the banner). However, unlike my exposed right side, the fuselage, metal tubes, covered with fabric, around the window area protected my left lower flank from the elements; thusly, only my left shoulder and head were exposed to the swirling winds that washed over me.

To say the least, it was a pretty breezy place and really noisy. Consequently, to protect my hearing from being damaged by the noise, I flew with earplugs and a snug-fitting ear-covering headset with a boom mic. There was no heater. Usually, it was hot enough, given the sultry summer days, and I flew low enough to stay warm; I usually flew in jeans, sneakers, T-shirt, ball cap, and aviator sunglasses (and this was before Top Gun . . . coolness knows no bounds). When the occasional summer "cold" front blasted through and the winds came from the north/northwest—chilly winds, relatively speaking—I would stick my left arm out the window and warm it in the exhaust . . . I figured the radiator effect of warming the blood in my left arm would warm the rest of me. In a psychosomatic sense, it worked!

With the sun still well below its zenith, I taxied 97B onto runway 16 for takeoff. There were a couple of ways in which she could be alighted from the tarmac. One was a rather boring three-point takeoff. In it you kept the stick back in your lap to keep all three wheels on the runway (two mains and the tail wheel) and when flying speed was achieved, she simply lifted off. The second way of elevating her was to perform a "wheels" takeoff. With this method, you lifted the tail up as soon as you applied full power and rolled only on your main wheels.

The faster you went, the more nose-down stick you applied. In this manner the aircraft stayed on the runway until well past the point when flying speed was achieved and when the stick was pulled back, like a homesick angel she would leap into the air. And so it would be today, in keeping with my imagined belief that 97B was descended from a World War II fighter and we were heading out on dawn patrol, that we would do a wheels takeoff. After all, I never saw a Mustang do a three-point takeoff! But more realistically, I thought this type of takeoff was a more stately and dignified way for her to depart to her winter's roost.

As the throttle was moved to wide open, the airy cockpit conveyed the exhilaration of the moment by allowing swirling air and raucous engine noise to envelope me. Initially, only my feet were busy. As the takeoff roll progressed, I would alternately feed in left and right rudder—sometimes rudely, sometimes gently—to keep her tracking straight down the runway. Since there was very little crosswind that morning the rhythm of the feet was kept to a minimum and 97B tracked as true as she ever had. But fancy footwork alone though would not get this girl flying. As wise as she was, she still needed to have her ailerons and elevator tended to. At a speed I could only tell by feel through the stick and rudder pedals and not numbers on the airspeed indicator, I eased the tail up to get us on the mains. The faster we went the sound of the engine was slowly being drowned out by the rush of the wind swirling past at ever-increasing velocities. As a symphony increases in crescendo, as it nears its finale, each musical instrument adding to the whole, so too were all the elements of this takeoff, adding to the excitement—the breeze freshening, propeller spinning, fabric rustling, cylinders firing, control stick coming alive, rudder pedals dancing, heartbeats, breaths, glints of sunlight filtered by old aviator sunglasses, perspiration in the usual places, the seductive smell of burnt avgas, sea air, and roasted coffee. All were feeding this festival of sensation as we neared the climax that was liftoff. Adding more nose down elevator to hold her on the ground, I was enjoying the delayed takeoff, relishing in the emotion of the moment and in the feel of 97B. She wanted to fly, but I didn't—not yet. I was tasting, coming alive with feelings of nostalgia, four years' worth, and enjoying this last dance, not wanting it to end, knowing it would. This was my moment as a connoisseur. I was at the table with 97B, and this was to be our last supper together. Finally, at a speed well above which she could have lifted off, I gently pulled the stick back to slowly lift her off. I was enjoying being here, at this moment, as I had enjoyed all the past moments, when two distinctly different machines—one biological, one aeronautical—combined to take flight. In more than 750 hours of flying 97B, the thrill of flight was still as exciting as it had ever been.

Like an overladen Mustang, with a full load of fuel and ordnance, we slowly climbed away. However, only because I wanted to climb slow and not due to any lack of spirit from 97B. I elected to climb to a few hundred feet because once I was over the Atlantic Ocean, which was about half a mile from the departure end of the runway, I was going to descend to wave-top level for the initial part of my journey.

One of my first flight instructors, Jack, was occasionally exasperated while teaching me how to fly because I had a tendency, when I was flying VFR, to take a very circuitous route to my destination. It drove him nuts. After more than one very circuitous cross-country flight, Jack told me one of the reasons aircraft are better than cars is because they can go from point A to point B in straight lines. He said I reminded him of the kid in the Family Circus cartoon who, when sent on an errand, would visit every part of his cartoon's neighborhood while getting to his destination. My retort to his sternness was that's why I liked to fly in the first place! I loved the view that the birds have and the freedom to flit about; getting to a destination was secondary to me, the journey was the gift.

Every Thursday morning in the summer, 97B and I would take off and fly to Cape May to pick up the paychecks for the ground crew and myself. That flight was my license to meander about "my neighborhood." I probably tripled the straight-line distance to Cape May as 97B, and I investigated all the nooks and crannies of the local area from above. I cherished those flights.

The first part of my neighborhood was the Atlantic Ocean off of Absecon Island (Atlantic City sits on top of Absecon Island, as do the cities—from north to south—after Atlantic City: Ventnor, Margate, and Longport). After crossing the beach, 97B and I swooped down to wave-top level, thirty feet or so, and headed southwest to parallel the beach about half a mile offshore. I always avoided flying directly over boats, and I avoided the beaches as there were too many people on them, even at 8 a.m. On this flight, 97B and I meandered about offshore, investigating buoys and lobster pot marker flags. There was no real reason for why I flew where I did over the ocean that day, or any other day for that matter. I simply enjoyed the moments spent flying my meandering path to whatever place struck my fancy. The ocean on this day was very flat with no perceptible swells, which may be the reason a lifeguard had rowed his rescue boat exceptionally far offshore. I decided to check out the boat; since it was so far offshore, I thought there might be a problem. That was my excuse anyway, playfulness was the real reason. I put the boat on my right side, about fifty feet out, thirty feet below and passed by at a hundred miles per hour. I waved to the lifeguard, and he waved back, each one of us surrounded by our mediums of choice and each enjoying this splendid morning while contemplating only what lay in the here and now.

After passing the boat I stayed low and flew down the length of Absecon Island, just offshore, enjoying the calm air and the feeling of speed at thirty feet and 100 miles per hour. Because most of the summer residents had returned to their winter roosts, there were not many boats motoring about. The contrast between that moment and the week before was amazing. Normally, in the summer, these waters would be filled with dozens of boats, particularly on such a beautiful day. A lot of these vessels entered the ocean through the Little Egg harbor inlet between the southern end of Absecon Island and the northern end of Ocean City.

As I approached Ocean City, I turned in toward land and headed towards the inlet. Since there were so few boats, I decided to fly over the waves of the inlet. I have no idea why I did this. I would do it when I could, but I cannot consciously give you a good reason as to why I thought it was cool to do this, but I did think it was cool to fly over the waves. To be sure, if my engine quit, I'd be swimming, maybe even body-surfing to land. The inlet was about a mile or two wide, and I was about a half mile out to boot. What is really odd is that every time I flew over this area I always thought the exact same thing.

Once past the waves of the inlet, I was now flying near the Ocean City beaches. While there is only a mile or two physically separating the two barrier islands, in terms of culture, they were light-years apart. Atlantic City, with all the glitz and glamour of its casinos, gave way to the family-centered way of life that the residents of Ocean City cherished. Atlantic City's skyline was chiseled with skyscraper type buildings beckoning those with dreams of getting rich quick, while Ocean City's low-slung and rather sedate profile was more boring and less intimidating. The contrast between the cultures was as stark as the difference in skylines.

Ocean City is a mostly residential, summer resort with the main commercial district occupying a few blocks of real estate on the north end of this roughly seven-mile-long island. In the late 1970s, the winter population numbered around 20,000 people; however, in the summer it swelled to more than 200,000. It was, and still is, a dry town; no alcohol was/is served in any commercial business. Surfing, fishing, boating, and water sports in general were the major summer activities. As boring—or exciting, depending on your personal preferences—as this may sound, Ocean City did have one attraction that brought thousands of people to it year after year . . . the boardwalk.

The boardwalk stretched for two miles over the beaches of the north end. It was about 100 feet wide in the main, middle section, tapering to thirty feet or so at the ends. The boardwalk was, and still is, a world unto itself. Unless you've actually been to it, it's hard to imagine the attraction that wood planks laid above a beach can have to thousands of people who come back year after year to walk upon them. The "boards" was a microcosm of a world that had never gone bad. There were arcades and shops and restaurants upon restaurants and amusement rides and, of course, the never-ending procession of attendant hotels, all of which laid on or near the boards so as to disgorge their guests in steady streams onto the boardwalk to feed the never-ending parade of people. Whatever troubles existed in your life disappeared when you walked on the boardwalk. The surfer dudes and their groupies, the boy next door along with the girl across the street and their parents and siblings and friends, all seemed to come at some time in the summer to get away from the realities of life. During the day, Ocean City's beaches beckoned tourists by the thousands, but at night, the boardwalk was the cultural and to some, spiritual, center of the city. If you lay on the beach in the day, you walked on the boards at night. It was the happy days year after year for many thousands of people.

Earlier, I had said that Atlantic City Airport was the womb of my aviation career, well now it can be said that the Ocean City boardwalk and its immediate environs was the womb of my pubescent teenage years. Because I had been so fortunate to live so near such a wonderful environment, I spent most of my teenage summer days and nights in, on and around the boardwalk. What my father couldn't teach me when we had that "father-son talk," my experiences in Ocean City did. With its beaches, surfing, movie theaters, arcades, amusement rides, and most important of all, girls, you had all of the ingredients necessary for endless summer romances. Yes, I had been hypnotized by Frankie Avalon's corny Beach Blanket Bingo movies. I fell in love more times than I can count, and out of love just as much while socializing there . . . spurred on by hormones and in the hopes of finding my "Annette Funicello." I had under-the-boardwalk kisses and on-the-beach romances. I had entire relationships that started, endured and ended upon the boardwalk and its immediate surroundings. And throughout all those growing years, with all the relationships and all the neon nights on the boards and the sun-drenched days on the beach in front of them, there always seemed to be aircraft flying by. From the simplest banner aircraft, towing its sign, to a military fighter slicing the air with its speed and noise, to the Coast Guard helicopter checking out the girls' tans, and everything in between, they all went by. Could it be that all these pilots (except the banner pilots of course!) were paying homage to some long past memories of some hot summer nights?

Considering this was quite possibly the last time I would fly 97B, I decided to pay my respects to both her and the boardwalk by flying the same route that the previous Romeos and/or Juliets flew before me and that had caused me to look up when I was immersed in my sea of love (almost six years after this flight I paid a tribute to 97B by flying a similar route, farther out to sea though, at 350 knots in a F-4 and then later in a F-16). I flew from the inlet to arrive just off the beach, outside the breaking waves, and abeam the boardwalk. I had large "N" numbers on the side of my aircraft, and I was worried about some double-chinned (one chin from God, the other from fat) FAA bureaucrat wrecking my career by telling me I was flying dangerously close to people, but on this day, I risked it. I owed it to 97B, all those memories of romance and friendships, and to myself. I flew along the entire length of the boardwalk at fifty feet, just outside the breaking surf, rocking my wings, saying hi to whoever was looking, and thinking about how I was going to miss my simple life of flights, nights, beach bars, beach babes, and buddies.

I contemplated going for a second run down the boardwalk, but I decided two runs was too much. One run was the dignified way to exit, and so I turned tail to the boardwalk's end and headed again for the open sea.

I frolicked about offshore, generally heading southwest as I flew the length of Ocean City Island; I was now contemplating the next act in my neighborhood journey. I had to cross from the sea to the land. I say "had to"—actually, that was BS. I didn't have to do any of this . . . I wanted to!

This was my "gift," this flight and every flight, and I was going to do what my mentor, Jack, hated most, and I was going to be pretty darned good at it too! That was my quest.

The reason I had to cross from the sea to the land was my desire to fly down the intracoastal waterway. This waterway lies between the mainland of New Jersey and its barrier islands, the islands of Absecon and Ocean City. (These islands are anywhere from two to three miles off the mainland and are much longer than they are wide, and they run from the southern-most tip of the state north to near Asbury Park.) There was a lot of water and marsh in between the two, and I loved to fly down a particular stretch of waterway that meandered like a snow skiing slalom course. I discovered it three years earlier, but because a lot of boats were usually on it in the summer, I couldn't fly low over it very much, except on the rare occasion, like that day!

The problem was, all the barrier islands were fairly densely inhabited. The homes and businesses on them created an invisible barrier to low-altitude flying because the regulations stated that you couldn't fly closer than 500 feet to any man-made object/dwelling (over thinly populated areas that is, 1000 for more heavily inhabited lands). A couple of islands up north had stretches of nature in their seemingly endless sea of homes, but down south, it was pretty packed. Except for one island . . .

God put the town of Strathmere where it was, for me, I am sure. The transition from crowded Ocean City to lightly colonized Strathmere was just too good to be true, so surely there had been divine inter-vention. Yes, there was an inlet, a break between the islands where water flowed, a small inlet, maybe half a mile wide that I could have flown over to avoid people and buildings, but there was a bridge that crossed that narrow bit of water, and on that bridge was a toll booth. I did not want to have a toll booth collector get all worked up if I flew low over his/her bridge and then consequently call the "authorities." Discretion, I thought, was the better part of valor on this day.

So, I flew just off the beach, just outside of the breaking waves looking for my moment to fly across. Only the northern end of this city, for about five blocks, had any sizable development; the rest of the city, until you got farther south toward Sea Isle, was very sparsely inhab-ited—probably because the island was quite narrow where I wanted to cross, with only one north/south road being able to fit within the confines of the island at this narrow "waist." The day was surreal in its brilliance and climate, and because of this, there were quite a few beachcombers walking about, scavenging for bits of driftwood or shells, or in search of charging up their spiritual batteries. I too was in a spiritual mood, and in this mood there was the matter of keeping a certain continuity to this flight . . . climbing above 100 feet was not a part of this continuity. So, like a seagull flitting about looking for food, I was flitting about looking for a break in this human wall. I flew toward Sea Isle, which was very populated, and then backtracked up north again, cursing the people like my feathered friends surely must when they want to alight on a beach and humans are there. Finally, after turning once again southward, I saw a break and went for it. Staying low, but far enough away from the people to make me feel I was legal, I flew quickly over the thin strip of barrier island and out over the backwaters.

I must stop my story at this point and explain something to you, reader, which must be starting to become glaringly obvious . . . my seeming obsession with low-altitude flying. In the early days of my flying, I never flew lower than 800 feet, except when in the process of landing. I loved flying for the view and wasn't all that fussed about going back from whence I came. Then one day, Jack picked me up in the Florida Keys where I was attending summer camp and flew me back to New Jersey in his Luscombe. With 65 horsepower, she was not exactly a screaming banshee in climb, particularly since Jack was, to be polite, still carrying some baby fat. That trip is a story in and of itself, so too, for that matter, was my life with Jack. But to get on with this, we flew from Florida to New Jersey pretty much at 100 to 500 feet all the way. We flew along the coast, avoiding dwellings and people, and climbed up to 1000 feet only when we had to turn inland to land and get gas or lodging for the night. It was a wonderful trip. I was seventeen at the time, and when I started towing banners and got 97B as my "ride" I began my low-altitude forays. Also, banner towing itself is done at relatively low altitude, particularly when zooming in for the pickup, so I was kinda used to flying low, and Jack did teach me some principles so that I wouldn't bust my ass.

Continuing, once over the back bays and marshes, I flew to the entry spot of my slalom course. It wasn't hard to find as the beginning was marked with an out-of-service railroad bridge. I should add that it was exactly in the very waterways below me where my sister and I learned, thirteen years before this flight, how to water ski.

At 100 feet and 100 mph, it wasn't too hard to stay within the confines of the waterway. Marsh grass formed the lateral boundaries of the serpentine course and the channel was wide enough, and the meandering turns gentle enough to allow me to easily maneuver without any radical aerobatics or gyrations. Since my earliest days of flight instruction, I had been taught to be gentle on the yoke/control stick and flight controls in general, to include use of the throttle. Even when the speed of flight control movement—be it the ailerons, elevator, or rudder, or a combination of all three—was of the utmost urgency, it was hammered into me to be fast but smooth. So, as I careened above the waterway, I practiced what Jack had been pounding into me. I was like a seagull looking for food, graceful in movement, however, quick, yet deliberate in direction. Yes, I know, I was supposed to be flying a P-51 Mustang, but I also loved to watch seagulls fly, so I was pretty flexible in my imagination.

I was really enjoying this union of man and machine. The winds were so light that nary a bump of turbulence was felt. I would start a turn and feed in rudder and ailerons and as soon as that turn was completed, I would have to do just the opposite. I also increased and decreased power to maintain 100 mph. There were "straightaways," however at 100 mph, and owing to the rambling nature of the water's course the time spent wings level was brief indeed. I thought that this "course" should have been a mandatory flying lesson as it required sooo much continuous movement and coordination between the stick and rudder pedals. Finally, because of the waterway's serpentine flow, with the confines defined by the mainland and the outer islands, we flew a very circuitous, hence long, route that enabled 97B and I to do some heavy-duty bonding.

Soon, all too soon, the nature of the waterway changed, the turns becoming more angular and narrow. God was softly, gently, letting me know that I had to end this mischief. I was now down to where the Cape May Airport banner pilots picked up their banners.

Unlike my operation up north, where I picked up my banners within the confines of an airfield, the guys in Cape May had to fly a couple of miles from their aerodrome to drop off and pick up from a farmers' field that lay close to the marsh and very close to the Garden State Parkway. I had been to this field many times in the past three years. Usually, every couple of days in the summer I would either tow a banner into this field or pick one up. And, as I previously mentioned every Thursday I would fly down to Cape May to pick up the payroll checks. Of course, given my nature, before landing at the airport and after taking off for my return trip home, I had to investigate the early morning goings-on of the ground crew at the towing field! So, I usually flew a surreptitious approach to the field and would swoop down upon the place as if coming in for a banner pickup . . . it was my way of saying "Hi!" and "Good-bye!" You could definitely tell the seasoned ground crew kids from the newbies by the effect of my low-level passes. The veterans didn't miss a beat in their movement, save for turning toward me and waving. The greenhorns, however, usually dove for cover! Oh, I almost peed my pants many times during those wake-up calls! What can I say . . . I was abused as a kid . . .

Shedding feathers and changing back into Mustang colors, 97B and I headed for the towing field. I was sure it was devoid of banner kids and everything else except memories. I approached from the east-north-east. The barely diluted rays of the sun highlighted the marsh and trees ahead making them appear to be closer than they were. I used an old piling that long ago housed an object for water navigation of some sort as my marker for helping me find the field. I was flying at about twenty feet over the marsh, and since the towing field was on the far side of some thirty-foot-tall trees, I needed some landmarks to help me find it at low altitude. With the Air Force theme song playing in my head, I set up for my attack! I approached the old piling at 100 miles an hour when I saw a bird, a large bird, alight from what appeared to be a nest that had been built under the cover of some wood adorning the piling's top. What was odd was that this bird was not heading away from me, she (I assumed it was a she) was heading directly toward me. I was dumbfounded to think that this bird of prey—I took her to be a hawk—had the gumption to go beak to beak, no pun intended, with a much larger bird of prey . . . 97B.

I don't know the distance between us when I first spotted her, but what I do know is that we were now wrapped up in a proverbial game of chicken. I can only assume this bird was guarding a clutch and was going to fight to the death to protect it. I decided to see if she was going to back off from her intercept course on me, so I continued flying directly toward her, gritting my teeth and lowering my head. She did not waver in her determination and aim. I knew that if we collided, particularly if she hit me in the windscreen, we were both gonna' lose. If she hit me anywhere, it would not be good as I'd have to explain the damage to the owners, and anyway, I didn't want to damage either bird. I can only wonder what thoughts were going through her head . . . did she think I was the mother lode of all turkeys and that I was dinner? Whatever . . . I do know that what is supposed to separate man from animal is reasoning thought, so at about 100 feet from this recalcitrant creature, I reasoned that I didn't want to die, so I turned abruptly away.

It didn't bother my pride to be the first to flinch; I'm proud I did. I saved two birds, and now this duel of avians was over.

Once the shock of the moment wore off, 97B and I collected ourselves and descended back into our role of the lead mustang on the invasion of the Normandy beaches during D-Day. As I said previously, finding the field was a little tricky from low altitude. Trees protected its eastern and northern flanks, making it impossible for me to see the field from where I was, but there was a small pond with a prominent set of reeds just before the trees on the northern flank. Also, the trees on the northern flank of the field had been cut to half of their height to allow the banner aircraft to stay low on their approach for pickup.

I spotted the pond with its reeds and then picked up the lower cut trees, which are south of the pond. I was coming in on a forty-five-degree angle to the opening from the northeast and was in a good position for the attack. Approaching the parkway that parallels the taller trees on the eastern flank of the filed, I pulled up kind of quickly to gain some altitude so I could swoop down into the field . . . this was so exciting! I apexed at 100 feet in the climb and then began a left descending turn. About 100 feet before the low trees, I was established on "final" and wings level. I cleared the low trees by ten feet or so as I continued down at 110 mph in a mock banner pickup. I pulled up into a twenty- to thirty-degree nose high climb after my low-level pass. I knew that I had no banner attached, so I immediately rolled left to begin a turn for another pass.

I always did two passes, and that day was no different. I flew a tighter-than-normal pattern rolling into sixty degrees of bank for my turn to final. I rolled out, as on the previous "attack," and proceeded to perform another mock banner pickup. I certainly didn't need the practice, I was just having fun.

Banner towing was fun. In the four years that I towed, I never got bored of the job, and for the most part, though it seemed the aircraft were frail and could break easily, they were actually very reliable.

I'd be lying if I said I didn't get the crap scared out of me a couple of times. The worst occurred when I accidently stalled and did a half turn spin right after picking up my first banner of the 1979 towing season. I was able to recover from the stall/spin with more than enough altitude to continue to fly and tow the banner on its run. But I have to admit, I knew I had nearly died, and my feet were shaking uncontrollably for at least fifteen minutes, as I towed the banner on its run. After landing, I sat for a long time in the cockpit, contemplating a different summer job. The banner kids thought I had done that "maneuver" on purpose and begged me to do it again.

What saved me was 97B. Oh sure, Jack and my father pounded some basics into me that no doubt allowed me to unconsciously react the way I did and keep from crashing, and I thank God for those guys and their instruction. However, on the flip side . . . I should have died. I stalled and spun at less than 300 feet. I should have been a statistic in the National Transportation Safety Board files. But I wasn't, I didn't crash and burn. God, knowing I could be a twit and wanting to protect his gosling as he left the nest provided me with His hand for protection. His hand was in the shape of an aircraft 97B. In her I could flit about here and there and do loops and rolls and spins and stalls and buzz barren beaches and tread near big thunderstorms all the while being protected and covered by His insurance policy for me.

I should have died in that stall/spin. Godless people can call it physics, I call it a divine 97B . . . don't try and change my mind.

Continuing with the flight at hand. With my second simulated strafing pass complete, my Mustang and I were ready to land. We were approaching the edge of the neighborhood, and the playground was empty. There were no banner kids to harass, no weekly paychecks to pick up, no banners to be towed. I didn't want to land at Cape May Airport. I didn't want to leave the womb, the cockpit of 97B, the comfort and security of which I had known for 750 hours. I was maturing, and even though I didn't want to grow up, the tide of nature, of life, was against me. Nothing lasts forever, if it did, it wouldn't be precious. My precious hours with 97B were almost at an end, and as sad as this sunset with 97B was, a dawn on new flying adventures was just beginning to break on a distant horizon to the west; 97B would be the mother of my instincts for all follow-on flying adventures. What she taught me, the aeronautical wisdom, would form the nucleus for everything I would do in subsequent aircraft and for that knowledge alone I thank God for the time He gave me with her.

We, 97B and I, landed at Cape May Airport to no fanfare, pomp or circumstance, and I taxied up to the other banner aircraft and shut down. I suspect 97B had a lot of gossip to catch up on with the other aircraft; such is the way in which I had personified her.

I said my goodbyes to the owners and their charges, people with whom I had worked for four years . . . good people.

After my goodbyes, I walked over to my father. He had flown in to pick me up in a light airplane and was waiting to fly me back home. I couldn't look back at 97B, and as I walked to the "other" airplane, I had tears in my eyes and a pain in my heart. I wanted sooo badly to take her with me, 97B, as I embarked upon my new horizon.

My dad asked me if I wanted to fly the other aircraft home . . . I said no. It is the only time in my life I have ever refused to fly. It was just too soon to try and meld with another aircraft.

Prologue

It is inconceivable for anyone to understand how much I loved flying 97B. Not only did I fly her during the day, towing banners, but I would often fly her in the evening after dinner. There was a certain barrier island north of Atlantic City, cut off from all the others and without any human habitation, save for an occasional boater who beached upon its shores. That island was my playground. I strafed it (pretend), bombed it (again, pretend), chased seagulls over it, and did touch and goes on it. After terrorizing the island's seagulls, I would fly over to the marshes near my house. My father was invariably outside, eating grilled chicken and drinking a beer—or two, or three, etc. Upon hearing the sound of my airplane, he would stand at the end of the street and watch while I performed aerobatics 3000 feet overhead. The whole neighborhood would watch at times . . . I thank the Lord I never ploughed into the ground doing some of the acrobatic maneuvers I did. While I did like to fly at the lower altitudes, one evening I decided to see how high I could get 97B. We climbed all evening it seemed. I flew long, lazy racetrack patterns over "the neighborhood" as we climbed . . . and climbed . . . and climbed. Finally, at 11,000 feet, I'd had enough of climbing. The sun was setting. When I looked about, I could see what I thought was all of the known world! The view was spectacular. When you live your days in the trenches, it's nice to stick your head up once in a while, but this was a little too much neck for me. I was feeling like I was out of my environment, particularly after seeing a couple of airliners pass a little above me on their way to New York. It took a long time for me to descend, and when I finally landed, it was after dark; that was the only time I flew 97B at night (she didn't have instrument panel lighting).

I have written this story forty-one years after my last flight in 97B. I have flown many aircraft since her, and I have loved each type of aircraft flown since . . . F-4, F-16, and MD-11/10, B-777, et al, to name a few. But what I have never achieved since flying 97B is the intimacy of flying one aircraft for 750 hours and four years. 97B was a school, a classroom, a dynamic learning environment that taught me the basic principles of flight. To some degree, everything I have learned while flying her I have applied to all of the aircraft that I have flown since, whether they were fighters, transports, jet engine, or turboprop. I will never know another aircraft as well as I know 97B. That is why I thank God for my hours in her.

Flight to Berlin

Early in the new millennium I flew an MD-11 into Hong Kong's Chek Lap Kok International Airport. It wasn't the first time I'd flown there, nor was it to be my last. Actually, I was on the third day of a 13 day trip and I'd been doing this, international flying, for over the past 12 years so I can't say I expected this layover, nor any of the others that were to follow in the next few days, to hold any great excitement. I had the mentality of, "been there, done that, got the tee shirt," and, though I do love the vibrancy of Hong Kong, those layovers were simply a means to an end. So, as we drove to the hotel and I stared out the window at nothing in particular, I figured this layover would merge with but a thousand others lost in my memory forever. By the end of the evening however, I would be grossly wrong in that assumption.

Upon our arrival at the usual hotel, located very close to Hong Kong Harbor and on the Kowloon side, my First Officer's China doll of a girlfriend was waiting for him and they excitedly left, arm in arm, for parts unknown. We had almost three days worth of a layover so Lord knows where they were headed. Don't ask, don't tell.

With dinner time approaching and after checking in and changing, I headed downstairs to the local Cheers type pub called "Someplace Else" for a glass of wine and a quiet dinner. Since I was alone, I sat at a tall table in the bar area and ordered my drink while perusing the menu. At the bar, not ten feet away, was a very lively crowd of British origin, judging from their accents. As my drink was delivered, a young lady standing next to me and involved with the festivities, told me I shouldn't drink alone and invited me into their fold. Sensing they were aircrew I readily accepted her offer and was immediately swallowed up by them and came under their flag.

As we all talked and joked and they became acquainted with me and I with them, the natural order of life began to take over and their Captain and I gravitated to each other. With the coalescing of rank within the unit complete, I was invited by their Captain to dine with them at some obscure Indian restaurant buried deep with-in the recesses of the Kowloon district, not far from the hotel. To this day the actual location of this fine restaurant is a mystery as we took so many twists and turns in the backstreets and alleys walking there, that I wasn't sure if they thought the MI 6 was following us and were trying to lose their tail.

While we ate this very refined Virgin Atlantic A340 Captain, his first name was Richard, and I talked about the usual aviation related stuff. Awkward, first steps at polite civil conversation by this eloquent English gentlemen, were followed by my New Jersey Public School style of overly dramatic arm movements woven with lively voice inflections, crude verbal utterances, and the usual Jersey clichés and slang...ya know what I'm sayin'???. As the wine flowed though, the differences in communication blurred and a natural alcohol induced translation took place.

I'm not sure how talked turned from flying to fixing aircraft, but for some reason it did. But, when I say fixing aircraft, I don't mean on the ground, I mean in flight with the pilot acting as the mechanic. We each had a story to tell and since I brought the subject up I went first.

My story involved an F-111 crew who noticed, while flying a low level over the New Mexico countryside, that their number two engine oil pressure indicator indicated zero, meaning there was no oil pressure in the engine. The pilot of the aging fighter/bomber aircraft did not believe the gauge and asked the weapons system operator (WSO), who sat immediately to his right, to take out his screwdriver and swap the number two gauge with the oil pressure gauge from the number one engine. The WSO, for some unknown reason, did have a screwdriver on his person and did indeed swap the gauges. Imagine their surprise when the different gauge gave the same indication! Shortly thereafter they were rewarded with a seized number two engine and an abbreviated low level followed by a single engine approach and landing. I'm sure their Squadron Commander was very curious as to why they didn't follow the normal checklist procedures.

Though my story got a few chuckles from the Captain and his First Officer, his story, even though told in typical stoic English prose, made me laugh so hard I almost relieved myself then and there and still caused effluent to spurt from my mouth; it is singularly the funniest aviation story I have ever heard and yet, as you will read, its moral should be taken very seriously by everyone who flies an aircraft.

Richard's story began in a previous life, before he went to Virgin Atlantic and while he was flying as a 737 First Officer with "Bee Cal" (British Caledonian). On the day of his tale he was flying from London's Gatwick airport to Berlin, in the old days, when there were two Germanys and three air corridors that aircraft from the "West" had to fly in for entry and exit into the airports of Western Berlin.

They had been flying in the high twenties (29,000) for the initial segment of the flight and as they neared East Germany they were cleared to descend to 9,000 feet in preparation for entry into one of the corridors. As they descended, the Captain, who was pilot flying, asked Richard to turn on the radar as there was low cloud and he wanted to survey the undercast in front of them.

The radar, however, would not turn on. Richard did everything he could think of to coax it to life, from incorporating the Captain's suggestions, to trying CPR (hitting it), and finally to pulling and resetting the applicable C/B (circuit breaker) but, to no avail; the CRT display wouldn't even display a flat-line, indicating a fate worse than death.

The Captain, however, knew better and would not accept the terminal condition of his radar and told Richard to take control of the slowly descending 737. Producing a screw driver from his flight bag, the Captain loosened the four screws on each corner of the combined radar control and display unit and slipped it out of its receptacle which was immediately in front of the throttles and between the two pilots on the pedestal.

After pulling the radar box out, he undid the cannon plug that integrated it to the aircraft and cleaned the connectors on both sides.

Haste was of the essence, as they were approaching the cloud tops, and Richard said that all through this process the Captain said nothing. Richard made the radio calls as well as fly the jet as the captain, now mechanic, tended to repairing his aircraft.

After a quick but seemingly thorough cannon plug cleaning the two ends were mated to each other and the surprisingly long black box was placed back into the metal cave in which it normally resided... but... the radar box only went halfway in before it stopped moving. No amount of coaxing by the Captain could get it to go in any deeper. With the full weight of said Captain pushing on the black box it would not move any deeper then when it initially stopped. Realizing it was hopeless, the captain attempted to pull it out. There too he was met with frustration as it would not budge. Since pushing is easier than pulling, and given his previous pushing attempts, with more force being applied than his pulling, physics seemed to working against him.

Though he showed no signs of panic, according to Richard, evidently he felt as such since he asked Richard to see how far the throttles would move forward before they hit the very protruding radar. A ten percent increase in RPM was all they could get from the engines with this newly configured cockpit, not near enough to maintain level flight.

The aircraft was now in a grey area with regards to the definition of their flight status...being more than a powerless, twin-engine airliner but less than a powered glider; they could control to some degree where they were going to land, but, to be sure, they were going to land, somewhere, and shortly if they couldn't get more thrust from the engines.

With no warning as to his intentions the Captain produced a crash axe and started whacking at the radar set. Not a word was uttered as Lizzy Borden hacked away. Richard continued to fly and talk as the radar set was demolished before his very eyes. If it was inoperative before now it was truly decimated. The CRT imploded and bits of metal and glass sprayed about the cockpit. Though it didn't take forty whacks to do it in, it took more than Richard thought it should have to loosen it from its moorings but, given the onslaught from a Captain with a quest to save his aircraft, it stood no chance and eventually it slid fully into the front pedestal, even smaller in stature then before.

Shortly after the mutilation was complete the Captain took control of the aircraft as they entered the air corridor from the west to the east and the rest of the flight was about as routine as you could get, according to Richard. Upon landing and clearing the runway he asked Richard to write the radar up in the log book.

To say Richard was shocked is an understatement, even in British terms. Richard said he gave the appearance of being busy as they taxied in and after blocking-in he asked the Captain what he should say in the write-up. Now, fully realizing his responsibilities, Richard said the captain took the log book and said he should actually make the write-up. Not waiting for a reversal of that thought, Richard gave him the log book and jumped out of the cockpit to greet the passengers as they deplaned, wanting to escape the scene of a massacre.

Every now and then Richard peeked into the cockpit and saw the maintenance log upon the Captain's lap and a pen in his hand. After an indeterminable amount of time and thinking that the captain was writing a novel, he emerged from the cockpit ready to go to operations to prepare for the return flight.

Richard said his curiosity as to how the Captain wrote-up the smashing of the radar was killing him, so as he walked down the steps of the stairs from the aircraft, he, Richard, feigned that he needed to get something from the cockpit so he pardoned himself and ran back up the steps. His excitement to read how the Captain explained the series of events that led to a mutilated radar set was at fever pitch as he excitedly opened the aircraft's maintenance log.

"Radar inop.," was all the captain wrote.

Sky Rage

Attending USAF Pilot Training was one of the finest years of my life. Besides the camaraderie I shared with my classmates, I had some very memorable times, both in the air and on the ground during those 49 weeks of flight training. Williams AFB, nicknamed Willie, and located in Chandler, AZ (it is now closed) was where I spent an exciting year learning to fly the USAF way.

Willie was a great place to both train and live. The days were usually sunny, and with a dry climate and little rain it made for excellent visibility and great flying conditions year-round. And when not flying, there was so much to do with regards to the outdoors; the mountains for fishing or camping, tubing on the Salt River, the SCAR (Saguaro, Canyon, Apache, Roosevelt) lakes for boating, and the history of the Wild West alone was fascinating. Being from New Jersey, I felt like it was still the Wild West, I mean people walked around with six shooters in holsters for Pete's sake. If you saw that in Jersey, where I'm from, you'd assume the guy's name was either Vito or Vinny and it might be the last thing you saw.

So, I'm digging seeing the mountains as I drive to and from work, or when I flew over them when I was training in either the T-37 or the more high performance T-38. There was not one thing about being in pilot training while at "Willie" that I didn't like… except RSU duty.

RSU was an acronym for Runway Supervisory Unit. The RSUs at Willie were small, mostly glass, tiny little buildings that were situated on each end of both the T-37 and T-38 runways. The view out the RSU windows was expansive which afforded a person inside of it to see 365 degrees around them, as well as up high in the sky.

The RSUs were used to monitor the local jet traffic flying from two of the three runways at Williams AFB. Willie had three fairly long runways: the western one (they were oriented northwest/southeast) was used exclusively for T-37 training; the middle one was the tower's and used for straight-in approaches or transient aircraft; leaving the eastern most runway for T-38 operations.

Three people occupied the RSU during normal training days, which were Monday through Friday, or anytime there was a large volume of jet training occurring that day or night. Two instructors and a student worked a roughly four hour shift, of which there were two to three (shifts) a day, depending on the time of year. I honestly didn't know if the instructor's had to be "special" (identified as above average pilots/instructors) to be bestowed with the opportunity to spend time in that Suzie Bake Oven, but I do know from personal experience there was nothing special required of the students. We had no say in whether or not we were going to be shoved in there. It was the typical, age old, military tradition of assigning "extra" duties to all the students as we worked our way through those 49 weeks.

When the students were in the T-37 phase of training they would pull duty in the T-37 RSU, likewise the same thing when they were in

T-38 training. It was the student's job, while in the RSU, to record the takeoff and landing times of every T-37/T-38 that took off and landed on their respective operating runways. I can't say it was tedious, nor even hard, though it could get busy. We were taught a simple, tried and true method for keeping track of the extensive number of jets as they flew. The reason the times were recorded was to keep track of the aircraft. If one went missing, generally the only way to know, in a timely manner, it was missing was to note that an aircraft departed but never came back (Cross country departures were recorded by the tower). Also, there were times when the SOF (Supervisor Of Flying, located in one of the OPS buildings) wanted to know what time a certain aircraft departed, a solo student usually for example, just to keep track of it/them/whomever.

The division of responsibility between the two Instructors in the RSU was distinct. One Instructor, let's all him Controller One, was responsible for monitoring the traffic at the approach end of the respective runway in which he was controlling and the other Instructor, call him Controller Two, was responsible for the landing/departure end of the same runway that Controller One was monitoring. Together, these two communicated about what traffic they had in their areas of responsibility and with that information they managed the flow of traffic in the immediate pattern, or on the outside downwind. Realistically, most times the aircraft themselves managed their own patterns, adjusting to whatever aircraft may be a potential conflict, but Controller One, the approach side of the runway, did check to make sure all the aircraft who were landing had their gear down as they turned final, whether they were doing a touch and go, or full stopping.

There were two training profiles for flights that departed Willy (not including those aircraft that were heading out on cross country flights). A few jets stayed in the pattern, never leaving the local area for the entirety of their mission as they did pattern after pattern, touch and go after touch and go, or practice instrument approaches, finally full stopping once their fuel ran low. Most aircraft however, initially took off and departed to the east and flew into one of the many MOAs (Military Operations Area) which were large volumes of special use airspace where the students practiced whatever maneuvers they were to practice, aerobatics or formation flying for example, during their phase of training. After completing their maneuvers, the aircraft returned to the pattern to either land right away, or practice overheads and landings until then too, their fuel ran low and they did a full stop landing.

The normal procedure for arrival and landing on the T-38 runway began with flying up "initial", meaning to fly directly on the runway's centerline, at 1500 feet AGL (Above Ground Level) above it. Once you were over the beginning of the runway, the numbers, you would "pitch out", meaning you'd roll the jet rapidly to the right (at other airports it might be a left turn) to maybe 70 degrees of bank, or slightly more, and then pull back on the stick with the intention of performing a level turn while pulling approximately 4 to 5 Gs. You wanted to this turn, "break turn" as it's called, to be tight enough so as to stay close to the runway as you turned, but not too tight. You held the turn level until you were now heading in the opposite direction from which you just came, with the runway now on your right side. If you pulled too hard, too tight, it would put you too close to the landing runway while on downwind so, when it came time to turn back towards the runway to land, you could possibly overshoot, go beyond the runway to the west, which could cause a conflict with the center runway. Once you turned 180 degrees you were now on "downwind". You flew level, 1500 feet, on downwind until the landing runway was at your 4 o'clock position, or thereabouts, and when it was you began a descending right banked turn, pulling the aircraft to "on speed" AOA (you didn't really look at the airspeed indicator, since you flew AOA (Angle of Attack) until touchdown. You played the turn from downwind to final so as to arrive a mile out from the runway at 300 above it and pointed directly at it and hopefully on centerline. When I say "played", you may have to turn tighter than normal, not to exceed on speed AOA. In order to turn tighter you added power, flew a bit faster, and steepened the bank and added more G which causes the turn to be tighter. Consequently, if you were really wide on the downwind, you may have to use less than on speed AOA and not turn as tight, not be as steep in your bank turn, as you adjust power to moderate your rate of descent. The objective was to roll out on centerline, facing directly in the direction of the runway while continuing a descent towards landing. You lowered your landing gear and flaps while on downwind. Once on final you tried to fly a three degree glide slope while maintaining an "on speed" AOA indication until touchdown. Your desired touchdown point was about 1000 to 1500 feet beyond the beginning of the landing runway.

Once the T-38 landed it could do one of two things upon touching down. Firstly, and most logical, was that it stay on the ground, with its nose in the air and was aero-braked, decelerating, until the aircraft's nose wheel dropped to the runway whereupon the brakes were applied and the aircraft turned off the runway at its end. Or, secondly, after touching down the aircraft would lift off, takeoff, again and then "pull" what is known as a "closed" pattern, or the student/

Instructor could "re-enter," meaning turn to a wide downwind, on the outside pattern and come back up initial for another overhead.

One HUGE caution about flying the overhead was the descending turn from downwind to final. You really wanted to make sure your base to final turn wasn't so tight that you exceeded your approach and landing AOA. If you pulled too hard in that final turn, without regard to maintaining an "on speed" AOA, you could cause the jet to lose too much lift and in doing so it would rapidly descend to the ground and might rock, "roll", back and forth rapidly while descending, causing an out-of-control situation to develop. If you got into this "behind the power curve" situation, you needed to immediately roll wings level, add max power (full afterburner), reduce back stick pressure to lower the AOA and as your airspeed increased, try to arrest your rate of descent so as to not hit the ground. Many military, and civilian, accidents have occurred in this final turn, with many deaths.

One a brighter note, though it may seem like it was hard or complicated to do this arrival and landing procedure, it was easy once you practiced it a few times. It was a very efficient way in which to land many aircraft in a short period of time on the same runway. Also, making things even more expeditious, you were allowed to land with another aircraft on the runway if that aircraft was 6,000 feet or more ahead, or, if it was offset from the runway centerline (left/right side) you could shorten that distance to 3,000 feet.

So that's a description of how T-38s (and T-37s too, but slightly different procedures) operated in the pattern at Willie. And that's where the students spent quite a bit of time with their instructors, learning how to land via the overhead pattern.

So, during a normal RSU shift the inhabitants of that small little building might get to see hundreds of overheads and touch and goes.

I think for me the best part of being in RSU was when the F-5s, that were associated with the locally based 425th TFTS (Tactical Fighter Training Squadron), came in and landed, or did the occasional low approach to closed pattern and full stop landing. The F-5s usually came up initial as a two ship; very rarely did they arrive from whatever MOA they trained in as single ships (one aircraft), though it did occur.

The F-5 "Tiger" was an outgrowth of the Northrop T-38, a much more formidable outgrowth. It was a lightweight fighter jet, single or two seat, with much bigger engines and much better performance. The 425th TFTS operated the F-5s in order to train foreign pilots, using American Instructors, on how to fly and fight in the F-5; most of the foreign students were from the Middle East.

It was evident from watching their patterns that the F-5 had much better performance than the T-38. Sometimes, when a F-5 pilot was performing a closed, or break turn, they would definitely fly a tighter pattern than the T-38s, but then the F-5 pilots had more experience and many of the students in the T-38 were not exactly aggressive, nor were their instructors. It was cool to watch the kind of performance the F-5s demonstrated on occasion, at least to a neophyte like me, and one day I hoped I could be as aggressive as some of those guys.

Finally, with regards to the F-5, the USAF did operate it in a few, small, very special, and elite squadrons. The pilots that flew these F-5s were called "Aggressors" and it was their assignment to travel around the USA and to fighter bases overseas and expose the American Fighter Pilots to Soviet style tactics. Mock dogfights and air battles, with the

Aggressors as the enemy were flown against the unwitting USAF Fighter pilots. The Aggressor pilots were extremely good at their job and they defeated and humbled many, many American Fighter pilots in these mock air battles. The objective of the USAF in forming and implementing the Aggressors was the belief that if American Fighter Pilots were exposed to the Soviet Style tactics before ever going into war, than they would be better prepared for what a Soviet trained fighter pilot would do in combat and therefore stand a better chance at surviving and indeed, neutralizing the threat. It was excellent training (In later years I would have many dogfights with these most excellent fighter pilots).

Because the Aggressors were so relatively new to the USAF when I was in pilot training and their expertise and exploits so legendary, anytime the topic of them was raised, whenever a few of us pilots were gathered together, the Aggressors commanded the highest degree of respect and were revered…if not idolized…in those conversations; simply put, from what I heard those guys walked on water. Oddly enough though, and this is what I found funny, most of those Instructors, if not all, whom spoke of the Aggressors' amazing war fighting abilities had never met, let alone flown against one.

So, I'm doing my second T-38 RSU tour of duty. I was in the formation phase of T-38 training, in other words I was nearing the end of my year of training and I was excited about the next phase of my USAF life. I was sitting "in the box" on this cloudless and relatively cool, by Arizona standards, day with the normal compliment of two Instructors. Controller One, the dude that watched the approach end of the runway, was obnoxious as hell. OH Em Gee, he was a "Check Section" Instructor, which meant, in his eyes, he was "SPECIAL." The

Check Section guys gave check rides to both students and Instructors alike and some of them were on power trips in which they felt superior to the rest of us aviators. Maybe they were great, I don't know, but most of the ones I met before this guy were very nice and didn't seem to process any super powers.

As we sat in the box and watched the T-38s, and occasional F-5s do their thing in the pattern that day, Mr Check Section continually made disparaging after disparaging remark about almost every T-38, or even F-5, that flew. I could tell Controller Two, by the roll of eyes when I looked at him, was maxed out with Controller One's almost continuous cynical jabs at the pilots in the pattern.

As our time "in the box" was nearing an end, and the T-38 traffic became non-existent, a single F-5 came flying up initial…and I mean flying. Normally T-38s and F-5s came into the pattern at 300 knots Indicated Airspeed. But, this F-5, much faster. I don't know how much, but he was hauling ass as my father might say. He broke swiftly and sharply over the numbers and pulled hard in the turn. He must have been doing 7 Gs in the break since his rate of turn was so fast, with an increasingly decreasing radius of turn. As he broke Controller One remarked at how aggressive this "cowboy", as he called him, was flying. Since this was the only aircraft in the pattern, Controller Two was watching this lone F-5 do his thing as I watched in awe. I'd never seen an F-5 turn that aggressively. Then, instead of rolling out on downwind as everyone else did, this F-5 immediately, once he had turned 180 degrees, began an immediate, and steep, descent while rolling into a steep right bank as he turned back towards the landing runway. As required by regulations, the pilot announced, "Gear down, full stop" while continuing his pattern. I can't express to you how aggressive this pattern was. I'd never seen another aircraft fly this "tight" of an overhead and I couldn't believe an aircraft could fly this way without crashing. I was convinced this guy was going to overshoot the T-38 runway and would have to go around for another pattern.

All of mine and Controller Two's observations and our vocal awe (we were saying things like, "holy crap that's a tight turn!" and, "How is able to do that!?") on this aerial demonstration were not lost on Mr. Check Section (Controller One). He was mumbling incoherently as the F-5 seemingly violated every known law of aerodynamics as it maintained its steep descent and bank as it neared the runway's altitude and heading.

As the F-5 was on very short final and almost aligned with the landing runway's heading, Controller One said, "F-5 on short final, go around, unsafe!"

Immediately, the F-5 rolled out and you could see the gear begin to retract. As the gear came up and the aircraft began to level off, it rolled slightly left and began heading directly towards the RSU. I think we were all crapping our pants upon seeing the flight path of that F-5. I thought he had lost control and was going to crash on or near us, but, at about 20 feet above the ground the wayward jet leveled out and straightened out to head in the same direction as the runway.

The aircraft was now just in front of the RSU, 20 feet up, and about 50 feet away…I mean we had a full view of that jet. It was now, as it flashed by, in about a 30 degree left bank, not turning, slightly nose up, and no doubt the pilot was holding it on a slight knife edge that he began silent, but loud….communication. His O2 mask was hanging down, his visor down and he looked right at us while flipping us the bird…middle finger up. Immediately, upon seeing the distinctive markings on the jet, you could tell it was an Aggressor F-5.

It was the first case of aerial road rage I'd ever seen and so far, the only case I've ever been a witness to. It was impressive to say the least. After his RSU flyby, in afterburner I might add, since it was so loud, he rolled wings level and headed down the runway, descending to maybe 10 feet.

"I didn't know it was an Aggressor, I didn't know it was Aggressor!!" yelped Controller One after the F-5 pilot communicated his displeasure with being sent around. Neither I nor Controller Two said a thing… we were speechless.

A few seconds after passing the RSU the F-5 pilot requested a "Closed" and Controller Two immediately approved it. With that approval the Aggressor pulled initially very steeply nose up and then as his nose achieved about 45 degrees in pitch he banked sharply right and performed another impossibly tight pattern. Not another word was said as we sat and watched this amazing display of airmanship. How and why that jet didn't crashed, I'll never know.

Years later, when I was an Instructor in the USAF F-4 Fighter Weapons School and coming back from a BFM mission in clean jets, with my student as number two. For some reason on that day, that sortie, I thought about that F-5 guy as I came up initial. So, feeling a bit "frisky", I pitched out ridiculously aggressive in my break turn, well, at least that's what my Squadron Commander said as he sat number one, waiting to depart from the same runway I was landing on and watched me. I thought I was doing what all fighter pilots should do, as I flew a tight pattern, and touched down still in a slight left bank, never having fully rolled out of my final turn. As a good wingman, my number two did the same. I was grounded for two weeks.

The moral of the story? Even though imitation may be the sincerest form of flattery, it doesn't necessarily mean it's the best way to express it. Still, my hat is off to that F-5 guy, whoever, and wherever you are... you are my hero.

Smoking Hot Jet

Seven days after my first solo in the iconic T-37, while in USAF pilot training at Williams AFB, in Chandler, AZ, I found myself strapping in for my second solo flight. To be sure I was excited. The T-37, "Tweet" as it was affectionately called, was a small twin engine jet trainer that'd been in the USAF inventory since the late fifties. Maybe when it first came out as a brand spanking new Air Force jet trainer were the crews that flew it awestruck. But, by the time I began training in that little sucker, early 80s, it was kicked round as the ugly sister to the more beautiful and much better performing T-38 Talon.

But, your first jet is always your favorite. OK, not really, at least not my feelings with the Tweet. But I had been flying a 150 horsepower Super Cub for four years prior to entering the USAF, so to me, the T-37, with its twin 1000 lb thrust Continental jet engines, was a big responsibility. I took each flight, solo, or with an instructor, as a very serious affair and I felt extremely blessed to be training in jets in the USAF.

The T-37 was relatively small, mid wing, and sat quite low to the ground. It had side by side seating and a big plexiglass canopy, hinged at the back, that allowed easy access to the cockpit. The two smallish jet engines that powered it were nestled in the fuselage, slightly below each wing, with the exhaust exiting behind and below the trailing edge of the wings and right next to the fuselage. The instrument panel, as compared to modern jet aircraft, looked as if someone took all the displays, dials, lights, knobs and handles needed to operate the aircraft and threw them against the panel and installed them where they hit the panel. Random is a word that comes to mind on the placement of some of the lights, displays, knobs, etc. There was nothing ergonomic about that instrument panel, but, hey, it was a jet and I was strapping in to go on my second solo flight.

In as much as "Willy", the nickname of Williams AFB, was a place where USAF pilots learned to fly, it was also, as we were told in our in-brief prior to the beginning flight training, a place where the USAF trained its Air Traffic Controllers. So, we were warned that sometimes the controllers will make mistakes so be skeptical, and cautious if some of the ATC directives/clearances seemed unusual or maybe not safe. In a way you kinda had the blind leading the blind at times when you had a solo student pilot being controlled by a controller in training. It was when "another" more authoritative voice came over the radio to counterman a training controller's more tentative instruction, when you knew the Supervising Controller had taken command of the situation.

After strapping in and starting those extremely high pitched, constant noise, variable thrust engines on the Tweet, I was ready to taxi for takeoff. It was a fairly long taxi from where my Tweet was parked to the active runway. During this period of time in its operational life, Willy was very busy. T-38s, T-37s, and F-5s were mixing in with each other daily as they either taxied for takeoff or taxied back to their parking spots after landing, so you had to listen up to the controller's verbal taxi instructions while being wary, wondering if their instructions were tainted with some mistake.

I called ground with ATIS and told them I wanted to taxi for takeoff. They cleared me to taxi to runway "three zero left" (30L) which was the normal T-37 runway. I had about a mile and a half, at least, to taxi to get to the assigned runway. Since the air conditioner on the Tweet was not very effective, we taxied with our canopy fully open. It was early summer and we were in the desert, so it could get quite warm.

To be sure, I was nervous as I prepared for this flight, but yet cocky too as I taxied out. I'd done well on my first solo, getting 3 excellent grades in all 3 areas in which you were graded. So, having broken the ice with that first solo, I was looking forward to breaking the bonds of gravity yet again flying by myself and without some instructor jumping on my ass about something I was normally screwing up.

About 2/3s of the way to runway 30L, and after having just turned left onto another taxiway, ground called.

"T-37 Solo (not my actual call sign), your aircraft is smoking," said ground control in a very casual tone and inflection.

"Roger ground, jet engines do smoke," came my immediate response, thinking this was a brand new controller in training, and he'd not spent much time around jet aircraft.

"Ahhhhh, T-37 Solo, be advised that your aircraft is smoking much more than normal," came this different, deeper, and more authoritative voice from ground control; obviously the person training the previous controller decided to intervene and reaffirm the trainee's less firm observation.

And just when I'd begun to suspect something actually might be wrong with "my situation," though I was not sure what, another voice came over the radio, and it was not ATC's.

"Hey Ace!" came the familiar voice over ground control's frequency, "Look over your left shoulder." That voice belonged to one of the instructors in my flight (the USAF breaks up large groups of students and instructors into smaller groups called "flights). He was with his student and taxing right behind me.

Since it was an instructor from my flight and he spoke with such an authoritative voice, and a bit of sarcasm, since he used the term "ace," I felt very compelled to do as he commanded… so, I looked over my left shoulder.

"Holy Shit!!" was my first thought as I saw a very thick plume of whitish smoke being exhausted from the left engine. It seemingly filled the entire sky behind my jet, bloody hell, no wonder why ground said my jet was smoking. All cockiness immediately left me, with a modicum of fear replacing it, and I immediately told ground that I was going to stop and do an emergency ground egress, shutting down both engines just before leaving the jet. I never waited for ground's reply nor for another word from the instructor with his student, who was now taking another taxi route to the active runway.

As the smoke rapidly dissipated, and my nerves settled, I stood off the taxiway to the side of my little Tweet; I could hear the sound of "tinks" as hot metal cooled on the aircraft as the last wisps of smoke vaporized in the warm desert air. Other T-37s, T-38s, and F-5s taxied by as the pilots in them looked over at this pathetic student, still wearing his helmet, and standing by his disabled Tweet.

A few minutes after shutting down and wondering what in the hell happened to my jet, while also wondering if I'd "FUBAR'ed, a maintenance truck drove up, along with an airport firetruck and then a crew van. I told maintenance what happened…"smoke"….and then filled out the maintenance log with the exact same thing I told maintenance, "smoke."

Walking into our operations, after leaving my parachute and helmet in the life support room, I met with a SOF (Supervisor Of Flying) who wanted to know what happened. I told him in as much detail as I remembered, though I was still in a bit of shock as to what happened myself.

"Lotsa' smoke," I told him, adding I thought the left engine might be on fire.

"No, the engine wasn't on fire, maintenance said that the pork chop seal at the aft end of the turbine had failed and was dumping oil into the hot exhaust at the back of the engine. There was no fire, but I'm told it put out a lot of white smoke. Call it a day Lieutenant"

"Yes Sir," I simply responded and headed back to my flight room.

"Jet engines do smoke?" said the Assistant Flight Commander, Capt. Palmgren, laughing as he met me in the crew room. "Did you really say that?" he asked laughing.

"Yes sir, I did," I said, looking down at my boots. "Not exactly the smartest thing to say over the radio was it Sir?" I asked, almost rhetorically, not wanting to hear his answer.

"Not sure if I'll ever forget that wise ass comment Roger. But then, you are from New Jersey. Nice job, though shutting down and ground egressing. We'll put you on the schedule tomorrow for another attempt at your second solo."

As he turned and left the room, I could hear him mumble, "Jet engines do smoke, I'm gonna remember that for a long time."

Of Fighters and Thunderstorms

I've had many, many encounters with severe thunderstorms around this globe of ours. In most cases, I've just deftly deviated around the weather using the aircraft's onboard radar. But there are some times when the massing of the cells is so great and extensive in area that avoiding the tempests by a wide area is almost impossible. In those instances, where avoiding the weather with a wide margin is impossible, you have a few options: (1) You can divert and land short of the thunderstorms and wait for them to pass; (2) Perform a huge, fuel-consuming deviation around the entire area of weather (if possible); (3) Hold over an area away from the storms and wait until they pass (assuming you have enough fuel) and then proceed to your destination; and (4) Lastly, pick an area of the weather that looks the least bad between the cells and fly through it, knowing you may fly very close to a cell but also believing that it's not going to be too bad of a ride.

One very notable encounter I had with a tremendously huge line of thunderstorms, with some storms topping out above 50,000 feet, occurred when I was leading a flight of four Phantoms. I elected to use option 4, as just described, and I have to tell you, I initially thought I had made a mistake in my decision to penetrate through the weather once I was actually in it.

The genesis of this thunderstorm encounter started from Nellis AFB, located near Las Vegas, Nevada. Eight of us, four front-seaters and four WSOs had flown into Nellis to pick up four F-4s. We did delay a couple of days in order to fly some local area missions, to include flying low levels and dropping bombs. On the day of departure, heading back to McGuire, we left in the early morning since we planned on flying a low-level to Kirtland AFB, in Albuquerque.

As a portent of the day to come, nearing Silver City, New Mexico, we had to abort the low level due to low clouds, rain showers, and generally poor visibility over the mountains of Western New Mexico. A weather abort was called on the radio and we all popped up above the clouds and reformed in route formation. As we were joining back up, we continued our climb to 17,500 feet and proceeded directly to Kirtland, all 4 aircraft landing uneventfully about thirty minutes after aborting the low level.

After refueling and flight planning, it was our desire to then fly a low level from Albuquerque (Kirtland) to Peterson Air Force Base, located on Colorado Springs Airport, in Colorado Springs, Colorado. We were to spend the night at "C Springs" and then fly non-stop back to McGuire the next morning. The USAF weather briefer in Kirtland said that the clouds where we wanted to fly our low level "should" be good enough for the required 5000-foot ceiling and the required five miles viz. I'd flown that low level once before and the flight amongst the Sangre de Cristo mountains was spectacular, so I was praying for a redux on this flight.

Since everyone in the flight was very hungover from the "last night in Vegas" festivities, no one wanted to actually lead the flight to Colorado Springs. My squadron commander said that his heading indicator was "acting up and unreliable" so therefore he needed to hang on the wing of whoever was leading. The guy who led the flight from Nellis to Kirtland said he'd already led one flight and therefore took himself out of the running. Steve, the number 4 guy was not legal to lead anything other than himself because he was a brand spanking new Phantom pilot.

So that left yours truly.

With bleeding eyes and throbbing head, I quickly did the required flight planning for the flight to the low-level start point (we'd preplanned the low level while in Nellis) and then briefed the boys on the entire flight. After about two hours of ground time, we departed the fair skies of New Mexico and headed north by slightly east in a loose route formation bound for a rendezvous with destiny.

It was very evident as we entered the skies over South-Central Colorado that it was looking pretty grim for being able to fly a low-level. Flying at 29,000 feet, the clouds were scattered and broken immediately below us but the lower I looked the thicker and more numerous the cloud layers to the point it was pretty much solid cloud from 15,000 feet and below. I knew in my heart this was going to be a waste of time, descending in the hopes we could find clear air but, I did it anyway if only because we were supposed to land at Colorado Springs and spend the night.

I called the boys into close, fingertip formation, and down we went into the relatively smooth, but extremely moisture-laden air mass below. Using our own aircraft's radar and the watchful eye of Denver Center's more all-encompassing weather radar to search the area in front of us, we descended on the eastern side of Colorado Springs, where the flat, great plains spread eastward.

The air traffic controllers at Denver Center were amazingly compliant, as we descended. I asked Center if we could go to this latitude and longitude or that one while we descended in the hopes of finding clear air, or at least a 5000-foot ceiling so we could fly the low level, and not once was the controller bothered by my requests, if anything he was extremely helpful, giving me PIREPs (Pilot REPorts from other aircraft) to help in my ability to assess whether or not we could fly the low level. Somewhere approaching 3,000 above the ground we broke out of the heavy clouds and were under a very dark and dreary overcast with rain showers visible almost everywhere you looked; it was immediately obvious once underneath the clouds that we would not be able to fly the low-level.

Now my attention turned to thinking if C Springs was the best place to land. So, I immediately headed in the direction of the airport, about ten miles to the west, and once I could actually see the environs of the field, I saw a dark and hugely pregnant cloud drifting over the airport and giving birth to drenching rains.

I sent the flight to a private UHF frequency as soon as we were established in VMC conditions because I wanted to talk to the boys about our options. Prior to going to the discreet UHF frequency, I had called Colorado Springs tower and asked them for their runway condition and indeed they said the runway was wet. I knew that, but I just wanted confirmation on what I was seeing as I put our four-ship in an orbit about eight miles east of the field.

Thanks to my father's training early in my career, prior to departing Kirtland AFB I had checked the actual weather and forecasts at a few of the surrounding major airports that we could reach from our intended destination of Colorado Springs. Because the weather was so bad at Colorado Springs, I dared not attempt a landing with the F-4s since it was pouring and the runway was thoroughly wet. At sea level, landing on a wet runway was not a big deal, even in the warmth of summer but, Colorado Springs is around 6000 feet above sea level, and the density altitude combined with the wet runway put our landing roll at the extremes of the field. If one of the drag chutes failed to deploy upon touchdown I doubt the Phantom could've been stopped without engaging an arresting cable. On most military fields taking a barrier isn't a big deal, but I was worried about all 4 aircraft having to take the cable and in C Springs the arresting cables were in the overruns of the runway . . . they were not meant for normal or frequent use.

Though the weather was bad and precluded us from flying the low level, and caused me concern about landing at Peterson AFB, by the grace of God on that day we were flying with three external fuel tanks. On most missions in the Phantom we normally carried a single high-speed centerline, external fuel tank capable of carrying 4000 pounds of jet fuel, but the F-4s we'd picked up at Nellis had been configured with three external tanks. The two external wing tanks we were carrying that day added 5000 more pounds of "gas" to our normal complement of 16,000 pounds of fuel. This added luxury gave me more options as to where we could go and took some pressure off of my decision to divert rather than land at "Pete" field.

While in the orbit below the clouds, and talking on the UHF radio, as if I was face to face with the other guys, I told them of my concerns with regards to landing at C Springs relatively heavyweight, with a wet runway and high density altitude, and I asked them for their thoughts. I specifically told the squadron commander if there was anything he wanted us to do, or place to go, and assuming it was safe, I'd defer to his desires. He said he was okay with whatever I decided so I briefed the guys on the weather at the various airports for which I was briefed before we departed Kirtland AFB and told them that since we still had a lot of fuel, we had quite a few options. I did add that McConnell AFB was my preference over Tinker (Oklahoma City, Oklahoma), Buckley (Denver, Colorado) or Salina (Salina, Kansas), but said I was open to thoughts. No one dissented about going to IAB, McConnell AFB.

My decision to go to McConnell was based upon its actual weather and the forecast. I also knew from previous flying experience that it would take about 6000 pounds of fuel to fly from Colorado Springs to McConnell (the wind would be at our back, too, which would help) and finally, I knew that around McConnell were other airports, relatively close, that could also be used if for some reason the weather crumped at IAB.

Fuel, in a fighter aircraft, is always a critical issue. It's often said that fighters take off with emergency fuel from the start. Though that may have been true in the early days of jets, it isn't at all like that nowadays with the newer fighters and their more fuel-efficient low bypass turbofan jet engines. The biggest reason it's thought that fighters take off with low fuel is because, quite simply, a lot of the practice missions flown require high power settings and consequently use prodigious amounts of fuel rather quickly. Also, let's face it, fighter pilots tend to push the limits of their fuel supply to maximize training time spent on each mission, so it was normal to push fuel reserves and land with twenty minutes of JP-4 in the tanks; on a good weather day, twenty minutes is fine. I have to fully admit though there were a few times when the weather suddenly became horrible, even though forecast to be good, and I had no choice but to fly an instrument approach down to minimums with no viable alternate airport to which I could divert. It's not a life enhancing experience to push the limits of your fuel, but sometimes you had no choice.

The F-4, if left in full afterburner right after takeoff, could consume its entire 12,000-pound internal fuel supply in about nine minutes, or so I've been told; to be honest I've never tried. In fact, in A/B the fuel is consumed so fast the external tank(s) cannot feed quick enough into the main tanks to keep them filled. The fuel flow indicators do not record the accurate fuel flow of the Phantom in full afterburner due to limitations on the fuel flow indicators themselves.

But while flying cross-country, and at much less power settings than full afterburner, the external tanks can easily keep the main fuel tanks full until the external tanks run dry. On this day, with my four-ship leveled off somewhere around 33,000 feet, a nominal cruise fuel flow of 7000 pounds per hour was the norm, not the eighty thousand pounds per hour while in full A/B. Normally I would set 520 knots true airspeed as my target cruise speed and as fuel burned off and lightened the aircraft's weight you could pull the power back to hold 520 knots, and then you could expect to see a 6000-pound-per-hour burn. So, for cross country planning purposes I would flight plan fuel burns at 7000 pounds for the first hour of cruising flight and then six thousand pounds for the remainder of the flight. With three external tanks, like we had on this day, we had 21,000 pounds of fuel which gave us roughly three hours of endurance at normal cruise speed and at the higher flight levels.

Normally, carrying all of that fuel is a pain in the butt as it weighs the aircraft down and limits your maximum combat/training maneuvering capability and G available due to the external tank airspeed and G restrictions. Today, however, we were just going cross-country and flying low levels and not going into combat as we went from AFB to AFB, so this extra 5000 pounds was realllllly nice to have, particularly today. (You can always selectively jettison the external tanks if you need to.)

As we started our climb and headed toward McConnell, we left Colorado in the rearview mirrors (both cockpits in the F-4 have rearview mirrors). My external tanks had just fed out as we began the divert and I was now using my internal fuel, 12,000 pounds. But, since this is not a perfect world not all pilots move their throttles in the same manner and when you are flying in formation the lead aircraft usually has the most gas, at any given time, assuming you are flying as we were, cross-country (combat is a different situation altogether). The wingman will normally have slightly lower fuel levels than the lead aircraft and the more junior the wingmen, the lower his fuel is than lead's since they usually haven't learned the varying techniques of fuel conservation as a wingman. As soon as we diverted and started a climb to the flight levels, I took a fuel check. As expected, number 4, the newest pilot member of the squadron, was almost a thousand pounds lower than me with wingmen two and three somewhere in between. As I said, I knew from past experience it took about 6000 pounds of fuel to fly the distance we needed to fly to get to IAB, not including deviating for weather though. So that would put us on the ground with about 6000 pounds, 5000 for number four, assuming he could keep his throttle bursts under control. If he started burning too much gas, I could make him the lead aircraft, and the rest of us would fly off of him, thusly allowing him to conserve fuel because he wouldn't have to continuously move his throttles to stay in formation position. Since I didn't expect there to be a wall of water with an attitude enroute to McConnell that I would have to deviate around, I figured we had plenty of gas.

As we climbed from 3000 feet AGL (about 9,000 feet MSL) to FL 330 (33,000 feet MSL) I sent my number 2 aircraft off in search of the real weather at McConnell and cleared him off the ATC freq. we were working on. (Since my number 2 wingman's head [I mean his actual physical head and body, along with his backseater's] was only about five feet off of my left wingtip in close formation as we climbed through some pretty thick cumulonimbus clouds, I was not too worried about losing him, in a physical sense, hence the reason I cleared him off frequency in the first place.)

If you are wondering, my numbers 3 and 4 aircraft were similarly stacked off of my right side, three being a mirror image of number 2, and number 4 flying off of number 3's right wingtip in a similar position as he, three, was on me. The proper term for this is called fingertip, and it's used for flying multiple aircraft, up to four, in weather when the visibility is poor and/or when arriving in the landing pattern for an overhead break.

As we climbed to FL330 in fingertip formation, somewhere in this climb, since the clouds were so moisture-laden, very thick, and with extremely poor visibility number 4 lost sight of number 3 and had to initiate lost wingman procedures. The WSO in the number 4 aircraft was very experienced and capable and he was able to talk his junior pilot through the procedures and eventually number 4 ended up about a mile behind and slightly below the rest of us. Using his radar to follow us as we climbed, eventually the thickness of the clouds lessened, and 4 was able to visually see the three-ship ahead of him and rejoined the flight.

As we crested the highest of the low clouds we were momentarily blinded by a brilliant but welcome sunshine. My number 2 man, after my backseater gave him the appropriate fingers to tell him what frequency we were on . . . and BTW, not the type of road rage fingers you might get while driving in New Jersey traffic . . . informed us that indeed IAB was clear, but . . . there was a severe storm front barreling its way toward the base, with the requisite thunderstorms, and we needed to hurry.

Dang. That USAF weather guy in Kirtland AFB needed some remedial training since he didn't forecast this massing of thunderstorms in Kansas.

As we climbed and headed east at .88 Mach_the clouds that had been below us since entering Colorado gave way to clear skies with only scattered clouds down low. But on my entire right side, from the extreme southwest and then then going in front of me to the extreme northeast, I could visually see the wall of weather and had no doubts about the ferocity of the storms. The experience of my years flying out of McConnell and many previous weather penetrations were still indelibly etched into my weather wisdom synapses.

My two biggest concerns, now that I knew we had a hugely imposing line of thunderstorms to penetrate, were: (1) Could I find a hole through which to slip my flight of four aircraft without being tormented by turbulence?; and, (2) could we get to the aerodrome before the weather hit?

With an old worry behind, landing at Colorado Springs, and two new ones ahead, I again sent my number 2 man off the active ATC freq. and told him to contact McConnell AFB tower and ask them, quite literally, what it looked like out their window, particularly to the west, from whence the weather was coming, and to give us an estimate as to how much time we had before the front hit. Two answered with a quick, "Roj," and off he went, at least in terms of the UHF radio spectrum (the F-4 had only one radio for ATC or inter-flight communications; it worked only in the UHF band).

I will pause from this narrative and marginally educate you on the F-4's radar and its ability for painting weather.

Simply put, the Phantom's radar was not made for weather interpretation or avoidance, but even so, once enlisted in that role and once you learned how to interpret the radar returns, it actually did quite well. All fighter aircrafts' radars are made for locating and tracking other aircraft, big or small, or for ground mapping, or both. Weather avoidance was a complimentary capability due to the nature of the radar and its design. A F-15/16/18 had to use a different, pulse, mode with their radar to "see" weather, whereas the F-4's radar could be used in its normal air to air mode. With that said, the ability for the F-4's radar to see through any thickness of clouds, electronically of course, was not a problem. In fact, the energy put out by the Phantom's radar was so much, because it was designed to detect aircraft at a long distance,

I wouldn't be surprised if water evaporated as it hit the radome while we flew in rain (kinda like a microwave boiling water). And on that thread, whenever I led a four-ship of F-4s and we were in close formation, I knew all of the guys had their radars on and their antennas were sweeping left and right (up to sixty degrees either side of center) and I wondered why in the hell with all of that RF energy passing through, around, and bathing me that my kids didn't come out looking like a Picasso painting.

Once level at 33,000 feet, Andre, my backseater, tilted and gained the F-4's radar. I had a repeater of his scope in the front seat, so as he manipulated the radar's search area, we talked between ourselves about what area ahead looked the best for penetrating. At first the wall of clouds seemed impenetrable. From sixty degrees left of the nose, to sixty right, all we could see was a mass of commingled storm cells. But I knew from experience, and I explained this to my charge in the WSO's seat behind me, that from a distance though the weather can seem solid, as you get closer, due to limitations in the specific design of each model of radar (F-4, F-16, F-18, etc.), you should see gaps between the cells; some are big gaps, some are small, and some of these gaps can close up as you approach them, so you need to be prepared to turn around if a hole suddenly closes.

As we got ever closer to the backside of the storms, I continued to talk to Andre about techniques on how to interpret the weather returns on the scope and about how best to tilt and gain to optimize said returns and understand the nature of the weather at which we were looking. Andre was so new to the F-4 he'd not had a lot of thunderstorm avoidance experience, so I figured this would be excellent learning for him.

After many minutes of lip biting on my part, I saw that there was a decent size gap between two monstrous cells just north of Wichita. I asked Kansas City Center for a lower altitude, as we approached the weather from the west, since I wanted to stay in the clear as long as possible and the clouds at the higher altitudes were encroaching upon us; I wanted to make it easier on the wingmen by staying in clear air as long as I could.

I did communicate to my wingmen the area of weather that Andre, and I thought would be the best bet for getting through relatively unharmed and they all concurred that it looked like the best area too.

As previously mentioned, the line of storms was marching in a northeast/southwest tilt. I'm sure this slant, in relation to magnetic north, made not a difference to Mother Nature, global warming, or the price of rice in China, but to me it was a royal pain in the butt because my ace in the hole through this mess was about twenty miles or so northeast of IAB, and this meant more fuel spent getting through to the front of the weather and then backtracking a bit southwestward to get to McConnell.

In preparation for entering the clouds, I took another fuel check to give me a heads up on everyone's fuel states. As expected, number 4 was still the low man, holding at one thousand less than me with 5000 pounds total. Since we were only twenty-five miles from our destination, that wasn't too bad, but we still had to fly another twenty miles or so eastbound and then come back southwest, so at best, number 4 would have 3000 pounds on landing . . . thirty minutes at our nominal burn rate of six thousand pounds per hour. If we had to divert to Tinker AFB or Tulsa, both about ninety-five nautical miles south of Wichita, they would land with about 1,500 lbs. of fuel, at best. Not optimum, but since Tinker and Tulsa were clear, I'd let them lead us down there so they could conserve fuel.

I have to say, as we approached the ominous-looking clouds, my optimistic "fat" fuel supply suddenly was looking pretty thin if not right on the edge between risking an end run around and getting in to McConnell or diverting to Salina, which was to the north of us about sixty miles. In fact, if Tinker AFB was not sporting the good weather it did have, I would have done just that, gone to Salina. But, with clear skies, light winds, and no thunderstorms in the area, Tinker was my alternate from IAB once we got on the other side of the storms.

We were now down to 10,000 feet or so, and descending. My wayward number 2 man came back on freq and said the field was VMC (Visual Meteorological Conditions) with mostly broken clouds at around 2000 feet and excellent visibility under the clouds, however, tower estimated we had about twenty minutes before the leading edge of the storms hit the field.

I slightly rocked my wings to bring the boys back into fingertip, as they had been flying in route formation, in preparation for entering the clouds...and then my radar quit.

Crap.

Can you believe it? Of all the times for it to stop working. At first I thought it was my front seat, repeater radar that was the culprit but, in fact Andre said he lost his scope too. I literally, as you might see on TV docudrama, hit my scope in the hopes that it might act like CPR and bring it back to life...unlike TV though, no such luck.

Announcing over the radio "gadget bent," the code words for an inoperative radar, my wingmen immediately picked up the slack and began giving me headings to fly to avoid the bad stuff while my WSO troubleshot our busted radar set.

Since we were only at 9000 feet as we started to enter the clouds, I saw, visually, what my radar had (before it quit) confirmed was a pretty decent hole in the mountains of cloud in front of us.

My visual clue that this area was the place to penetrate as we approached the ankles of these monstrous storms from the west was the ripped-up clouds in an otherwise uniform wall of white. It literally looked like the two cells we were about to fly between were fighting over a white veil and consequently tearing it to shreds, from the ground up. In their fight, they were leaving tattered bits of cloud in this one geographical area alluding to a weak spot in the storms; or so I was betting, hoping, and praying.

As direct sunshine quickly became obscured by cloud fragments, I couldn't help but take a few deep breaths to try and break the tension within me, as the last time I did this I damn near flew into physical hell on Earth. (That's another story for another day.) I wiggled my toes and fingers and looked over my left and right shoulders at my wingmen to check on their position. Like little ducks nestled in close to mama, they were right there, rock solid and staring at my aircraft, the pilots in each, making continuous and mostly small adjustments with their throttles and ailerons and elevators (stabilator on the F-4) and rudder to stay close enough to see me in the clouds, but yet far enough so as to not hit me. Sometimes these adjustments follow each other in a mixed order, sometimes they are simultaneous, most times they vary between those two extremes. It's a continuous, delicate and minute dance of the flight controls and engines to maintain position on mama duck. Flying on the wing is hard work and mentally very tiring as you must also be thinking about what is coming up and trying to maintain a modicum of situational awareness as your flight progresses.

As bright day quickly turned dark, due to the thickening of the clouds, my wingmen were constantly reassuring me via the radio that the heading we were on looked good on their radars for weather avoidance. Wichita Approach Control had long ago told us that we could deviate at will since there was not another aircraft within forty miles and to let them know when we were turning direct to McConnell. According to my wingmen it would take about ten miles or so to get through the worst of the weather and then we could start edging to the right (south then southwest).

Into the gathering darkness we motored on, at 300 knots, in and out of clouds of varying thickness, and I won't lie and say that I didn't feel a bit uncomfortable flying into this mess without a radar. Sometimes we would blast through thin "whispies," mere remnants of much larger clouds, or maybe they were developing storm embryos, not yet full term . . . who knows. But no doubt our wake turbulence and engine effluent was blasting them apart and either hastening their disappearance or aborting their development. I can't say it bothered me either way . . . I've never had a strong emotional attachment to clouds. At other times we passed through the connecting clouds between the thunderstorms, where I'm sure our passing did little to disturb the nature of the weather behind us. The whole experience was surreal because as we were alternately flying through thick cloud, thin cloud, or no cloud we were seeing almost continuous lightning bursts all around. Some of the lightning was suffused, embedded within the clouds, and acted like an X-ray machine since you could see the outlines of the clouds within the clouds . . . if that makes any sense. At other times, ragged streaks of lightning, clear in definition were observed, causing me to think I was in Dr. Frankenstein's laboratory where monsters were jumpstarted to life by arcing bolts of electricity shooting through the air.

As we flew through the skies of Oz, I calculated how much fuel we would have upon our arrival. I had the airfield's TACAN tuned in and it was showing the distance and azimuth to the airport for situational awareness purposes. I was doing my best guessing at this point, as I had no exact idea as to when we could turn toward the runway. I was figuring though, just to give you an example of the extremely difficult mathematical calculations that fighter pilots use in flight (I'm be facetious), the following—we were doing roughly six miles a minute, 360 kts. ground speed, and were about thirty miles northeast of the destination. I figured we had another six miles, one minute, to go before we could turn southwest toward the airport. So, guessing that we had thirty-six miles to go, and at six miles a minute, that would equate to a fuel burn of around 600 pounds (100 pounds per minute, or 6000 pounds per hour, times six minutes of flying time equals 600 pounds. Now, add an extra 400 pounds for slop and then subtract that 1,000 pounds of fuel from the 5000 pounds number 4 said he had when I started this calculating…well, so, I figured the wingman with the lowest fuel state should be on the ground with around 3,500 pounds of JP-4; not too bad actually.

And, with that said, though I dearly wanted to fly at 500 knots to make sure I beat the encroaching weather, neither our fuel supply nor the wingmen could take it (the faster you go the more sensitive the flight controls and though I've flown on someone's wing in fingertip at 450 knots, it's not fun, particularly in the clouds). I figured 300 knots was the best compromise between fuel consumption and beating the storms, so it was at that speed in which we soldiered on.

Just as I was deep in thought in those aforementioned and extremely complex math problems, the sky all around us immediately brightened, signaling our passage through the worst of the weather. To be honest the entire time we ran the gauntlet between the two massive cells the turbulence was, at worst light, so it was indeed a good area for us to have penetrated, and really the passage through was a bit anticlimactic.

Once we broke into the clear, I immediately kicked the boys into a loose route position so they could relax a bit.

Now that we were through the mess of angry clouds, I put the TACAN bearing pointer on the nose and pushed up the power to accelerate to 350 knots. I felt so much better now that I could once again see the amazingly stratospheric ascending and impressive wall of cumulonimbus, this time from the eastern side.

I was now very confident that we would beat the storms to the field, but now I had a new worry, and oddly it was not the towering clouds above us but low-lying clouds below.

If you remember, earlier in the flight my number 2 man said that the field was reporting a 2000-foot broken ceiling. What I was looking at as we headed southwest was a mostly overcast (actually undercast, since the clouds were below us) sky; I wondered just how low the clouds descended.

I had figured earlier, based upon the earlier cloud report, we could fly up initial as a four-ship and then pitch out and land . . . a fairly expeditious and fuel-thrifty procedure. But if we had to split up, plan B, for individual ILS approaches, some of us weren't going to make it before the weather closed the field.

Plan "B" was not on my top ten list of things I wanted to do, so I asked Approach what McConnell was reporting for weather. Their latest report was almost an hour old and it jived with Tower's of a broken, 2000-foot ceiling. Since I was seeing that it wasn't that, I asked Approach for lower. Bringing the boys back into fingertip formation, we re-entered the clouds and descended to four thousand feet. At four grand, we were solidly encased in white and I asked for lower again. Since there didn't seem to be any other aircraft flying, my request was quickly granted, but even at 3000 feet we were still in the muck.

I had pretuned the ILS to runway 19 right's frequency while in the thunderstorms, so I asked for and was cleared to intercept the localizer as we approached the field from the northeast. We were now eighteen miles out and still firmly in the clouds' grip. I asked approach to take me down to their min. vectoring altitude. That altitude was about 2,500 feet and at that altitude, about 1,500 feet above the ground, I could see breaks in the clouds and the ground below. Upon seeing the ground and noticing the visibility was pretty good underneath the clouds, I immediately cancelled my IFR clearance and descended to get fully into the clear air. With my cancellation to Approach, they bid me sayonara and told me to go to tower's frequency.

At twelve miles out, and lined up on runway 19 right, I told Tower where we were. They cleared us to land on the right side (McConnell AFB has two parallel 10,000-foot runways).

Since we were only about a thousand feet AGL we could not fly up initial and pitch out as I initially had planned, we had to do straight-ins from this altitude. Just seeing the runway made me feel incredibly relieved and took a ton of bricks off of my chest. But I could see lightning to the west and a roll cloud out there . . . until we were all safely on the ground we weren't home free yet. With the new wrinkle, low clouds, spoiling my arrival and landing plan, and not wanting to break up for ILS approaches, I told number 4 to "drag."

If you remember, number 4, at least the front-seater, was the "new guy," so I was sure he had no idea what "drag" meant. When I first talked to tower and saw the low ceiling I told them we were going to do a "shotgun" approach. This was vernacular that came out of my ass as I hadn't used the term "shotgun approach" in a couple of years. But we used to do these oddly named approaches when I was on active duty for the exact reason I wanted to do one now . . . low cloud and straight-in approaches while in a formation. In essence, all you did was have the wingmen, in turn, starting with number 4 and then number 3, etc., slow down as rapidly as possible to landing/approach speed at two-mile intervals, or thereabouts. Since I was the lead aircraft, I flew on at 300 knots as each aircraft rapidly slowed and hopefully this would give us the required 3000-foot (offset, alternate sides of the runway) spacing we needed to land behind each other. In theory, and practice, it worked well, but it was not something we did a lot in my guard unit in Jersey.

Since I had told tower we were going to do a shotgun approach, I knew that would key the other flight members as to what my plan was and with that said, though I knew the number 4 "pilot" was clueless as to what this meant, I knew his backseater was not and I hoped he would brief the "greenhorn" on what the plan was. When I told number 4 to "drag" at twelve miles, the word "drag" being the command to slow down, I was looking directly at him to see what his reaction would be . . . I really, really hoped that they would immediately slow down as I didn't want to have to brief this over the radio at this point!

To my immediate relief, no sooner had the "ga" sound of drag gotten out of my mouth than number 4 was dropping back rapidly, his speed brakes fully deployed. That was a relief . . . the rest of the guys I wasn't worried about.

And so it went, at roughly two mile increments, I dropped the guys off one by one with number 2 leaving me as we approached six miles to go via the TACAN-indicated DME.

At that point, I was doing 300 knots; the final approach/landing speed was around 150 knots. While the Phantom may seem like a flying brick to some, it does have a pointy end, and merely pulling the throttles to idle and going to fully deployed with the speedbrakes isn't going to kill 150 knots or so of excess speed in four miles (the TACAN is located midfield, about 5000 feet from the approach end of either runway). Though my father never trained me to fly fighters, he did show me how to go down and slow down via cross controlling the flight controls of an aircraft (also known as "slipping") and I am here to tell ya, the F-4 can be cross controlled quite easily. The first fifty knots I "killed" using speedbrakes and slipping the aircraft; using a lot of left aileron to fight against a lot of right rudder which caused the aircraft to fly somewhat sideways on its way to the runway. Keeping the speedbrakes extended, the next 100 knots were lost with the aid of the landing gear and full flaps which were extended at their 250-knot limit. By the time the runway met the wheels I was on speed and well within the normal touchdown zone for landing; I had four thousand pounds of JP-4 remaining in the tanks.

As we rolled out on our landing roll into a strengthening headwind, I could hear number 3 ask tower if he could land on the left runway because he was having trouble getting spacing on number 2. Tower approved this and as I turned off the right runway, and headed east, toward the left runway, number 3 rolled past the intersection I was approaching.

Crossing the runway after number 3 went by, I taxied to the transient ramp to park after being cleared by tower. As I shut down my engines on the ramp number 4 was taxiing into parking.

As Andre and I got our bags out of the travel pod (a long since converted napalm bomb canister that we used to carry our personal effects) and closed the canopy, I felt some plump-sized raindrops hit my head. By the time number 4's canopy was closed, the wind had shifted from the south to out of the west with a roll cloud fast approaching the western edge of the airfield while lightning segregated the very blackish western sky. As soon as we walked into base ops, the monsoon started in earnest with sideways pelting rains and amazing displays of lightning accompanied by very loud and sharp reports of thunder. Settling into seats at base ops in preparation to going to the base hotel, I casually asked number 4 how much fuel he had when he landed . . . 3000 pounds he nonchalantly said; just enough I thought . . .just enough.

Landing Blind

Of all the flying my father did while a Captain at Meteor Airlines, he said he loved the European flights in the DC-4 the most. He told me many stories of his European and other worldwide adventures, but I'm sorry to say that the finer details of most of them have been carried away by the gentle breezes that eavesdropped upon our conversations.

There is one story, though, that I shall never, ever forget. If anything, what my father told me had to do to get his aircraft and crew safely to the ground, while on the following story's flight, truly defined his supreme aviator persona and gives much credibility about how he was always at his best when things were at their worst.

This amazing adventure began when my father and his crew were flying into Châteauroux-Déols Air Base, France, on a late fall's evening in 1956.

When telling me about his escapades while flying in Europe, my father often mentioned a seemingly ubiquitous and perpetual fog as one of the main or supporting characters in his tales. However, when I began to fly to England, and other destinations in Europe myself, I can't say I ever saw anything close to those Jack-the-Ripper, menacingly thick, London-type fogs that infiltrated many of my father's experiences. With each trip over there being devoid of even a heavy mist, I began to wonder if the old man was radically embellishing his stories to make them more profound.

But serendipity came to the rescue of my dad's integrity while I was on a trip to Wales, UK, in June 1997 and visiting an old coal mine. An elderly tour guide said that back "in the old days," almost every home and factory in England, if not in all of Europe, used to burn coal for heat and/or production of goods. This dependence upon coal for home and industrial related heating started in earnest with the beginning of the Industrial Revolution in the mid- to late-1700s and continued until legislation in the mid-20th century mandated cleaner burning fuels.

Further explaining the link between coal and fog, the guide said that when the homes burned coal for heat, usually during the colder months, and if the air was moist (humid) all this particulate matter floating about in the atmosphere was ripe for being coalesced. During the day, while the sun was high and the temperatures fairly warm the sky would appear very hazy, but at night when the air cooled malicious fogs would come out of hiding and appear ominously across entire counties, if not even countries. To add even more mayhem to this brew, if a low-pressure system was bringing in the moist air, it often brought with it an inversion. This was particularly bad as the inversion caused the warm coal smoke to settle back on the neighborhoods from whence it came, thusly polluting the polluters with a double dose of their own poisonous exhaust. These inversion-enhanced fogs could be so thick there were times when you couldn't see across the street. The dangerous health effects from these acidic fogs are pretty obvious, and in 1956, Britain enacted its first Clean Air

Act, but the actual cleaner air wouldn't come until well after my dad's regular trips over there ended.

So back we go to the fall of 1956 as we re-immerse ourselves in my father's story . . .

As the Meteor DC-4 neared Châteauroux Air Base, the whole of Europe was blanketed in low clouds and fog. Just getting into Shannon, so said my dad, was a dicey affair as they had gone down to minimums in mist and drizzle as they approached; after departing for Châteauroux, the weather finally did go below minimums.

As they continued to their destination and checked the weather, their alternate, London Heathrow, went below minimums as did all the other alternate airports that they normally would have used while flying into Châteauroux : Prestwick, Brussels, Frankfurt, Paris, etc. Everywhere they checked, the weather was below minimums.

Amazingly enough, the weather at their destination continued to hover just above minimums, so they held out hope that they would be blessed with a relatively easy arrival.

Not.

As they were being vectored for a GCA, Ground Controlled Approach, the radar controller told them that the weather had just gone below minimums for the approach; in fact, he said it was WOXOF (ceiling and visibility zero)

Their options were now very limited. As they held over the field, they used their radio to talk to the meteorologists in the military base below them and checked the weather at various airports in Europe. As the weather reports from around Europe began rolling in from the

Teletype, it was becoming intuitively obvious that they were screwed. Every airport within range of their now somewhat-depleted fuel supply was reporting weather that was either at or below minimums, and those airports that were much farther away but with weather that was decent were forecasting rapidly deteriorating conditions.

In the final analysis of the weather aspects of this flight, the good news was that they had the fuel to go somewhere. But, the bad news was they simply had nowhere to go that was better than where they were now when time was factored in, at least according to the forecasters.

In his evaluation of a game plan for a successful conclusion to their flight, my father said he "knew" Châteauroux Air Base. He was the captain on the company's first flight to the base and continued to fly there month in and month out. He knew its runway, the controllers, and the lay of the land around the airport. He felt comfortable there. So, after evaluating all the weather information, the facilities of the other airports with similar weather, and looking at all the other options available to them (there really weren't any), my father said he was going to shoot a GCA approach to a blind landing.

Probably the biggest factor in causing my father's reticence to leave Châteauroux was the fact that he trusted their GCA controllers. He said the GCA, in his opinion, was the greatest invention since paid toilets. But then my father had many, many moments of fleeting hyperbole where he said a lot of things were the greatest invention since paid toilets, so I am not actually sure where on the pecking order of superlatives the GCA actually stood. And to be honest, as I write this, I never quite understood what it was about paid toilets that made my father love them so, as I never got into an in-depth conversation with him on the subject. But I can tell you on this night, the GCA was right up there with beer, aircraft, and paid toilets.

Briefing the crew on the approach, he said he would monitor what heading it was that kept them on course as they neared "minimums" and once the controller said they were at minimums (whereupon the controller would no longer give directions) he would hold that heading as best as he could until landing. Concurrent with managing the heading, he said they needed to hold whatever average rate of descent it was that kept them on glideslope and continue with that descent rate once the controller went silent. Continuing, he briefed the boys that they had a lot of fuel so if the first approach was not going well, they could go around for another try, and another, and another until they nailed the numbers as precisely as they could. He finally added that there was very little wind that would affect them on this approach, so at least they had that going for them. Looking on the bright side he said, "Since it is dark, we have a good chance of seeing the runway lights before we land." There was not one dissenting voice among the crew for my father's game plan.

They got vectored out of the holding pattern and onto GCA final. With their gear and flaps down and slowed to final approach speed, they established contact with the final GCA approach controller. This controller told the DC-4 crew that they were approaching the glideslope and to not acknowledge further radio calls. Upon seeing the bright greenish dot, which was the actual raw data radar, return of the Meteor DC-4 on his cathode ray tube (CRT) reach a downward descending, much lighter green line that represented the three-degree Glideslope of the GCA, the controller said, "Begin descent." With that call, the flight engineer pulled off a bit of power on the engines, and my father lowered the aircraft's nose so as to begin a 500 to 600 feet per minute rate of descent toward an intensely black abyss.

Thus began an approach whose success or failure would define my father for his lifetime.

As they flew down an invisible, radar-derived glideslope into a night so thick with fog that some trains would refuse to leave their stations, the only way the crew on the DC-4 knew they were actually airborne was due to the various readings on their flight instruments indicating such. Vestibular, inner-ear sensations belied their actual aircraft's flight path and movement, causing the pilots to think they were in either a left bank or a right bank, pointing steeply toward the ground, or climbing rapidly when in actuality, they were wings level and in a precisely controlled descent. To land on the runway would be magic, but secretly, my father said any landing close to the runway and its relatively flat environment and one that didn't spell catastrophe for the crew would have been acceptable in his eyes; hence the adage, "Any landing you walk away from is a good one."

The GCA controller's radarscope is split into two distinct presentations. The top part of the display, the glideslope, is represented by a slightly descending whitish green line on one part of the controller's radarscope, the length of which is measured in miles and altitude (horizontal and vertical axes, respectively). Below the glideslope is an absolutely straight horizontal line that indicates the final approach course to the runway, again represented in miles from the runway. The GCA controller, by cross-referencing the bright-green dot on the CRT, uses his/her radio to give heading and descent information to the aircraft, such as, "Turn right to 271 degrees, on course, slightly high on glideslope," etc. With each radio call by the controller, the pilot of the aircraft would turn in the appropriate direction and maintain that GCA-directed heading as best he/she could. Were it just a heading that the pilot had to fly, the GCA would be a relatively easy approach to fly. But to get down below the clouds, you flew a glideslope too. So, adding another dimension, the vertical, puts a little more dynamic stress on the approach and both the pilots' and controllers' respective duties. However, unlike the azimuth, where a specific heading was given to fly in the vertical plane (no pun intended), the controller simply states where the green dot is in relation to the glide slope line on the CRT and trend information. So, a GCA controller's calls might go like this:

"MATS 4, no need to acknowledge further radio calls, check gear down, six miles from the runway, on course, approaching glide slope."

"Begin descent, come left to 270, going slightly right of course."

"On Glideslope, come left to 269, slightly right of course."

"Going slightly high on Glideslope, come right to 270, on course."

"Holding slightly high on Glideslope, on course."

"Four miles from touchdown, on course, on Glideslope, you are cleared to land."

"Come left to 269, going slightly right of course, going slightly below Glideslope."

"Come right to 270, on course, slightly below Glideslope, correcting."

"Three miles from touchdown, on course, on Glideslope."

And down you flew, increasing your descent rate, or slowing it to try to match the glideslope as best as you can, and making little "baby steps" with the flight controls to maintain the controller-directed headings and descent as best as you can.

When I began to fly these approaches myself in the USAF, I thought the attention to detail in flying would be too difficult for me to handle and that I would fail miserably. But after some practice, I felt comfortable enough to fly the approach down to minimums; but beyond that, I wanted to see the runway for landing. The thought of actually flying the GCA blind, to landing, caused me to shudder every time I flew a practice GCA (or the two "real" weather GCAs I flew in an F-4 while going into Navy bases).

I cannot imagine what it was like for my dad to fly at 120 knots in a lumbering DC-4 on that miserable night. The F-4, and then the F-16 that I flew in the USAF, flew at 165 to 145 knots, respectively, and they were nimble and responsive and had ejection seats. I knew if worst came to worst, I could punch out (eject) and get a nylon letdown. Not so for the old man and his crew. Their asses were tied to whatever fate their skills and the controller's were able to achieve. Those are the times when no amount of pay is enough and when you secretly, or openly, wished you had thought about your career choice with greater detail and forethought.

The pilots flying these approaches back then did not have the luxury of an autopilot to use for the actual approach, autopilots being used only for cruise phase of flight during this period of aviation development. Consequently, the approaches were manually flown, using the pilot's hands, legs, feet, eyes, ears, intuition, and brains to guide the aircraft to a safe landing. Flying this type of approach takes attention to detail to the extreme when it comes to manipulating the flight controls and interpreting the aircraft's flight instruments. The control yoke, which controls movement of the ailerons and elevator is constantly being manipulated by the pilot to meet the parameters required to stay on course and on glide slope. If the heading is one degree off the pilot will make a slight bank, to correct, and then bank back slightly to hold the bank angle and then add input to the ailerons in the opposite direction to roll back to level flight to hold the new heading once achieved. In tandem with aileron movement, the rudder pedals may or may not be pushed depending upon their need to maintain coordinated flight. The elevator, too, is adjusted if the aircraft is slightly high, or low, on the glide slope. In this case, the yoke is either pushed, or pulled, gently, in order to lower or raise the nose in order to increase or decrease the rate of descent, or ascent, in order to get back on glide slope. But, almost immediately after the yoke is pushed or pulled in order to get on the correct glide path, it is readjusted again, ever so slightly, so as to remain on the correct glide path. The throttles are constantly manipulated too, usually in concert with an increase or decrease in elevator input to maintain the correct airspeed for the approach. Every input of one flight control can slightly, or greatly, depending upon which flight control it is and to the extent it was moved, upset the aircraft's heading or rate of descent or airspeed and thusly require a corrective movement of the other flight control(s). For the approach to be successful, unyielding attention must be paid to the flight instruments and GCA directives and then the required flight control inputs made to cause the aircraft to conform to the proper flight path while maintaining the correct approach speed. There is a rhythm that develops between the hands and feet of the pilot, somewhat mimicking those of a conductor as he/she directs the orchestra to its crescendo. In a similar way, the pilot, the leader of his band of brothers (the other crew), directs his thundering aircraft to its climax, which occurs with a successful landing; to say the least it's mentally exhausting and requires a tremendous amount of cognitive and fine motor skill.

The GCA controller was the key to the success of the approach. He/she was part-human and part-machine since they had to know their own ground radar's idiosyncrasies, as well as those of the aircraft they were controlling. If that wasn't enough, they had to be able "read" the temperament of the sometimes emotionally fickle pilot(s) with whom they were talking. Some pilots were "mechanical" in their flying, and when the controller said turn to this heading or that one, they would "snap" to it and correct now. Other, more laid-back flyboys may be more lackadaisical about their corrections. In every case, the controller would have to adjust his/her instructions and anticipate appropriately for each different aircraft and/or pilot flying so as to be able to safely guide their charges home. Finally, as they goaded the green dot across their scopes, they had to keep in mind that that little "blip" on their scope represented a real aircraft in which sat real people who could die in a firestorm of debris if they were accidentally flown into the ground.

So, as I said, not only did they have to be masters at mechanical ingenuity, these GCA controllers had to became instant Dr. Phils as they sensed the pilot's reactions to their instructions, gauging whether they were guiding a type A personality or a type B. My father said a good GCA controller was worth more than his weight in gold; after I began flying GCAs in the USAF, I couldn't have agreed with him more.

The approach itself on that black, mucky and moisture-laden night, according to my dad, was about as good as you could get when it came to being "On course, on Glideslope."

Once they reached minimums, the controller told them they were going below minimums and should be able to see the runway. They did not.

So, downward they flew into an opaque, completely black, and misty kind of fog hell. Though his duties officially ended at 200 feet above the runway, the GCA controller provided guidance to the limits of his radar and display screen. Amazingly, the DC-4 continued on course, but went slightly above glideslope as they neared the runway—but still, they pressed in for the landing.

When flying, there are times when fate can quickly descend upon you and be either like a soft and gentle paramour, wanting to free you from harm—or conversely like a truculent ex-spouse from hell, intent on your destruction. This night, in my father's case, fate was caressing him sweetly, as if he was in a dream in which a delicately framed and lightly perfumed French beauty wrapped herself around him, whispering barely audible romantic exhortations in his ears in between her gentle good-luck kisses.

My dad said this night was even darker than any he'd ever experienced, and his eyeballs hurt from looking desperately for any kind of light as they got close to the runway. It was all to no avail and the landing was totally blind and the touchdown, when it came, unexpected. They knew, via reference to the altimeter, they were getting close to the ground and then very shortly after the glance at the altimeter they glimpsed the diffused illumination of one runway light, which came into view on the left side cockpit window, and then they touched down.

The actual touching of the gear to the concrete was not harsh with the ground effect slowing their sink rate just a bit before the actual smack of the gear against the concrete. Temporarily shocked by the landing, they all sat there wondering if this was the actual touchdown or a prelude to greater mayhem. But when they saw the runway's lights, ever so faintly, out of each side of the cockpit, the pilots swung into instinctive action to slow their forward progress. They landed on the left side of the runway, close enough to cause my dad to urgently steer right as they slowed, but how far down the runway's length they couldn't tell. The brakes were applied in direct proportion to my father's ability to keep the wheels from skidding since he feared they might go off the runway's end.

Silence infiltrated the cockpit once they stopped as each man thanked whatever entity he thought was responsible for their safe arrival.

The ironic part of the whole approach is what happened after landing—when the copilot finally regained his composure enough to announce to tower that they had landed. The controller didn't believe him. He said you'd have to be crazy to land in such a fog. So, a surreal conversation ensued for a couple of minutes between the tower and the aircraft, where one did not believe the other had landed, even though the one claiming he had landed had actually landed and couldn't understand why the other didn't believe them. The stalemate was broken when the radar shack called the tower to verify that the DC-4 had actually landed and not crashed somewhere, as the aircraft was not showing up on their radar. Tower finally acknowledged to the radar shack that they were talking to an aircraft that claimed they had landed somewhere on the airport, but they weren't exactly sure where.

Because of their unease about their exact position and just plain inability to see the runway lights and markings well, my father told the tower that he would not taxi off the runway unless a "follow me truck" was sent to guide them. In anticipation of this request, the controller said they had already dispatched one and that he should be there shortly. As they waited for their shepherd, all the aircraft's engines were shut down. That they did this, shut down the engines, was fortuitous.

The arrival of the "seeing eye Jeep" was announced to the Meteor crew by a rather violent jolt to the aircraft; the airman had run into the right main wheels of the DC-4 while he was looking for it! It is a good thing that the engines had been shut down since the jeep driver would possibly be sporting a new haircut. My dad said they deplaned to find the source of the bump and discovered a rather perplexed and unhurt airman shaking his head, as he examined his Jeep. With the aircraft's tire taking the brunt of the impact, no harm was done to either vehicle and after coming to his senses the airman slowly guided the DC-4 to its overnight roost.

Made in the USA
Las Vegas, NV
04 February 2023

66856610R00184